FIRST SERIES

ANTIQUE COLLECTOR'S DOLLS

by

Patricia R. Smith

Edited by: Karen Penner
Price Guide Editor: Kim McKim of Kimport Dolls

COLLECTOR BOOKS

Published by Collector Books
Box 3009
Paducah, Kentucky, 42001

ANTIQUE COLLECTOR'S DOLLS

Dedication

To the collector who sees and reflects love through dolls, and does not care what nationality the dolls are!

To Karen and Paul Penner for their hours spent helping to trieve and retrieve dolls from
shelves to camera and back to shelves, and their good nature and kind thoughts.

COVER DOLL

"FY" Nippon pouty. Refer to "FY" section for full description.

Acknowledgments

The author wishes to give special thanks to those whose dolls appear in this book:

Pearl Clasby
Margaret Esler
Margaret Gunnel
Verena Holzley
Donna Maish
Jay Minter
Karen Penner
Kimport Dolls
Ralph's Antique Dolls
Ellie Watson
Kathy Walters

All dolls are credited with the owners name, with each picture. My special "thanks" go to
two extremely busy people, Kim McKim and Ralph Griffith..the old saying still holds true,
"If you want something done, ask a busy person." I have taken the liberty to include into
this book a story on Kimport Dolls that was prepared for Region 5 of the United Federation
of Doll Clubs because this book will reach into areas not as close as Region 5, and I know
you will enjoy the fascinating story of the McKim family. I would like to say, publicly,
"thank you, Kim" for access to your invaluable doll library.

All photographs were by Dwight F. Smith except those of the Donna Maish Collection,
whose photographer was Ron A. Hensel and Ellie Watson, who took her own picture.

Dolls from the Margaret Gunnel Collection were dressed by Mary Frazier.

Other Doll Books by Author:
Modern Collector's Dolls
Armand Marseille Dolls
Modern Collector's Dolls, Second Series

About the Author
PATRICIA R. SMITH

SCHOOLS: Page School for Girls, Los Angeles, California
St. Mary's, Santa Barbara, California
Nevada State, Nevada
St. Theresa, Kansas City, Missouri

DEGREES: Pedogogy
Adult Psychology
Child Psychology
Dogmatic Theology
Apologetics
Literary Methods

OTHER: "Famous Artists" Course, studying art layout and design. A commissioned artist, who specializes in "faces" and religious art.
Studied with "Famous Writers School" in Connecticut on fiction aspects.

WORK: Has worked in Occupational Therapy Departments in Psychiatric Wards. As Assistant Advertising Director for large catalog order firm. Member of Ad Club. Worked as substitute teacher in local school system.

PUBLISHED: Articles and short stories on such varied subjects as: "Teen-age Dating", "How to Sculpture A Face", "Comparative Religions", "The Art Of Being A Wife", "Safety Afloat", "That Life-Jacket May Save You", "What It Is All About (USCGAUX)", "The Day That Tim Drowned", "What Is Religion?", "The Ins and Outs of Ceramics", "You Can Paint".

HOBBIES: Archery, Boating, Sewing, Collecting dolls.

ORGANIZATIONS: National Field Archers Ass'n, U.S. Coast Guard Auxiliary, Council of Catholic Women, Lake of the Ozarks Yachting Assn'n. Independence Gay Ninety's Doll Club. National Federation of Doll Clubs.

CONTENTS

How To Use Price Guide

The main and of utmost importance to any doll is the head. The quality of the bisque and not damaged in any way is the determining factor for which prices should be based. That means no hairline cracks, cracked or broken shoulder plates, eye chips, any mends or repairs, etc., and that the quality of the bisque is very good to excellent.

The most desirable dolls are completely perfect, original, in original boxes and never played with. But prices based on this assumption are unrealistic because the ratio is an overwhelming 6,000 to 1. That leaves 5,999 dolls showing varying degrees of use...so the prices in this book are based on the quality of the head alone. These prices are for excellent quality bisque in perfect condition and with no defects.

Body rubs, a missing finger, a crack in a kid body, a minor repair to the foot, etc. (These are all minor, not major damages), play no part in the prices in this book and I have not gone into great detail on bodies, because who can say what is original or not. After all, many, many heads and bodies were replaced when the dolls were toys and for various reasons, bisque heads did break and were replaced; bodies broke and were replaced.

The prices in this book were not made up. They cover a 3-year study from mail order firms, ads, price guides and price lists from all over the United States and Canada. They are the now prices and any changes will be reflected in an index that will be included into Series II of "Antique Collector's Dolls," at future date.

If a doll is more than I have based prices on...that is, all original, in an original box and unplayed with...you can add 30% over and above these prices and get it!!!

Please let me repeat! The first and foremost importance is the condition and quality of the head of the doll you are thinking of buying or selling.

I will finish this by saying: Collector's set their own prices by the amount they are willing to pay for any certain doll!

I have priced all dolls by using the retail dealer's prices except for bisque. Since allowances must be made for the quality of the bisque, I have used a scale method of pricing: For example: "18" M-N would make the price of the doll between $800.00 and $900.00.

A	$50.00
B	100.00
C	150.00
D	200.00
E	250.00
F	300.00
G	350.00
H	400.00
I	450.00
J	500.00
K	600.00
L	700.00
M	800.00
N	900.00
O	1,000.00
P	1,050.00
Q	1,100.00
R	1,200.00
S	1,300.00
T	1,450.00
U	1,700.00
V	1,900.00
W	2,200.00
X	2,400.00
Y	2,700.00
Z	3,000.00

A Short History of Dolls

I would like to start by saying that, in my opinion, a doll book should actually be a catalog of dolls, in picture form, not paying attention to country of origin, original cost, etc. I feel that we authors should not select what dolls should be collected by placing them "in a book." The different and most difficult to find, or the most expensive dolls are fine, but all dolls deserve recognition, for somewhere they are in a collection or are a keep-sake from the past in some quite place. They were loved not because they were French, not because they were in elaborate clothes, but because they were there! Plus the fact that only a tiny 10% of all doll collectors are "advanced" collectors.

What is a doll and when did it all start? The word "doll" came from the Latin word "pupa," meaning girl. In French, "poupee" and in German "puppe" and then to English, "puppet." A 1696 French dictionary (Dictionnaire de-l'Academie) defines the word "poupee" as 'little figure of wood, pasteboard or wax, representing a child or a young girl, with which children play.'

When "dolls" first came into being is questionable, as it is most difficult to draw the line, archaelogically, between "graven images" and playthings...for example, items found in early Egyptian tombs, Aztec graves and other peoples, are actually "friends" or "servants," religious helps into the unknown land of death, just as the "boats" of Egyptian tombs were to "carry the passengers across the dark abyss" into eternity. But no matter, at some point in time "dolls" happened.

Dolls played an important part in the life of the child queen, Isabella, who was married to the King of England, Richard II, at the age of eight.

Prior to her marriage, Isabella was a French Princess and was born in the Louvre Palace in 1387. Her father was King Charles VI and mother, the beautiful Isabeau of Bavaria. Isabeau bore King Charles VI a total of 12 children and Isabella was the eldest.

King Richard II of England was a widower when he asked for the hand of the little Princess and at first was told she was too young to marry. King Richard II decided to send an embassy made up of 500 attendants and consisting of knights, earls, squires, and headed by the Archbishop of Dublin. The leading spokesman for the embassy was the Earl Marshall James.

After their arrival in France, it was not long before King Charles VI and Isabeau granted his offer of marriage to Isabella. But when the Earl Marshall James asked to see the Princess, he was at first refused because she was too young to make an appearance at public affairs...but with much persuasion, the Princess was presented to them and they were amazed at her poise.

Earl Marshall James knelt before her and said "Madam, if it please God, you shall be our lady and our queen."

Little 8-year old Isabella replied "Sir, if it please God and my father that I be the Queen of England, I shall be well pleased, for I am told I shall be a great lady."...and with this gave her hand to the Marshall to be kissed. With reflected grace and ease, she took him to present him to her mother.

Within hours the child Isabella was married by proxy to the King of England and, within a few days, King Richard II arrived with many titled ladies to attend his bride.

There was a formal wedding in France accompanied by many parties, and it would be fantastic to have seen this child's trousseau! About 42 inches tall, these clothes would be very small and very elaborate. It is said her jewelry was priceless.

After returning to England, Isabella was crowned queen in Westminster Abbey, and after the ceremonies and pomp ended the routine of daily life began. Isabella studied to continue her education, but every leisure moment was spent with her king-husband. He sang to her and played musical instruments for her and they spent many hours playing dolls together. There are paintings and drawings showing this adult king playing dolls with his child queen.

Between 1395 and 1398 King Charles VI of France sent dolls to his daughter, the Queen of England, to show the English Court the fashions which were being introduced to the French Court. Of course, they were not "play dolls" but actually "fashion mannequins" and made to the size of the Queen of England so she could see how she would look in the fashions. It is assumed that these were all wood dolls and jointed and about 52 inches tall.

Isabella's love and devotion to King Richard was very great, and it was a sad parting as he headed for the war in Ireland. Within a few short weeks, his cousin Henry of Lancaster had overthrown King Richard, confiscated the Royal Treasury, captured Richard and had him thrown into the Tower of London, and declared himself King Henry IV.

Isabella was 11 years of age and she was pushed from one place to another, one town to another, and with each move more and more was taken from her. She was forbidden to see her beloved husband.

Isabella was brought a rumor, late one night, that her husband had escaped. She rallied a small army of men and went out to meet him, declaring along the way, publicly, that she did not recognize Henry IV as King. The rumor was not true and Isabella's small army was scattered and killed. She was returned and guarded much more closely, and Henry IV had her husband and his cousin, Richard II, put to death.

During this time the French King Charles VI was trying to get his daughter returned to France and had been refused. It was a number of years before she was allowed to return.

Isabella returned to France and, at the age of 21, married the poet, the Duke of Orleans. She lived just one year and died at age 22 (1409). The Duke of Orleans wrote about his bride:

"Above her lieth spread a tomb
   of gold and sapphires blue
The gold doth show her blessedness
   the sapphires mark her true,
and round about, in quaintest guise,
   is carved 'Within this tomb there lies,
The fairest thing to mortal eyes!

1

Yes, there lay the beautiful child, a bride at 8, a widow at 12, and dead at 22, a child who played dolls with her King husband in the moments of love and tenderness they shared together.

We see evidence to fashions in 1450 when it was written about the bazaars of Paris "Those presents so dear to little girls, those dolls so charming and so marvelously dressed." And in 1571, the Duchesse de Lorraine, Claude de France, sent to the child of the Duchess of Bavaria, dolls, "not too large" and the "best dressed obtainable." Both Louis XIII and Louis XIV had a very large number of dolls and doll houses. As we can see, the "doll" was the toy of the rich and makes one wonder what the poor children were playing with.

During the late 1600's, dollmaking in Sonneburg, Thur (Saxony-Germany) grew by leaps, as the dollmakers received a "tax break" from the government. As early as 1705, dolls had become a large industry.

"Dictionnaire du Commerce" of 1723 says: "those beautiful dolls richly dressed and with beautiful head dresses are sent to foreign courts to exhibit the latest French fashions." In an exhibit of 1763, hairdresser Legros showed 30 dolls with the latest "hair dress" and, in 1756, there was an exhibit with 100 dolls.

A word here on early china heads. The rarest seem to be called "Biedermeyer" and were made as early as 1830. But during the years of 1835 to 1840, they were produced in the greatest quanity. The character of these china heads is a small black spot on the crown of the head, where the wig is attached. They came on cloth bodies with china arms and legs. Collectors are prone to call any "bald" head china a "Biedermeyer."

At Sonneberg, by the mid 1800's, wood dolls were still most popular, also papier mache heads on kid bodies, poured wax over other materials, china heads (made mostly in Denmark, Prussia and Austria). In 1855 there came a patent to put glass eyes in porcelain heads and, by 1857, gutta percha and rubber were being used, also jointed bodies and "Frozen Charlottes."

Bisque headed dolls began to become very popular in the 1860's, both tinted and untinted. The untinted often were pressed (pouring molds did not come until later) into the same or identical molds used for papier mache and china heads, and generally had molded hair. These were mainly put on cloth bodies. The tinted bisque were largely of the lady type with wooden or kid bodies.

These were usually dolls dressed to show the current fashions in European capitals. To have the latest fashions was important to European nobility. Fashion display dolls date back many centuries and were not always bisque. For example: there were china heads by Sevres, dressed by Lanvin. Not all fashion dolls were ladies, some were dressed as children, plus the same doll could be used as a "play doll" as well as showing the latest fashions.

Many collectors and dealers use the term "fashion" or "French Fashion" for any adult-figured doll and this seems to be incorrect. There seems to be enough evidence that the majority of these were merely "mother" or "lady" dolls and were play dolls, not often seen in fashionable clothes. A "fashion" doll is not a type of doll at all, just a use for any doll.

Germany became the capital of dollmaking long before France, and almost all the dolls heads before the 1860's were made in Coburg, Nurnberg and Sonneberg. France imported dolls from Saxony (Germany), wax dolls from England and porcelain heads from Bavaria, Prussia and Austria. France had always excelled in clothing for the dolls. It was this period (1860's) that pierced ears and heels became fashionable. Before 1860 dolls usually were unable to sit down.

Actually from 1852, with Huret, Paris "began to produce dolls" but not too successfully until the 1860's.

In 1852 Mademoiselle Calixte Huret, Paris, began making jointed bodies of gutta percha (the same thing that is used today to cover golf balls), using imported German china heads. These dolls were dressed with complete wardrobes.

In 1855 Monsieur Griffier patented a "talking doll," but maybe the first talking doll was by M.M. Aelzel in 1827 (patented). In 1855 M. D'Autremont was using India rubber for dolls. During this same year Jumeau devised a firing color process.

During the 1860's many French companies were doing new things, such as:

1860: A moving doll: Galibert. Musical and jumping doll: Herland. A swivel head: Huret and also Jumeau.
1862: Speaking doll: Steiner. A jointed doll: Briens.
1864: Jointed doll held together by rubber: Arnaud.
1866: Leather doll: Clement.
1867: 2 faced doll: Bru. A jointed doll: Joliet.
1868: A molded doll from a paste: Chamson. A molded doll: Hawkins.
1869: A jointed doll of cork: Madame Restignat. A flying doll: Boutard. A jointed doll: Leverd et Cie. A doll of artifical wood: Chavallier et Brasseur.
1870: A speaking doll: Chauviere.
1872: A singing doll (music box) Madame Bru, a metal frame/jointed doll: Pannier.
1874: A "grimacing" doll: Gerabon.
1875: A dancing doll: Schmetzer.
1876: A metal doll: Vervelle. A swimming doll: Martin.
1890: A tiny phonograph in the chest of a doll: Jumeau.

It should be noted here that French patents were issued from 1824 but items were not registered (trademarked) until 1885.

From this same period of 1860 to 1890, 30 short years, the Germans were very busy making dolls. Waltershausen, Ilmenau, Koppelsdorf, Ohrdruf were locations of procelain manufacturing companies, but the main center was at Sonneberg. This great growth was due to the fact that the government subsidized the dollmaking industry, and that industry grew out of a home work plan where even rural Germans were helping in all phases by painting, putting in eyes or assembling dolls...sometimes coming up with dolls that were out of proportion or not too well painted.

It should not be assumed that the "best" dolls are French, for a greater amount of "French" heads were actually made in Germany than collectors are willing to admit and if imported to France after 1890 would naturally bear the French markings...this leads to marks: "D.G." means "German Made;" "D.R.G.M." is the German abbreviation for a German company that was "incorporated;" "D.R." is "Deutches Reich." "Gebruder" means brothers. "Fils" means sons. "Cie" means company. "Maison" means "house of." "Dep" or "Deponirt" means "registered." In France "Dep." or "Depose" means "registered." "Marque Deposee" is "Registered Trademark" "Deposee" is "Trademark." "Fabrikmarke" or "Schutz Marke" means a "German Trademark."

The doll industry of the 1880's brought the change from lady dolls to those of children and babies...the bent leg baby body was not on the market until after 1905...and before the 1900's "babies" were generally a regular doll dressed in christening clothes or baby clothes. This period also saw the revival of sleep eyes and then the jointed all bisque dolls were introduced, also celluloid dolls. The 1880's brought a change from the flat top chinas (popular for 30 years prior) to the Rembrandt hair styles. In the 1890's the slightly turned shoulder heads became popular as did the china with bangs, also the dolls portraying Negros, American Indians and Orientals. Flirt eyes were put on the market as well as spring strung dolls, although the major part were still strung with elastic.

The 1900's introduced the "pet name" dolls which include Agnes, Bertha, Daisy, Esther, Florence, Helen, Mabel and Pauline. These were made by the German companies of Hertwig of Katzhutte and Porzellan Fabrik Co. of Veilsdorf.

It was in 1905 that the hair styles changed from a center part to a side part. Pierced ears declined in popularity and disappeared by 1920.

The 1890 Tariff Act stated that all articles of a foreign manufacturer would be plainly stamped, branded or labeled, in English, to indicate the country of origin. In 1909 the Payne Law was less liberal but still holding that the goods had to be "marked, stamped, branded or labeled without injury." Needless to say many took advantage of this loop hole, provided in both Acts, so unmarked dolls were permitted to enter the country after the 1890 Tariff Act and it cannot be assumed all dolls not showing maker and country of origin were made before 1890...plus the fact that many visitors to Europe brought or sent home many gifts and hundreds of "unmarked" dolls, never meant for export, entered the United States.

Picture Cross Reference

I made up this cross reference of photographed dolls for my own use and have used it so much. It has saved me much hunting and time, so I thought I would include it into this book for you.

My own file contains many more sources than is listed here, but I have chosen 22 books that may be "standard" items in the majority of "doll book libraries." If you have other books and illustrated price lists, etc., you can add them to this listing and the next time you see an ad, or wonder what a certain mold number looks like, refer to the list and you can locate that mold number and see the doll. I have not incorporated the index of this book into the following. The abbreviation used is shown after the full title of the book.

All Color Book Of Dolls, Kay Desmonde. (Color)
Antique Price Guide, Marlene Leuzzi (Leuz)
Armchair Museum Of Dolls, The, Olinda Tavares (Museum)
Blue Book of Dolls & Values, Bateman & Foulke (Blue)
Collector's Encyclopedia Of Dolls, Dorothy, Elizabeth & Evelyn Coleman (Cole)
Dimples and Sawdust Vol. 1-Selfredge & Cooper (D&S Vol.1)
Dimples And Sawdust Vol. 2.-Cooper (D&S Vol. 2)
Doll Home Library Series Vol. 1, Marlow Cooper (Cooper)
Doll Home Library Series Vol. 8 (Cooper)
Doll Home Library Series Vol. 15 (Cooper)
Dolls, A New Guide, Clara Fawcett (Dolls)
Dolls, Images Of Love, Selfredge (Im of L)
Handbook Of Collectable Dolls Vol. 1, Merrill & Perkins (M&P)
Handbook Of Collectable Dolls. Vol. 2 (M&P)
Heirloom Dolls, Brenda South (South)
Kammer & Reinhardt Vol. 1. Patricia Schoonmaker (K&R Vol. 1)
Kammer & Reinhardt Vol. 2 (Further Research) P. Schoonmaker (K&R Vol. 2)

Once Upon A Time, Ralph Griffith. (Ralph's)
Open Mouth Dolls, LaVaughan Johnston. (OM)
Portrait Of Dolls Vol. 1. Carol Jacobsen (P of D Vol. 1)
Portrait Of Dolls Vol. 2. (P of D Vol 2)
Wendy & Friends-Selfredge. (W&F)
The number following the abbreviation for the book is the page number on which the picture of the doll can be found. Example: Mold number 1099: D&S Vol. 2-103 (S&H Oriental) transposes to Page 103 in Volume 2 of Dimples and Sawdust by Marlowe Cooper. Shows a picture of a doll with mold number "1099" which happens to be an Oriental and made by Simon & Halbig. Another Example: You look for a mold number "17" and it says: 17: Cole 570. This means there is a picture of a doll with the mold number "17" on page 570 of Coleman's Encyclopedia.

Mold
#

0: Cooper Vol. 15-5; OM-64
1: Ralphs-21; OM14; Cole-323.

2: Cooper Vol. 15-12 & 36; Museum-57; D&S Vol 2-106 (lady); D&S Vol. 1-32 (C.O.D. lady) Cooper Vol. 15-12; Cole-319 (Indian)
3: OM-105; D&S Vol. 1-6 (A.M.); M&P-34D & 34I.
4: OM-11; 30&33. M&P-78 (Bonnet doll); M&P-44F&I (H. Hand.); Ralph's-12 Cooper Vol. 15-11.
5: W&F-68 (S&H); M&P Vol. 2-78G (Bonnet doll); Ralph's-8&14; OM-53; Cole-167&544; M&P Vol. 1-40M&42A (Heu)
6: D&S Vol 2-68 & 106; Im of L-49&52; OM-30&53; M&P Vol. 2-78R; M&P Vol. 1-40 (Heu); M&P Vol. 1-22E.
6X; Leuz-77
7: P of D Vol. 1-14 (J.D.K.); Museum-20 (S&H)
8: W&F-79 (Heu); Leuz-46; D&S Vol. 1-63; M&P Vol. 1-40D&42F
9: D&S Vol. 2-98 (Heu)

10: Im of L-51 (Heu); OM-32&103; Leuz-74; Cole-35&665.
11: W&F-22; Im of L-5; Leuz-45; D&S Vol. 2-29.
12: D&S Vol. 2-128; Im of L-27; Cooper Vol. 15-20; OM-21; D&S Vol. 1-60; OM-34 (S.F.B.J.)
13: D&S Vol 1-6 (J.D.K.); M&P Vol 1-40C (Ger. Heu)
14: W&F-40; D&S Vol. 1-61; OM-Cover; Pof D Vol. 1-23 (14P-Hilda)
15: P of D Vol. 1-12 (J.D.K.)
16: Im of L-5 (Heu); D&S Vol. 1-5&30.
16X: D&S Vol. 2-68; W&F-67.
17: Cole-570; Cooper Vol. 15-30 (man)
18: Im of L-58 (K&H); OM-54; M&P Vol. 1-74E (Googly)
19: OM-19, 53&75; Im of L-49; Cooper Vol. 15-29.
20: Leuz-99; Cole-259.
21: Blue-141 (R.A.)
22: M&P Vol. 2-86E (Bonnet)
23: Museum-59 (P.M.); Cole-521; M&P-Vole. 1-40F (Colored)
25: Blue-53 (C.O.D.)
27: OM-86; Museum-61.
28: Im of L-57 (R.A.); Cole-367; M&P Vol. 2-86D (R.A. Bonnet doll)
29: M&P Vol 2-86D (R.A. Bonnet doll); Blue-37 (Celluloid)
30: Museum-22 (Heu. Kopp); OM-80; Cole-255; Blue-29; Museum-57 (B3½)
31: Im of L-53 (Heu); M&P Vol. 1-48N
32: P of D Vol. 1-36; Cole-544
33: M&P Vol. 1-40P (Heu)
34: OM-54; Coopers Vol. 15-29; Im of L 34,38&70; M&P Vol. 1-32B
35: D&S Vol. 2-97 (Heu); M&P Vol. 1-40C (Ger. Heu); M&P Vol. 2-94C (Celluloid)
37: M&P Vol. 1-42A (Heu)
38: Im of L-34,38&70.
41: Im of L-53 (Heu)
43: Im of L-57 (R.A.); Im of L-53 (Heu)
44: Im of L-57 (R.A.); OM-60.
45: Cooper Vol. 15-19 (R.A.)
47: Cole-480
48: Cole-655; W&F-78
50: Im of L-28 (K&R); M&P Vol. 1-42B (Heu); M&P Vol. 2-94D (Celluloid)
51: D&S Vol. 1-63
52: Cooper Vol. 1-15&19 (S.F.B.J.-googly)
55: OM-31 (K&R/SH)
56: Cole-462
58: Im of L-61
60: Cooper Vol. 1-5&16; OM-79; Cooper Vol. 15-33; Cole-586; Blue-169 (S.F.B.J.); M&P Vol. 1-26D; Blue-100 (K&K)
64: M&P Vol. 1-26F
68: Im of L-51 (Heu)
69: Museum-24 (H. Hand)
73: Im of L-57 (R.A.); Cole-255
74: Im of L-74 (Heu); M&P Vol. 1-42A (Heu)
76: Blue-184 (K&H)
77: Cole 296; M&P Vol. 1-40P (Heu)
78: Cooper Vol. 15-7
79: M&P Vol. 1-22K
80: M&P Vol. 1-40P
85: Im of L-51 (Heu)
86: Cole-519
87: Im of L-53 (Heu); M&P Vol. 1-40N (Heu)
88: Im of L-50 (Heu)
91: D&S Vol. 1-97 (Heu); Im of L-54 (Heu)

92: Blue-23 (Phenix)
93: OM-85 (Phenix); Cole 202; W&F-14 (Phenix); M&P Vol. 1-30 (C.O.D.); M&P Vol. 1-40N (Heu)
94: M&P Vol. 2-78/0 (Bonnet Doll)
95: Im of L-62
99: Blue-79 (H. Hand)
100: W&F-74; P of D Vol. 1-36; Im of L-28; M&P Vol. 1-30z& 44G; Blue-101; All Color-46.
101: W&F-75; D&S Vol. 1-32; Im of L-28,29&75; P of D Vol. 2-86; Ralph's-24; Cole-344-493; M&P Vol. 1-33; All Color-46; Cooper Vol. 15-40; Im of L-29&73 (101X)
102: Im of L-30&C-43 (Colored Section)
103: Im of L-30&C-38 (Colored Section); W&F-67
104: Im of L-31 (K&R)
107: Im of L-73 (K&R); D&S Vol. 2-91
109: Museum-56; P of D Vol. 2-85; D&S Vol. 2-90; Im of L-32; Cole-283; All Color-48
111: OM-59
112: Cooper Vol. 15-29 (K&R); Leuz-107; Im of L-C-2 (Color Section); W&F-77; Im of L-33.
114: P of D Vol. 2-87; Ralph-24; Leuz-106&108; P of D Vol. 1-35; D&S Vol. 2-90,91&92; Im of L-33&34; Cooper Vol. 15-36&40; M&P Vol. 1-32F
115: W&F-68 (J.D.K.); M&P Vol. 1-32D; M&P Vol. 1-52A (Indian)
115A: D&S Vol. 2-91; Im of L-34
116: OM-26; Ralph-21; W&F-38; Im of L-35; Cole-344; M&P Vol. 1-34; M&P Vol. 2-78D (Bonnet Doll)
116A: D&S Vol. 1-6&92; Im of L-35; All Color-46
117: P of D Vol. 2-88; South-43; Ralph-24; P of D Vol. 1-35&36; Cole 345; D&S Vol. 2-91; Im of L-36; Blue-104; Cole 465
117N: OM-38; Im of L-36; M&P Vol. 1-32E
117A: W&F-75
119: K&R Vol. 2-19
120: K&R Vol. 2-13; Im of L-62
121: W&F-72; Im of L-37; Blue-103
122: K&R Vol. 2-10; Im of L-37; Cole 345
123: D&S Vol. 2-90; W&F-76; Im of L-38; Cole 363
124: D&S Vol. 2-90; Im of L-38; M&P Vol. 1-48B
126: K&R Vol. 2-12; P of D Vol. 1-27; Im of L-37&38; Cooper Vol. 15-41 (S&H); Cole-345; Blue-106&107; OM-110; M&P Vol. 1-32H
127: Cooper Vol. 15, 12&32; K&R Vol. 2-12; Cole-342; P of D Vol. 1-26 (S&H); Im of L-39&62.
128: K&R Vol. 2-16; P of D Vol. 1-15 (J.D.K.); Im of L-39
129: Museum-25
130: M&P Vol. 1-68C
131: Im of L-40 (Googly)
132: Cooper Vol. 15-10
133: Museum-29 (G. Krauss)
136: Museum-19
137: Cole-193
138: Blue-140 (R.A.)
139: D&S Vol. 2-65
140: South-40; Cooper Vol. 15-12
141: Cole-350
142: OM-74; P of D Vol. 2-74 (J.D.K.)
143: D&S Vol. 2-104; Im of L-59 (K&H); Cooper Vol. 15-33 (J.D.K.); D&S Vol. 1-63; M&P Vol. 1-30Y&34/0
146: P of D Vol. 2-84; Blue-110 (J.D.K.)
147: Musuem-52
148: P of D Vol. 1-14 (J.D.K.)
150: Cooper Vol. 15-11&12; W&F-48 (baby); M&P Vol. 1-68A

151: Im of L-41 (S&H); K&R Vol. 2-11; M&P Vol. 1-6C&40E
152: Museum-41; Cole-350
153: Im of L-41 (S&H)
154: OM-76 (J.D.K.); P of D Vol. 1-14; Museum-22; Cole-229&350; M&P Vol. 1-30V
158: Cole 361
159: Dolls-125; Blue-111
160: OM-53&160; M&P Vol. 1-76F
161: Im of L-58 (K&H)
163: Im of L-63 (Googly)
164: P of D Vol. 2-74 (J.D.K.); OM-53; South-52; Cole-229
165: Im of L-63 (Googly); M&P Vol. 1-48D (Googly); Cooper-52 (Googly)
167: OM-92 (K&H); P of D Vol. 1-40 (A.M.); OM-38 (J.D.K.); Cole-351
168: Museum-58; Cole-609
169: Im of L-58 (K&H)
171: OM-89 (J.D.K.); Cole-352
172: Im of L-63; Im of L-77 (Googly); Ralph-22
173: Cooper-52 (Googly)
175: M&P Vol. 2-92C (Celluloid)
180: Cooper Vol. 15-17
182: OM-14
183: P of D-55
184: Cooper Vol. 15-11
185: W&F-79 (Lady); South-44
189: Cooper Vol. 15-18
191: P of D Vol. 1-29 (G.B/SH)
192: Cole-364
193: OM-47
194: OM-24 (P.M.)
196: OM-18
200: South-52; W&F-78 (A.M. Googly); Cole-22&604; OM-6
201: D&S Vol. 1-8 (J.D.K. Celluloid); Im of L-60 (C.P.); Leuz-22; Cole-109; Blue-117
203: D&S Vol. 2-77; M&P Vol. 1-44i (FY); Blue-80 (M. Hand); Cooper Vol. 1-5&16 (S.F.B.J.)
208: Cooper Vol. 15-15; W&F-79; M&P Vol. 1-30F (J.D.K.)
211: P of D Vol. 2-79 (J.D.K.); Cole-352; Im of L-C-5 (Color Section); D&S Vol. 1-25 (Jumeau); Cooper Vol. 1-5 (S.F.B.J.-
212: Ralph-16
213: W&F-78 (Googly)
214: Museum-31 (J.D.K.); Im of L-34 (K&R/SH)
215: Cole-221
216: M&P Vol. 1-40L
20: P of D Vol. 1-15 (J.D.K.); Im of L-59 (K&H); Im of L-60 (C.P.)
221: P of D Vol. 1-15 (J.D.K. Googly); Im of L-77 (J.D.K. Googly); D&S Vol. 2-103 (Googly); Ralph-22; M&P Vol. 1-48 (Googly); Cooper-51 (Googly); South-53 (Googly); Cooper Vol. 15-15
223: Im of L-62
225: Im of L-C42 (Color Section-A.M.); M&P Vol. 1-34M
226: P of D Vol. 1-10 (J.D.K.); D&S Vol. 2-141 (S.F.B.J.); Cooper Vol. 1-4,6&19 (S.F.B.J.); Cole-587; D&S Vol. 1-56; W&F-30 (S.F.B.J.)
227: D&S Vol. 2-141 (S.F.B.J.); Cole-587; Cooper Vol. 1-6,7 & 17 (S.F.B.J.); Blue-166; M&P Vol. 1-22G (S.F.B.J.)
228: D&S Vol. 2-141 (S.F.B.J.); Cooper Vol. 1-7
229: P of D Vol. 2-77; D&S Vol. 2-140&141; Cooper Vol. 1-8
230: W&F-28 (S.F.B.J.); Cooper Vol. 1-8; OM-153
232: Cole-154
233: D&S Vol. 2-140&144 (S.F.B.J.); W&F-73; Cooper Vol. 1-8&17; Im of L-C20 (Color Section); M&P Vol. 1-34E.

235: Im of L-76 (S.F.B.J. Googly); W&F-30 (S.F.B.J.); W&F-73 (J.D.K.); Cooper-17&18
236: OM-96; Leuz-69; P of D Vol. 1-50,56&57 (S.F.B.J.); D&S Vol. 1-55 (Clown)) D&S Vol. 2-141,143&144; W&F-30; Cooper Vol. 1-9&18; M&P Vol. 1-20E; Blue-172; Color-40 (S.F.B.J.)
237: D&S Vol. 2-93,141&144; Cooper Vol. 1-9&17; M&P Vol. 1-22H&22i; Museum-30 (Hilda); P of D Vol. 1-19 (Hilda)
238: D&S Vol. 2-140&144; Cooper Vol. 1-10&11; Color-41
239: W&F-30 (S.F.B.J.); D&S Vol. 2-140&144; Cooper Vol. 1-11; Cole-502
240: Cole-595
241: W&F-27 (Googly)
242: Cooper Vol. 1-11 (S.F.B.J.)
243: P of D Vol. 1-14 (J.D.K. Oriental); Cole 353; Im of L-62; South-53&57
244: Im of L-27
245: Im of L-7; P of D Vol. 1-16,20,22&23; Ralph's-25; D&S Vol. 2-93 (Colored Hilda); W&F-27 (Googly); D&S Vol. 2-141 (Googly); Cooper Vol. 1-12,18&19 (Googly); Cooper Vol. 15-18; Blue-87 (Hilda)
246: K&R Vol 2-23 (SH/K&R); Cooper Vol. 1-12
247: P of D Vol. 1-12,56&57 (J.D.K.); W&F-28 (S.F.B.J.); D&S Vol. 2-143; Cooper Vol. 1-12&18; Blue-174 (S.F.B.J.); Ralph-25 (S.F.B.J.); Cooper Vol. 15-21
248: Ralph-26; Cooper Vol. 15-39 (A.M. Fany)
250: Cooper Vol. 1-12; OM-22; Cole-294
251: Blue-168 (Unis); Ralph-27 (Unis); Color-40; Cooper Vol. 1-13; Cole-43; Leuz-69 (S.F.B.J.); Cooper Vol. 1-15 (Unis)
252: Cooper Vol. 1-13&20 (S.F.B.J.); Im of L-71 (S.F.B.J.); Leuz-98; P of D Vol. 1-52; D&S Vol. 1-10 (Googly); D&S Vol. 2-20; Blue-173 (S.F.B.J.); Im of L-40&C6 (S&Q-Color Section)
253: Cooper Vol. 15-16 (A.M.); D&S Vol. 1-10 (Googly); W&F-30 (S.F.B.J.); Cooper Vol. 1-14 (Clown)
257: Museum-30; Cooper Vol. 15-20 (J.D.K.)
259: Cooper Vol. 1-14 (S.F.B.J.)
260: Cole-354
262: M&P Vol. 1-49 (E. Heu)
264: Cole-108
267: Cole-293; M&P Vol. 1-34F (A.M.)
270: Ralph-4
271: Cooper Vol. 1-15 (Unis)
272: W&F-74; Ralph-4
275: Museum-27 (Heu-Kopp); Blue-86 (Heu-Kopp)
278: Blue-74
282: Cole-177; Ralph-25
289: OM-42&43
299: D&S Vol. 2-140
300: Im of L-55 (Heu-Kopp); M&P Vol. 1-40i (Heu-Kopp); Museum-26 (Heu-Kopp
301: Cooper Vol. 1-14&15; Museum-66; D&S Vol. 2-22-142; OM-10&49; P of D Vol. 2-69; Cole-73, 586&655; Blue-170&183; OM-101; M&P Vol. 1-24A
302: Museum-26 (Heu-Kopp); M&P Vol. 1-22M
310: Cooper Vol. 15-20; Cole-431; D&S Vol. 1-1; M&P Vol. 1-48F (A.M.)
312: M&P Vol. 1-40H (Heu-Kopp)
320: Cooper Vol. 15-15,16,17,19&20 (Googly); D&S Vol. 2-104 (Googly); Ralph-19; Museum-41; M&P Vol. 1-48C (A.M. Googly)
326: W&F-74 (A.M.)
329: P of D Vol. 2-56; Cole-429
341: P of D Vol. 1-39; Museum-45; OM-23 (A.M.)

351: Museum-43 (A.M.); Cooper Vol. 15-39; M&P Vol. 1-36B (A.M.); Blue-125 (A.M.)
353: Ralph-19 (A.M. Googly); M&P Vol. 1-52F (A.M. Oriental); South-57 (A.M. Oriental)
370: Cole 428: M&P Vol. 1-44D; Blue-126; Museum-34&44; OM-78
372: M&P Vol. 1-44K (A.M.)
390: Cole-429; M&P Vol. 1-42E; Blue-124; Museum-32&39; Color-44; OM-15,23&75; South-56 (All bisque)
399: Im of L-56 (Heu-Kopp); M&P Vol. 1-34B (Colored); Blue-84 (Colored); Cooper Vol. 15-27 (Colored)
401: Cole-429; M&P Vol. 1-44L&73E
403: Im of L-40 (K&R)
407: Museum-27 (Heu-Kopp)
410: Cole-612
412: M&P Vol. 2-90D (Celluloid)
442: Cole 346
450: OM-105
451: Im of L-56 (Heu-Kopp. Colored)
452: Im of L-56 (Heu-Kopp. Colored)
455: Ralph-19
458: M&P Vol. 1-34L (K&H)
463: Im of L-56
500: P of D Vol. 2-80 (A.M.); Im of L-74 (A.M.)
514: Cole 290
520: Im of L-59 (K&H)
524: Im of L-60 (C.P.)
525: P of D Vol. 1-40 (K&H)
526: W&F-78; Im of L-59
529: Cole-546
530: Cooper Vol. 15-3 (S&H)
531: W&F-75
537: W&F-1 & cover (BSW); Im of L-cover
548: Im of L-58 (K&H)
550: W&F-79 (A.M.); Cooper Vol. 15-36 (A.M.); Cole-253 (S&H); M&P Vol. 1-32C (A.M.)
570: M&P Vol. 1-26C (A.M.)
571: Im of L-58 (K&H)
585: OM-97; Cole-44; Blue-19
590: W&F-72; Cooper Vol. 15-32; Im of L-C-22 (Colored Section)
600: M&P Vol. 1-40 (A.M.)
604: Museum-49; Cole-44
607: Im of L-45 (S&H Oriental)
608: OM-56; Cooper Vol. 15-13
624: P of D Vol. 2-56
625: Blue-116 (K&H)
639: South-38
673: D&S Vol. 2-100 (Heu)
696: D&S Vol. 2-102 (S&H)
701: K&R Vol. 2-20; Im of L-29 (Celluloid)
716: W&F-63 (Celluloid); Im of L-35 (K&R)
717: Im of L-36 (Celluloid)
719: Cole-209 (S&H); M&P Vol. 1-30E (S&H)
721: K&R Vol. 2-15 (celluloid)
727: K&R Vol. 2-15 (Celluloid)
728: Im of L-34 (Celluloid); K&R Vol. 2-15; Cole-347; M&P Vol. 2-90A (Celluloid)
739: Im of L-45 (S&H Colored)
759: Cole-571
790: Cooper Vol. 15-10
800: Cole-286&1429
833: Cooper Vol. 15-14
852: D&S Vol. 2-67

886: M&P Vol. 1-34P
887: Cooper Vol. 15-13 (S&H)
890: D&S Vol. 2-64
894: M&P Vol. 1-52G (Heu)
908: Im of L-42; M&P Vol. 1-30A (S&H)
927: South-41 (S&H)
929: D&S Vol. 2-19 (S&H)
939: Im of L-43; W&F-68 (S.H.)
941: Cole-569
947: Cole-595
949: Blue-159 (S&H); P of D Vol. 1-29 (S&H); Cooper Col. 15-28; OM-50&51; Im of L-43 (S&H); Cole 570; W&F-71; D&S Vol. 2-103
950: Cole-568
969: Im of L-42 (S&H); D&S Vol. 2-102
971: P of D Vol. 1-39 (A.M.); Museum-41; D&S Vol. 2-94
975: Blue-123 (O. Gans)
985: Cooper Vol. 15-28
993: OM-45
1005: W&F-78
1008: Cole-576
1009: Im of L-45 (S&H)
1010: Cole-569
1019: Museum-53
1039: Museum-20 (S&H); Im of L-44 (S&H); Cole 573; M&P Vol. 1-30D (S&H)
1040: D&S Vol. 1-7
1045: D&S Vol. 2-93 (Hilda-Colored)
1059: Cole-410 & 573
1061: Im of L-46 (S&H)
1070: P of D Vol. 1-21 (Hilda); Museum-53 (S&H); Museum-30 (Hilda)
1078: Blue-163 (S&h); Color-47 (S&H)
1079: Blue-160; D&S Vol. 2-29; Im of L-44; Cole-117&570; W&F-69
1080: P of D Vol. 1-27; Blue-157
1099: D&S Vol. 2-103 (Oriental)
1109: Im of L-44
1127: Cole-35
1129: D&S Vol. 2-102; Cole-572
1132: Ralph-2
1159: Blue-162; OM-35&36 (S&H lady); Color-42; Im of L-46 (S&H lady); D&S Vol. 2-102
1160: Im of L-46 (S&H); Cole-574&575; M&P Vol. 1-64B (S&H)
1199: W&F-80 (Oriental); M&P Vol. 1-52D (Oriental)
1249: OM-88; Im of L-46&47; P of D Vol. 1-29; Cole-541
1271: Blue-148
1272: Cole 548
1279: Im of L-47; W&F-68; P of D Vol. 1-29; M&P Vol. 1-44B; Ralph's-23
1294: Blue-158
1295: Cole 549
1299: Cole-573
1300: OM-102
1301: D&S Vol. 2-101 (Colored)
1303: Im of L-48; D&S Vol. 2-20 (Indian); D&S Vol. 1-24; D&S Vol. 2-101
1305: D&S Vol. 2-101 (S&H)
1310: Cole 177; Im of L-57 (R.A.)
1329: Im of L-48 (Oriental); P of D Vol. 1-27 (Oriental); Cole-572; Blue-99
1339: Color-43
1348: P of D Vol. 1-28

1349: P of D Vol. 1-27
1358: Im of L-48 (Colored); D&S Vol. 1-29; Leuz-112
1362: Museum-13; Blue-12
1388: D&S Vol. 1-29; Cole 575
1394: Cole-34
1420: W&F-78
1428: Cole-114; M&P Vol. 1-34J
1430: Cole-480
1468: Im of L-47
1469: Im of L-47
1488: Im of L-41; W&F-77
1603: Im of L-55 (Heu)
1616: Cole-576
1720: M&P Vol. 2-94A (Celluloid)
1728: M&P Vol. 2-92A (Celluloid)
1894: Blue-124; Museum-36,37,42; Color-43&45; OM-12
1897: Museum-35
1900: D&S Vol. 1-29 (Santa); D&S Vol. 1-31 (BSW)) Blue-71 (A.M.)
1902: OM-44
1904: Cooper Vol. 15-9 (ACM)
1906: Museum-53
1907: OM-10,14&39
1909: Cole 553; Blue-150
1913: Museum-56
1914: P of D Vol. 1-16&27 (Hilda)
1916: Cole-68
1919: Cole-480
1920: OM-69
1979: Im of L-107
2015: Leuz-104
2094: Cole-546
2096: Cole-547
2878: D&S Vol. 2-130
3200: OM-57&58
3500: Blue-126
4500: Cole-553
4900: Cole-553; Blue-151 (Oriental)
5500: P of D Vol. 1-42, Cole-47
5636: Cole-297
5689: Museum-28
6789: Cole-243
6897: M&P Vol. 1-30S
6969: Cole-297
7129: Im of L-52
7345: D&S Vol. 2-98; M&P Vol. 1-40J
7435: D&S: D&S Vol. 1-4
7602: M&P Vol. 1-40
7612: W&F-77
7622: Im of L-50
7644: M&P Vol. 1-40B
7665: M&P Vol. 1-40Q
7671: Im of L-53
7748: Im of L-50
7761: Cole-296
7825: W&F-71
8743: Cole-296
7911: M&P Vol. 1-42
7925: M&P Vol. 1-13
8178: M&P Vol. 1-48K
8192: Cole-298
8682: Im of L-75
8724: M&P Vol. 1-40R
8903: Ralph-13

9109: M&P Vol. 1-72J
10490: Ralph-11
10731: Cole-448
10727: OM-17
10954: M&P Vol. 1-74G
11439: Ralph-13
24011: M&P Vol. 1-30X
24014: Cole-42
45520: D&S Vol. 1-5; Cole-472
95469: Im of L-62
96643: D&S Vol. 2-96
421481: Cole-653
486986: M&P Vol. 1-48K
954642: Im of L-62
IV: Im of L-41 (S&H); Cole-575
X: OM-70
XI: Im of L-72; Cole-79; Museum-66
A: Ralph's-26; OM-83 (Alma)
B: D&S Vol. 2-100; Im of L-23; Ralph-17; M&P Vol. 1-34G (B.S.); M&P Vol. 1-76B (Baby Bud); Im of L-24; Im of L-8 (BL); P of D Vol. 2-50 (BF); P of D Vol. 1-40 (BSW); P of D Vol. 1-40; P of D Vol. 2-80; W&F-67&80; P of D Vol. 1-56 (BPG); Dolls-52 (Baby Gloria); Im of L-25 (BS); W&F-43 (BS); D&S Vol. 2-107; W&F-63 (Celluloid Baby Betty); Im of L-69 (BS Lady); Im of L-72 (Bonnie Babe); Cole-42; Cole-407 (BF); Cole-39 (Baby Darling); Cole-40 (Baby Glee); Cole-56 (Bebe Elite); Cole-34 (Baby Blanche); Im of L-24 (BF); M&P Vol. 1-20H (BS); Color-41 (BS); Color-52 (Baby Gloria); Ralph-5 (Baby Bud); Ralph-20 (Bonnie Babe); Cooper Vol. 15-35 (Bebe Bijou); P of D Vol. 1-40 (Bebe Elite)
C: Im of L-75 (CBD); Cooper Vol. 15-39 (COD-a/2); W&F-67 (Clover); Museum-46&58
D: Im of L-60 (Dolly Dimples); M&P Vol. 1-30C (Dolly Dimples); South-43 (Dolly Dimples); D&S Vol. 2-105 (D Lori); Cole-186 (DV); Im of L-16 (DL); Cooper Vol. 15-7 (Didi)
E: Cole-212 (Einco); Cole-213 (Eleonore)
F: Leuz-48 (F3 lady); Im of L-16 (FL)-Im of L-21-(FR); W&F-39; P of D-Vol. 1-39 (Floradora); W&F-39 (FR); W&F-42 (FB); Dolls-155 (Froebel-kan); Cole-223 (Fany); Cole-225 (Favorite); M&P Vol. 1-34N-(FB); Museum-32&38 (Floradora); M&P Vol. 1-44C (Floradora); M&P Vol. 1-44L (FY); Blue-63&64 (Floradora); Cooper Vol. 15-39 (Fany)
G: P of D Vol. 1-38 (GE); D&S Vol. 2-26 (GK); M&P Vol. 1-30U (G&S); Cole-265 (Grete); Im of L-70 (GK)
H: Im of L-71&C7 (Color Section); Leuz-22 (Hilda); D&S Vol. 1-30&55; OM-68; W&F-35; W&F-39 (HA); M&P: Vol. 1-12A&12B; Cole-293 (Hertzi); Cole-285 (Hanna); Blue-151 (Hanna); M&P Vol. 1-52E
I: Cole-320 (Italy)
J: D&S Vol. 1-56 (J-2); P of D Vol. 1-27 (Jutta); W&F-32; D&S Vol. 2-21 (JG); Im of L-25; Cole-480 (JJO); D&S Vol. 2-145 (JM); W&F-38 (JM); Cole-339; Im of L-24 (JJ); M&P Vol. 1-48F (Just Me); Ralph-21 (Just Me); Cooper Vol. 15-20 (Just Me)
K: W&F-63 (KRW-Celluloid); W&F-72 (KH); Cole 340 (K&K); M&P Vol. 1-44 (Kiddiejoy)
L: Leuz-45,103,109&141; South-39; D&S Vol. 1-63; D&S Vol. 1-56 (LC); P of D Vol. 1-38 (Lori); Cole-628 (Liane)
M: Leuz-100 (MOA); Leuz-103 (My Sweetheart); M&P Vol. 1-48G; Leuz-124 (MB-Japan); OM-6 (MOA); D&S Vol. 1-58 (Mimi); Cole-466 (My Girlie); Im of L-26 (M/C); Cooper Vol. 15-16 (My Fairy); Cole-402&594; M&P Vol. 1-28&29
N: Cooper Vol. 15-16 (Nobbi Kid); Cooper Vol. 15-18 (Nippon

Googly); Cole-304 (No 1)

O: D&S Vo. 2-76 (Our Fairy); Cole-460&481 (Olympia; M&P Vol. 1-76A (Our Fairy)

P: Im of L-64 (PD); M&P Vol. 1-48A (PG-Googly); Museum-47 (Princess); Leuz-77 (Paris Bebe); Leuz-80 (PG); OM-52 (P); Im of L-21 (PD); W&F-39; Cole-442; Museum-89 (Prize Baby); Cooper Vol. 14-6 (Prize Baby); Cole-490 (PRP); Cole-494 (Peterkin); Cole-501 (Poppydoll); Cole-506 (Princess); M&P Vol. 1-22E; M&P Vol. 1-30P (PRP)

R: Cooper Vol. 15-35 (R4R); Im of L-23 (RR); Cole-86 (RA); Cole-524 (Revalo); M&P Vol. 1-44H (RE); Blue-73 (Ruth); Museum-51 (Ruth)

S: Im of L-63 (SK); Doll-118; Ralph-7 (SW&Co); Cole-298 (S122); Cole-541 (Santa); Cole-566 (Sicoine); Blue-190 (Special); M&P Vol. 1-24D; M&P Vol. 1-44J (SC); M&P Vol. 1-30/0

T: Leuz-75 (Totot); Leuz-126 (TN); D&S Vol. 2-105 (TT); Cole-623 (Tynie Baby); Cooper Vol. 15-6 (Tiny Tot)

V: M&P Vol. 1-30B (Viola)

W: D&S Vol. 2-21 (Front of crown); Im of L-25 (WD); Cole-633 (WZ); Cole-649 (Wide Awake); M&P Vol. 1-30N (WD)

Y: W&F-48 (You Kid); Cooper Vol. 15-5 (You Kid)

BISQUE

All bisque dolls became very popular after 1880, although they had been around many years. You could still buy all bisque dolls well into the 1940's.

All bisque dolls can be of the "frozen" type, jointed at shoulders only, jointed at the shoulders and hips. Relatively few are also jointed at the necks (swivel heads) as well as shoulders and hips. Because so few are jointed at the neck, it is assumed that they must be French, although this may not be true!

All bisque dolls can be found with many types of joints... pegged, pinned, elastic strung. They also come dressed with molded on clothes, cloth clothes or no clothes. They can have open or closed mouths. They can have flat feet, be in high heeled shoes or have boots. They can have painted on hose or be barefooted. They can be boys, girls, no gender, comic, serious. They run the entire rainbow of hues of expression, quality of workmanship and nationality. Some are French, some German and many are Japanese. Entire collections and studies have been devoted to these "little ones" and more often than not, we still don't know who made them!

All Bisque--6½" All bisque with swivel neck. Glass eyes. Deeper red line between lips. Painted on stockings with maroon line around top. 4 strap black painted on boots. $150.00. (Courtesy Kimport Dolls)

All Bisque--4½" Sleep eyes. Jointed shoulders, hips and neck. Open mouth with molded teeth. Painted on long black hose with one strap shoes. $135.00. (Minter Collection)

9

All Bisque--4" Twins. Jointed shoulders, hips and necks. Open/closed mouths. Glass eyes. Marks: 620.0. $135.00 each. (Gunnel Collection)

All Bisque--6" All bisque. Jointed shoulders and hips. Red lines over painted eyes. Flat feet painted blue. Socks with green band. Original except bonnet. Closed mouth. Marks: 8095/2B, on head. 2B, inside of legs. 11, inside arms. $45.00. (Author)

All Bisque--4½" All bisque. Jointed shoulders and hips. $55.00. (Walters Collection)

All Bisque--4½" All bisque. Gray sleep eyes. Jointed shoulders and hips. Marks: 829/10/Germany. $65.00. (Clasby Collection)

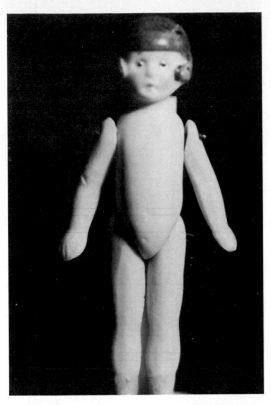

All Bisque--3" All bisque. Pin jointed shoulders and hips. Molded on skull cap. Molded on shoes/socks. Marks: 7½, on back also on inside of arms. Germany on inside of both legs. $25.00. (Gunnel Collection)

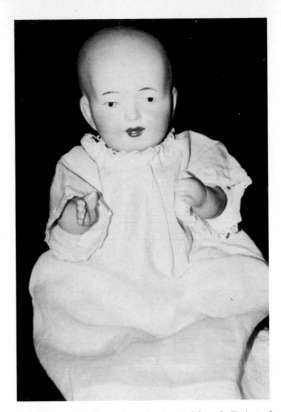

All Bisque--6" One piece body and head. Painted eyes. Marks: P2/1 ⚜ /Made in Germany. Made by Limbach Porzellan. $65.00. (Minter Collection)

All Bisque--4½" Sleep eyes. Closed mouth. Jointed shoulders, hips and neck. Molded on shoes and socks. $65.00. (Minter Collection)

All Bisque--7" All bisque with swivel head. Painted blue eyes. Open/closed mouth. Painted black heeled boots/white socks with blue bands, over the knees. Made by J. Verlingue and dressed by Otto Krause. Ca. 1915. Marks: J ⚓ V/France/Petite Francaise. $125.00. (Maish Collection)

11

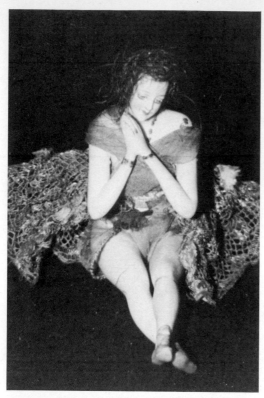

All Bisque--2¼" Seated French Ballerina. $95.00. (Courtesy Kimport Dolls)

All Bisque--6½" Bathing Beauty. Solid dome head with upper and lower lashes. Red line eyes. nostrils. Brown glued on mohair wig. Tiny perfect ears. Not a single mold seam mark. Marks: 405. $85.00. (Maish Collection)

All Bisque--3½" Bathing Beauty. Very delicate pink bisque. Black painted hair and stockings. "Snow" cap and suit. Marks: Germany & a #. $55.00. (Maish Collection)

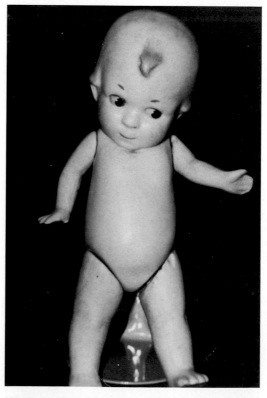

All Bisque--5" All bisque with slightly turned head. Marks: Germany/10950. $75.00. (Courtesy Kimport Dolls)

All Bisque--3½" All bisque. Jointed at arms only. Painted eyes. Marks: 8093/2/0J. $45. (Clasby Collection)

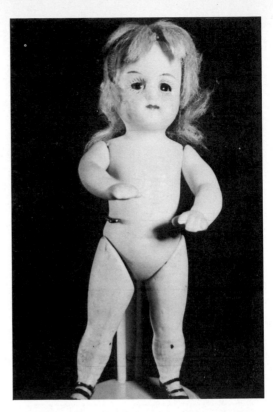

All Bisque--5" All bisque with open crown. Glass eyes. Jointed hips and shoulders. Molded on shoes/socks. Marks: 2/0/Germany/3547. $65.00. (Gunnel Collection)

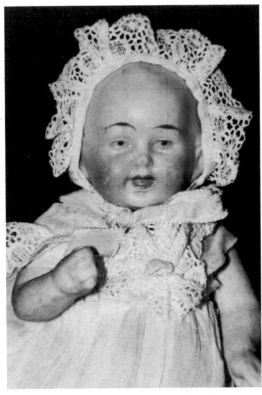

All Bisque--6" All bisque baby. Painted blue eyes. Open/closed mouth. Jointed hips and shoulders. Marks: 945/Germany. $100.00. (Courtesy Kimport Dolls)

All Bisque--3" All bisque baby. Crossed molded together legs. Molded bottle in hand. Jointed shoulders only. Marks: 747/Germany/8½B. $85.00. (Clasby Collection)

13

All Bisque--5½" "Dutch Girl and 3½" Dutch Boy." Marks: Boy: 840. Girl. $17.50. Boy $12.50. (Maish Collection)

All Bisque--6½" All bisque. Jointed at shoulders only. Marks: 665/15/Germany. $35.00. (Courtesy Kimport Dolls)

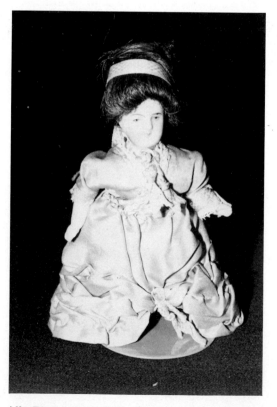

All Bisque--6" All bisque. Jointed shoulders only. Marks: 665D/Germany/15. $32.50. (Gunnel Collection)

All Bisque--3½" All bisque. Painted eyes. Jointed shoulders and hips. Closed mouth. Original clothes and wig. Marks: 600/5/0. $65.00. (Clasby Collection)

All Bisque--3½" Called "Amilia" Molded on caps/goggles. Painted eyes. Molded on high heel shoes. Both are original. Marks: 415/8. $115.00 each. (Clasby Collection)

All Bisque--4½" All bisque with pin jointed arms and legs. Marks: 170/2. $65.00. (Gunnel Collection)

All Bisque--4¾" All bisque. Closed mouth. Sleep eyes to side. Molded on brown shoes/white socks with blue bands. Marks: Germany/161-11. $60.00. (Gunnel Collection)

All Bisque--4½" All bisque. Sleep eyes. Closed mouth. Molded on hose and black Mary Janes. Jointed shoulders and hips. Marks: 150. Kestner seal on chest. $70.00. (Clasby Collection)

15

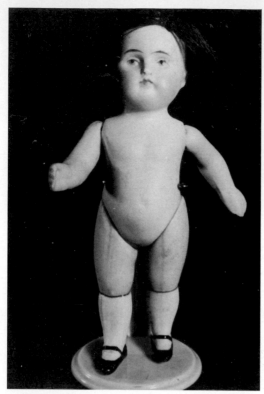

All Bisque--4½" All bisque with painted blue eyes. Painted on shoes and socks. Open crown. Marks: 150/4/0. $50.00. (Gunnel Collection)

All Bisque--5" All bisque with glass eyes. Jointed shoulders and hips. Marks: 150/4½/0. $70.00. (Gunnel Collection)

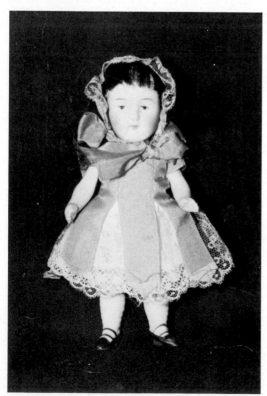

All Bisque--4" Excellent quality bisque. Jointed shoulders and hips. Open/closed mouth. Open crown. Original clothes. 2 strap brown shoes/ black line around soles with black ball over toes. Soles same color as shoes. Marks: 130, on head. $85.00. (Clasby Collection)

All Bisque--Close-up of 130, 4" all bisque.

All Bisque--4½" Jointed shoulders and hips. Painted features. Open crown. Original straw color mohair wig. Marks: 79/0 4/4, on head. $40.00. (Maish Collection)

All Bisque--2" Bisque Bather, in porcelain tub. Marks: Germany, on head. 1930. $15.00. (Maish Collection)

All Bisque--2½" All bisque. Brown sleep eyes. Jointed at shoulders only. Marks: Germany, on back. $50.00. (Clasby Collection)

All Bisque--3¼" Doll House Dolls. All painted bisque with molded hair. Jointed shoulders and hips. Marks: Germany, on back. The Collies are bone china miniatures, recently made. $20.00 each. (Maish Collection)

17

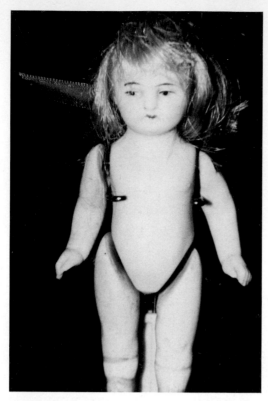

All Bisque--5" All bisque. Jointed shoulders and hips. Marks: Germany, on back. $45.00. (Walters Collection)

All Bisque--5" All bisque googly with blue inset glass eyes. Jointed shoulders only. Marks: Germany, on back. $60.00. (Gunnel Collection)

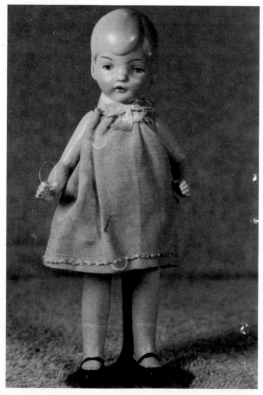

All Bisque--5¼" Doll House Doll. Painted bisque. Bent arms and extremely long legs. Marks: Germany. $20.00. (Maish Collection)

All Bisque--The Saturday Night Bath. The 2½" bisque bather in china tub is removable. 2 piece set: $15.00. The china furniture has both English and Japanese numbers and symbols. Ca. 1925-1930. The china Mammy is Aunt Jemina. (Maish Collection)

18

All Bisque--3" "Joe Cobb of Our Gang." Painted bisque. Marks: Joe Cobb, on back. $20.00. (Maish Collection)

All Bisque--4" "Prize Baby" Seal on chest. Jointed shoulders and hips. Glass eyes. Made by Armand Marseille for the George Borgfeldt Co. in 1912. $115.00. (Minter Collection)

All Bisque--4" "Snow White and 3" Dwarfs" All painted bisque. Marks: Walt Disney, on each piece. $15.00. (Maish Collection)

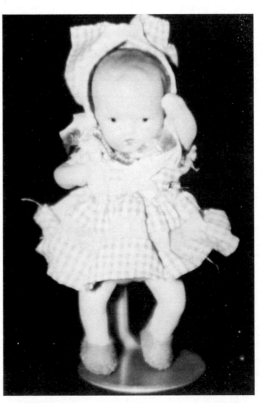

All Bisque--4½" All painted bisque with open mouth. Original. Marks: ◇ /G. $12.00. (Gunnel Collection)

19

All Bisque--2" Frozen type babies. Silver heads. Dressed in lace butterfly wings. $4.00 each. (Maish Collection)

All Bisque--2" "Teenie Weenies" Molded and painted. 1930. $6.00-$7.00 each. (Maish Collection)

All Bisque--3" Stone bisque. Wired arms. 1930. $6.00. (Maish Collection)

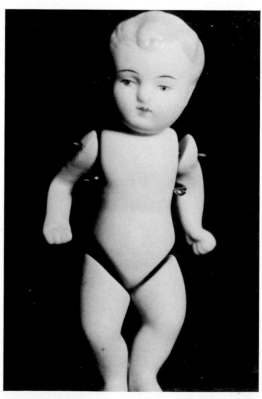

All Bisque--3½" All bisque with jointed shoulders and hips. Bent baby legs. $75.00. (Gunnel Collection)

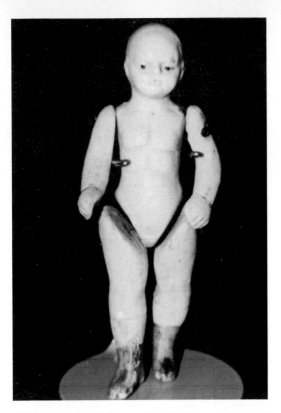

All Bisque--3½" Very old all bisque with bald head. Molded rib cage. Jointed at shoulders and hips. $50.00. (Courtesy Kimport Dolls)

All Bisque--3½" Bride and 4¼" Groom. The groom has molded, painted clothing. Gold rimmed glasses and tipped cane. Gray spats. Character dolls are slightly higher than others. $15.00. (Maish Collection)

All Bisque--3½" Boy. Molded clothes. 1935. $10.00. (Maish Collection)

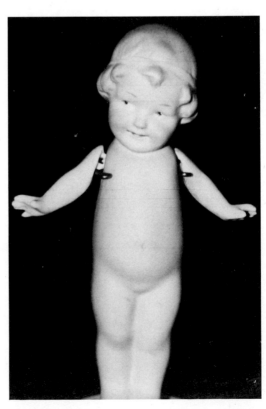

All Bisque--4" All bisque. $75.00. (Walters Collection)

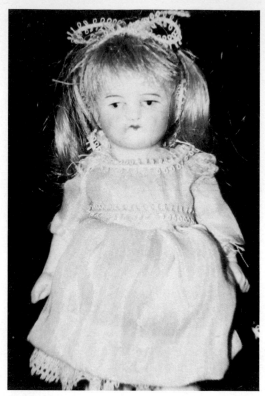

All Bisque--4½" All bisque. $45.00. (Walters Collection)

All Bisque--4½" with tie on arms. Ca. 1920. $12.00. (Maish Collection)

All Bisque--5" All bisque. Top of head cut out. Painted eyes. Molded on belt and dagger. Jointed at shoulders only. $40.00. (Courtesy Kimport Dolls)

All Bisque--5" Dutch girl and boy with pails. These were one of the most popular adornments of the 1920 to 1930 knick-knack shelves. Many different sizes and mold types. Current prices range from $6.00-$15.00 apiece. (Maish Collection)

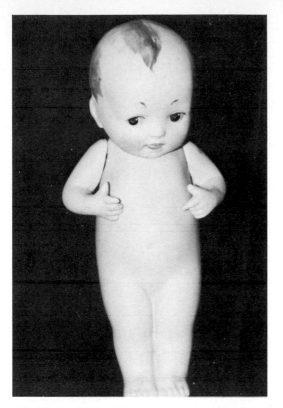

All Bisque--5½" All bisque with open/closed mouth and 2 painted upper teeth. Marks: none. $40.00. (Courtesy Kimport Dolls)

All Bisque--5½" Stone bisque with molded hair and painted features. 1930. $18.00. (Maish Collection)

All Bisque--5½" Tie on arms. Molded hairband-type. 1917-1930. $16.00. (Maish Collection)

All Bisque--6½" All bisque with jointed shoulders and hips. Painted blue eyes. Molded on shoes and socks. Marks: none. $35.00. (Gunnel Collection)

23

All Bisque--6½" Stone bisque with tinted features. Long sideburns. Molded ribbon. Glued on cloth playsuit. Only jointed at shoulders. 1930. $15.00. (Maish Collection)

All Bisque--7" All bisque. Jointed shoulders and hips. Painted blue eyes. Painted blue shoes/ socks with green band. Marks: Germany. $65.00. (Gunnel Collection)

All Bisque--7" All bisque jointed at shoulders only. $12.50. (Courtesy Kimport Dolls)

All Bisque--7" Frozen type with molded on clothes and puppy. "Coal scuttle" hat dates her from 1920's. $20-$22.00. (Maish Collection)

All Bisque--8" All Bisque. Molded on clothes. Jointed at shoulders only. $115.00. (Gunnel Collection)

All Bisque--2½" Unjointed. Marks: Japan. $6.00. (Gunnel Collection)

All Bisque--3" Molded on clothes. Marks: Made in/Japan, on back. $10.00. (Penner Collection)

All Bisque--3" girl and 2¾" boy. All bisque. Marks: Made in/Japan. Girl $7.50. Boy $10.00. (Courtesy Kimport Dolls)

25

All Bisque--3" Unjointed. Marks: Made in/ Japan. $6.00. (Gunnel Collection)

All Bisque--3½" Painted children. Marks: Japan. 1935. $12.50 each. (Maish Collection)

All Bisque--3½" Painted bisque children. Marks: Japan. 1935. $15.00 each. (Maish Collection)

All Bisque--3½" Painted bisque children. Marks: Japan. 1935. $10.00 each. (Maish Collection)

22" "Mein Liebling" (My Darling) Marks: K ✡ R/Simon Halbig/117a

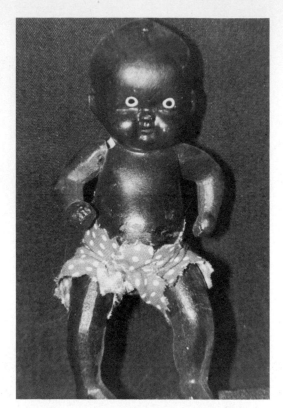

All Bisque--3½" All bisque. Original. Marks: Japan. $25.00 each. (Courtesy Kimport Dolls)

All Bisque--4" Painted bisque. Jointed shoulders and hips. Marks: Japan, on back. These dolls are being reproduced and sold around the New Orleans area. $6.00. (Courtesy Penner Collection)

All Bisque--4" Holes in head hold 3 tiny pigtails. Jointed shoulders and hips. Marks: Japan. $6.00-$8.00. (Maish Collection)

All Bisque--4" Painted features. Open mouth. Jointed shoulders and hips. Marks: Made in/Japan, on back. $6.00-$8.00. (Maish Collection)

All Bisque--4" Character toddler. Tinted features. Molded green hair ribbon. Glued on dress. Marks: Japan and maker's symbol on back. $15.00. (Maish Collection)

All Bisque--4" All painted brown bisque. Jointed shoulders and hips. Marks: Japan. $22.50. (Holzley Collection)

All Bisque--4" All bisque with pin wired arms and legs. Marks: Made In/Japan/C-38. $22.50. (Gunnel Collection)

All Bisque--4½" All bisque with molded hair bow. Jointed hips and shoulders. Marks: Nippon. $22.00. (Clasby Collection)

29

22" Simon Halbig. Marks: Wimpern (eyelashes) Seal in Red. Low on shoulderplate; SH 1080-8

21" Composition body. Open mouth. Marks: Bru Jne R-8

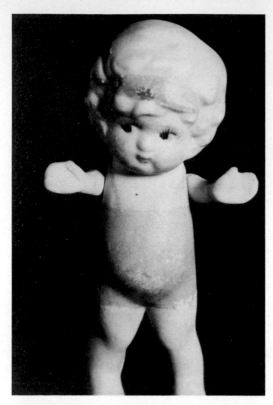

All Bisque--4½" All bisque. Jointed at shoulders only. Marks: Made In/Japan. $15.00. (Gunnel Collection)

All Bisque--5" All bisque. Jointed shoulders only. Marks: Made In/Japan. $15.00 each. (Clasby Collection)

All Bisque--5" Painted bisque with molded blonde hair with bow. Jointed shoulders only. Marks: Japan, on back and clothes. $6.00. (Penner Collection)

All Bisque--5" Jointed shoulders only. Marks: Made in Japan. $15.00. (Gunnel Collection)

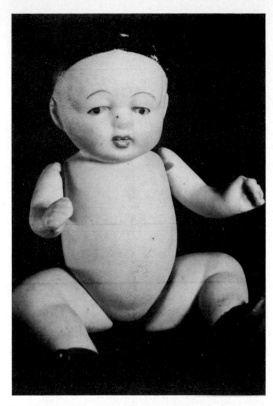

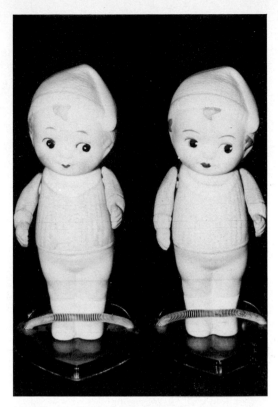

All Bisque--5" All bisque with open/closed mouth and 2 painted teeth. Black painted on skull cap. Feet are painted black. Jointed shoulders and hips. Marks: Nippon. $17.50. (Gunnel Collection)

All Bisque--5½" Jointed at shoulders only. Molded on clothes. Marks: Made In/Japan. $15.00 each. (Clasby Collection)

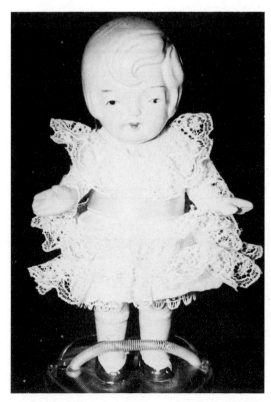

All Bisque--5½" Painted over bisque. Molded blonde hair. Marks: ⃝ Made In Japan. $20.00. (Clasby Collection)

All Bisque--5½" Jointed shoulders and hips. Molded blonde hair. Painted blue eyes. Molded and painted bow in hair. Marks: Nippon, on back. $20.00. (Minter Collection)

33

20" Flirty and sleep eyes. Marks: 1249/Halbig/Germany/Santa/S&H

All Bisque--5½" Molded hairband type. Jointed shoulders only. Stamped Japan on sole. $15.00. (Maish Collection)

All Bisque--5½" Original painted red suit. Pointed index finger. Impressed Japan on back. 5½" Same type with original green suit and slightly different posture. Impressed Japan on back. 1920-1930. $12.00 each. (Maish Collection)

All Bisque--5½" Molded Dutch girl carrying basket of flowers. Marks: Fan-Japan. $15.00. (Maish Collection)

All Bisque--5½" All bisque. Jointed shoulders only. Marks: Nippon. $10.00. (Gunnel Collection)

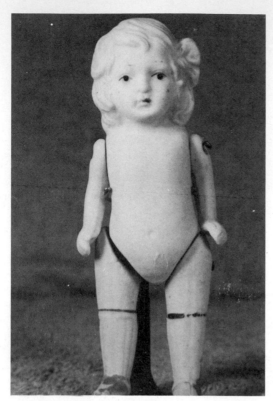

All Bisque--6" All bisque. Marks: Made In Japan/200. $13.50. (Courtesy Kimport Dolls)

All Bisque--6" Jointed shoulders and hips. Painted features, socks and red Mary Janes. Molded red hair ribbon. Original panties and dress sewn on. Marks: Made In/Japan S-1225. $18.00-$20.00. (Maish Collection)

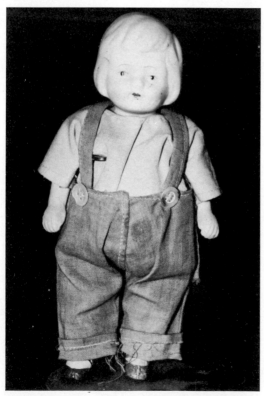

All Bisque--6½" All bisque. Painted eyes. Jointed shoulders and hips. Marks: Nippon. $22.00. (Clasby Collection)

All Bisque--6½" Nice quality with carefully painted features. Marks: Japn. 1920-1930. $20.00. (Maish Collection)

All Bisque--6½" "Jackie Coogan." Painted bisque. Marks: Japan and symbol. $25.00. (Maish Collection)

All Bisque--7" China luster glaze. This is a scarce doll as it is unusual to find a "Betty Boop" type with molded clothes and especially with pink luster. Marks: Japan on heel. $45.00. (Maish Collection)

All Bisque--7" All bisque jointed at shoulders only. Marks: Made/In/Japan. $15.00. (Courtesy Kimport Dolls)

All Bisque--7½" All bisque. Jointed only at the shoulders. Marks: Made In/Japan. $15.00. (Courtesy Kimport Dolls)

37

All Bisque--8" Nicer quality bisque. Deeply molded hair. Delicately tinted features. Tied on arms. Marks: Japan and symbol. ca. 1915. $22.00. (Maish Collection)

All Bisque--8" All bisque with molded blonde hair. Marks: Made in/Japan. $17.00. (Courtesy Kimport Dolls)

All Bisque--9" All bisque with jointed shoulders and hips. Open/closed mouth. Molded blonde hair. Marks: Ⓑ Japan. $12.50. (Courtesy Kimport Dolls)

ALT, BECK & GOTTSCHALCK

Alt, Beck & Gottschalck--They started a porcelain factory in 1854 (Porzellanfabrik Von Alt)
and made both the Bye-lo and Bonnie Babe for
George Borgfeldt Co. Many of their babies have
pierced nostrils.

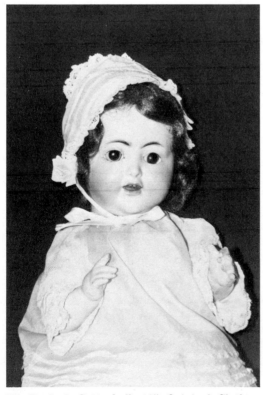

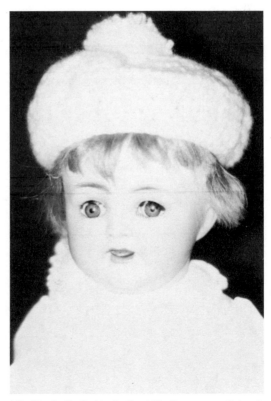

Alt, Beck & Gottschalk--13" Original Clothes.
Open mouth/2 teeth. Marks: A.B.G./1361/48/
Made in Germany/6. 13"-B-C, 19"-D-E. (Minter
Collection)

Alt, Beck & Gottschalk--14" Open mouth/mol-
ded tongue. Marks: ABG/1367/35-36. ca. 1930.
14"-B-C, 20"-D-E. (Gunnel Collection)

39

Amberg

American
Dolls
Mfg. Co.

Louis Amberg began business in 1878 and continued into the late 1930's. His major place of operations was in both New York City and Cincinnati, Ohio. He was a major doll importer and ran several different businesses, including the manufacture of dolls and toys. After dissolving his partnership with Ira Hahn in 1911, he became sole operator of the business.

In 1905 Louis Amberg copyrighted his own work, as artist, of the first known American copyright doll's head. This doll was called "Lucky Bill" and in 1910 he started using the tradename "Baby Beautiful Dolls." Many of these dolls were designed by Louis Amberg and some by artists such as Grace G. Wiederseim (Drayton) and Juno Juszko and he also advertised "unbreakable" dolls of composition.

In 1914, Jeno Juszko designed "New Born Babe." The "Bye Lo" baby copyrighted in 1923 was very much like "New Born Babe." The last doll designed by Juszko for Amberg was in 1915, the "OO-Guk-Luk," a portrait of a Zulu.

During 1915, Louis Amberg died and his son Joshua Amberg became head of the firm. This same year Amberg appeared with "Ambisc," all composition dolls. In 1917 Amberg had Reinhold Beck design "Fine Baby" and in 1918, "Amkid" shoulder head dolls were put onto the market. During 1919 and 1920 Amberg used some bisque heads made by Fulpher Pottery Co. and these were labeled "The World Standard."

In 1921 the Amberg factory burned and dolls were imported from abroad, and by 1924, when Borgfeldt advertised the Bye-lo, Amberg re-issued his "New Born Babe" with heads made by Armand Marseille. There was an infringement fight but Amberg lost because they had not complied with Section 18 of the Copyright Act requiring the full name and not just initials of the copyright owner on the doll. Some of the New Born Babe heads are marked with R.A. (Recknagel of Alexandrinethal), Hermann Steiner and Armand Marseille.

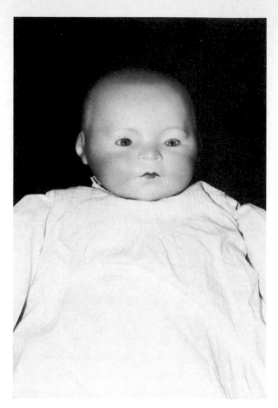

Louis Amberg & Sons--20" head. Cir. Cloth body. Marks: L. Amberg & Sons/Germany/88678. 20"--E-F. (Courtesy Kimport Dolls)

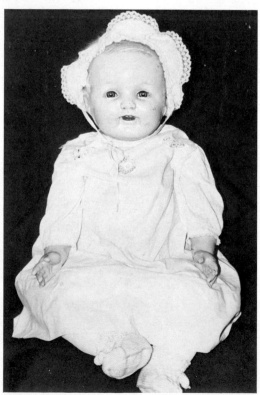

Amberg--24" "Vanta Baby" Cloth and composition. Lightly molded red hair. Sleep, partly closed, smiling tin blue eyes. Open/closed mouth with two painted upper teeth. Large legs. Molded to sit byself. Doll is spring strung. Advertising doll for Vanta baby garments. Marks: Vanta Baby/Amberg. 1927. $65.00.

A.D. Co.--24" Composition one piece shoulderplate. Painted features with decal eyes. Cloth body with composition arms and legs. Marks: A.D. Co., on head. Made by American Doll Mfg. Co. 24"-$65.00. (Minter Collection)

40

ARMAND MARSEILLE

Armand Marseille began in 1865 in Koppelsdorf, Thur and within a short time this firm had grown to have over 200 people employed. Son, Armand, now known as Hermann Marseille married the sister of Ernst Heubach of Koppelsdorf, a maker of doll heads, and it was in 1891 that Marseille began making doll heads in his own factory.

The Armand Marseilles produced dolls in mass, with thousands of heads firing in the kilns on any given day. The quality of some A.M. heads did not always equal that of other German manufacturers, such as Kestner or Simon Halbig because of the gigantic output of the artists, who paint each personality onto each head. The A.M. output was, at one time, larger than any other doll company and also included the greatest variety of bisque doll heads...with a great many excellent quality dolls finding their way through the hectic day of mass production competition and even wars. A.M. dolls must be judged on an individual basis of quality, not jut because they are "A.M.S."

A&M initials were used at a porcelain factory in Aich near Karsbad, Bohemia, by M.J. Moehling (1870-1936) and should not be confused with Armand Marseille.

There was also a French Marseille. Francois Emile Marseille, from Maisons, Alfort, France in 1888. His doll marks were an anchor. ⚓ There was no relation between these Marseilles.

Dolls marked "370" only means it is a shoulder plate. Those marked "390" only means they are socket heads.

For additional information concerning the Armand Marseille dolls, with detailed information, please refer to "Armand Marseille Dolls" by this author.

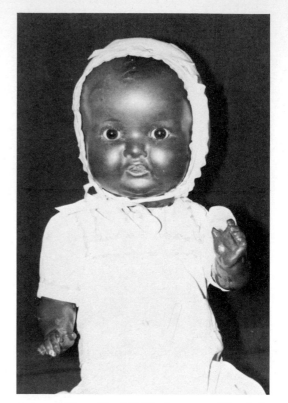

Armand Marseille--12" head Cir. "Baby Bobby." Solid dome with brush stroke hair. Brown sleep eyes. Open mouth/2 lower teeth. Marks: A.M/ 328. Ca. 1912. Some are also marked with a "G.B." and these were made for George Borfeldt in 1922. 14"--B-C, 20"--F-G. (Courtesy Ralph's Antique Dolls)

Armand Marseille--20" Black composition baby made after 1910. Marks: AM/Germany/518-6/K. 12"--B-C, 26"--H-I. (Courtesy Kimport Dolls)

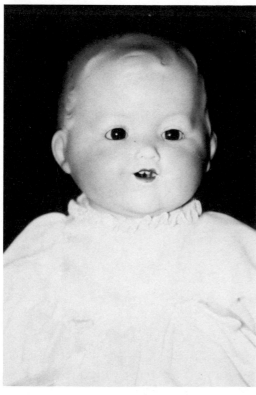

Armand Marseille--18" "Baby Love." Molded hair. Brown sleep eyes. Dimples. Cloth body with composition arms. Marks: A.M./Germany/ 352. Made for Cuno and Otto Dressel in 1915. 12"--C-D, 20"--F-G. (Minter Collection)

Armand Marseille--13" Open mouth/2 lower teeth. Marks: G327B/A2M/DRGM 259. Made in 1912 for George Borgfeldt & Co. 12"--A-C, 20"-- C-D. (Gunnel Collection)

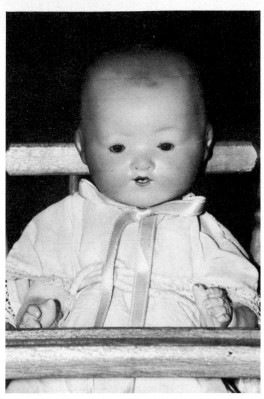

Armand Marseille--16" "Dream Baby" Open mouth version. Marks: A.M./Germany/351/2½K. Made for the Arranbee Doll Co. 1924. 7"--A-C, 20"--D-E. (Minter Collection)

Armand Marseille--12" Pápier maché "Dream Baby." Molded curly hair. Blue sleep eyes. Open mouth/2 lower teeth. 1924. Marks: U/A.M./Germany/351 2/0k. 7"--A, 20"--C-D. (Clasby Collection)

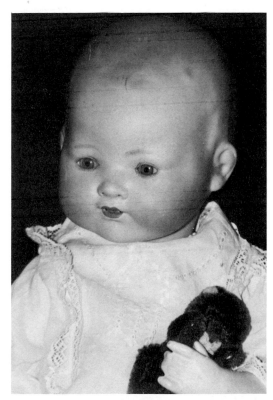

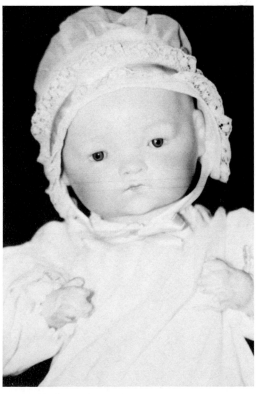

Armand Marseille--16" "My Dream Baby" made for Arranbee Doll Co. Marks: A.M./Germany/351. 14K. 1924. 7"--A-C, 20"--D-E. (Walters Collection)

Armand Marseille--15" "Dream Baby" Marks: Germany/341/4k/AM. Made for the Arranbee Doll Co. 1924. 7"--A-C, 20"--D-E. (Minter Collection)

43

Armand Marseille--15" "Dream Baby" Marks:
A.M./Germany/341/3. 7"--A-C, 20"--D-E. (Minter Collection)

Armand Marseille--20" Socket head. Molded
eyebrows. Open mouth. Marks: Made In
Germany/A4M. 12"--A-B, 26"--C-D. (Walters
Collection)

Armand Marseille--13" Shoulder plate. Marks:
∽ /AM8/0X. 12"--A-B, 26"--B-C. (Gunnel
Collection)

Armand Marseille--19½" Shoulder plate. Kid
body. Open mouth. Marks: A.M.95 5 Dep. 14"--
B-C, 24"--C-D. (Walters Collection)

44

Armand Marseille--11½" Papier mache body and limbs. Socket head. Marks: Made In Germany/Armand Marseille/D.R.G.M.246/1/A6/ 0M. 10"--A-B, 20"--B-C. (Walters Collection)

Armand Marseille--11" Googly girl. Marks: Germany/323/A3/0M. 7½"--F-J, 11"--J-L. (Minter Collection)

Armand Marseille--12" Googly boy. Marks: Germany/323/A4/0M. 7½"--F-J, 11"--J-L. (Minter Collection)

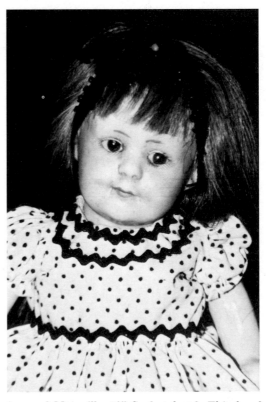

Armand Marseille--10" Socket head. This head was buried for many years and shows the effect of the damage to the bisque. Marks: Germany/ 550/A4/0M/DRGM. 10"--D-E, 18"--F-H. (Author)

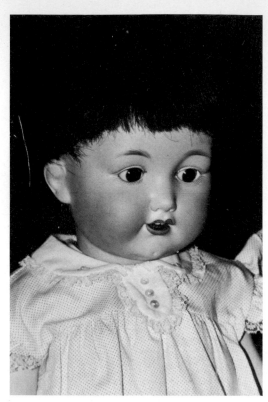

Armand Marseille--16" Made for Otto Gans. Ca. 1915. Marks: Otto Gans/Germany/975/A11M. 14"--A-C, 25"--C-E. (Walters Collection)

Armand Marseille--18" Shoulder plate. Marks: A.M./Germany/Sch 1901 1. Made for Peter Scherf, Sonneberg, Thur. 16"--B-C, 24"--C-D. (Gunnel Collection)

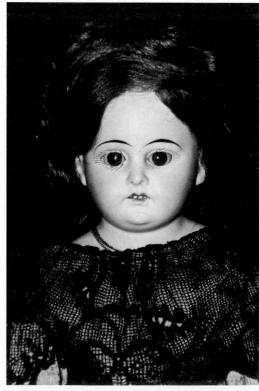

46

Armand Marseille--17" Lady doll. Shoulder plate. Kid body. Open mouth. Marks: 1894/A.M. 2/0 Dep. 11½"--A-B, 26"--C-D. (Walters Collection)

Armand Marseille--14½" Socket head. Composition body. Marks: 1894/A.M.1 Dep./Made In Germany. Childhood doll of Kathy Walters. 11½"--A-B, 26"--C-D. (Walters Collection)

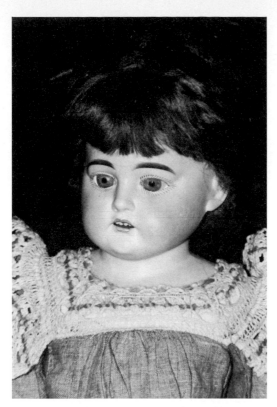

Armand Marseille--20½" "Bright Eyes"
Shoulder plate. Kid body. Open mouth. Marks:
1897/AM5Dep. Made for Cissna Co. in 1898.
12"--A-B, 26"--C-D. (Walters Collection)

Armand Marseille--18" Turned shoulder plate.
Marks: 2015/0½. One of the "Queen Louise"
series. Ca. 1895. 18"--C-D. (Gunnel Collection)

Armand Marseille--18" Shoulder plate. Open
mouth. Marks: 3700/AM2/0/Dep. Ca. 1897. 14"--
A-B, 24"--C-D. (Gunnel Collection)

Armand Marseille--17" "Alma" Shoulder plate.
Marks: Alma/5/0A.M. 12"--A-B, 26"--C-D.
(Penner Collection)

47

Armand Marseille--23" Shoulder plate. Marks:
Alma/2. Ca. 1897. 12"--A-B, 26"--C-D. (Gunnel
Collection)

Armand Marseille--17" Shoulder plate. Marks:
Baby Betty, in circle/DRGM. 12"--A-B, 26"--D-E.
(Penner Collection)

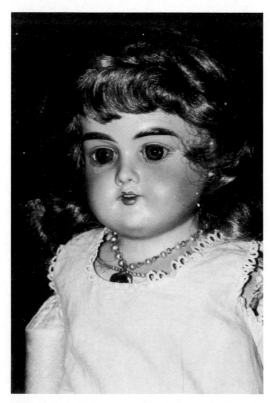

Armand Marseille--20" Shoulder plate. Open
mouth. Marks: AM Beauty/Made In Germany.
12"--A-B, 26"--D-E. (Walters Collection)

Armand Marseille--21" Shoulder plate. Marks:
Lilly/5/0. Ca. 1898. 12"--A-B, 26"--C-D. (Gunnel
Collection)

Armand Marseille--12" Shoulder plate. Kidalene body. Open mouth. Marks: Floradora/Armand Marseille/A7/0M/Made In Germany. 14"--A-B. (Walters Collection)

Armand Marseille--17" Socket head. Marks: Floradora/A1M. 17"--B-C. (Penner Collection)

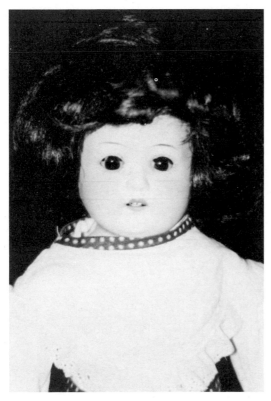

Armand Marseille--17" Turned shoulder plate. Marks: Floradora/Germany. 17"--B-C. (Gunnel Collection)

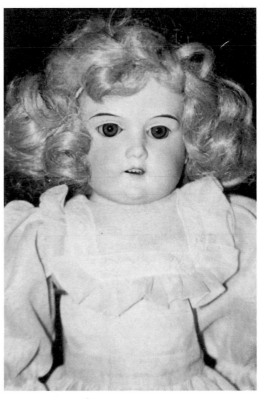

Armand Marseille--18" Shoulder plate. Marks: Floradora/AOM. 18"--B-C. (Gunnel Collection)

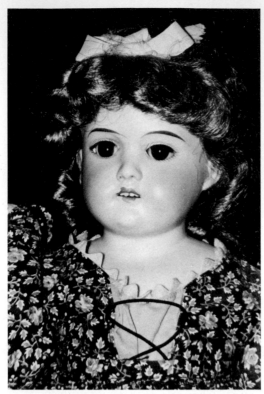

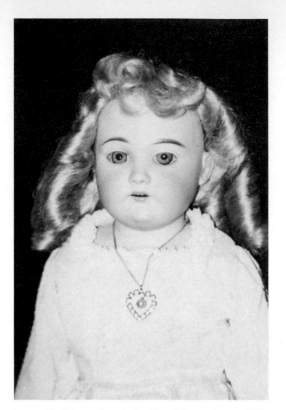

Armand Marseille--20" Shoulder plate. Open mouth. Kid body. Marks: Floradora/A.O.M./Made In Germany. 20"--B-C. (Walters Collection)

Armand Marseille--21" Shoulder plate. Kid. Deeply incised "X" on front crown. Marks: Floradora/A2½M/Made In Germany. 21"--B-C. (Gunnel Collection)

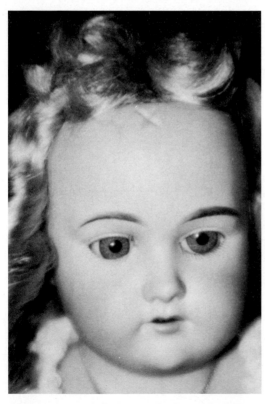

Armand Marseille--Shows deeply incised X on 21" Floradora.

Armand Marseille--26" Shoulder plate. Marks: Floradora/A5M/Germany. 26"--C-D. (Gunnel Collection)

14" Kestner. Marks: XV, on crown. B Made in 6/Germany/169

Armand Marseille--12" Shoulder plate. Marks: Mabel/16/0. 12"--A-B, 26"--C-D. (Gunnel Collection)

Armand Marseille--17½" Shoulder plate. Kidolene body. Molded eyebrows. Open mouth. Marks: Germany/Mabel/3/0. 12"--A-B, 26"-C-D. (Walters Collection)

Armand Marseille--25" "Mabel" One piece shoulder plate. Marks: Germany/Mabel/1. 12"--A-B, 26"--C-D. (Penner Collection)

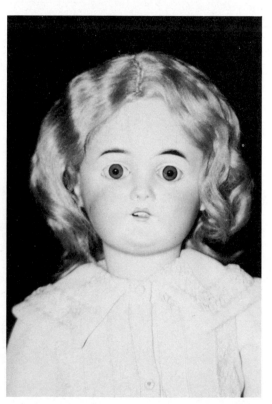

Armand Marseille--24" "Queen Louise" Socket head. Open mouth. Marks: 29/Queen Louise/100/Germany. Made for Louis Wolf & Co. in 1910. 12"--A-B, 30"--D-E. (Courtesy Ralph's Antique Dolls)

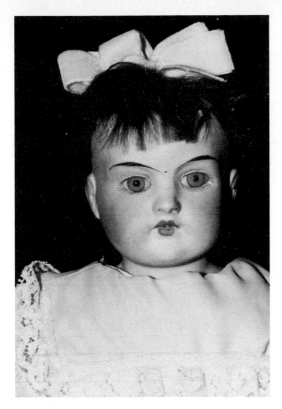

Armand Marseille--16" Shoulder plate. Kid/ muslin body. Marks: Armand Marseille/370. $50.00. 12"--A-B, 30"--C-D. (Courtesy Kimport Dolls)

Armand Marseille--17" Shoulder plate. Kid body. Open mouth. Marks: Armand Marseille/ ✕ /370/A.O.M. 12"--A-B, 30"--C-D. (Walters Collection)

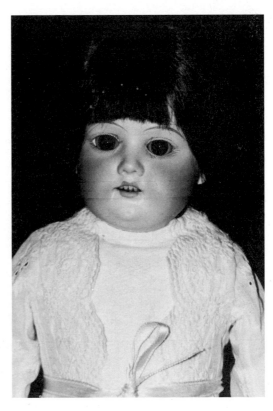

Armand Marseille--18" Shoulder plate. Open mouth. Marks: 370/AM2/0 Dep. 12"--A-B, 30-- C-D. (Gunnel Collection)

Armand Marseille--18" Shoulder plate. Open mouth. Marks: 370/AM Dep/Armand Marseille. 12"--A-B, 30"-C-D. (Walters Collection)

53

21" Marks: Eden Bébé/Paris/9/Deposé

14" Le Petit Parisien by Jules Steiner. Marks: Paris/A7-8 (X, inside head)
Body: Bébé "Le Parisien"/Medaille d'Or/Paris

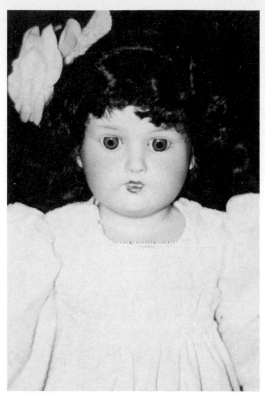

Armand Marseille--20" Shoulder plate. Open mouth. Marks: 370/AM1 Dep/Armand Marseille/Made In Germany. 12"--A-B, 30"--C-D. (Gunnel Collection)

Armand Marseille--22" Shoulder plate. Open mouth. Lashes. Marks: 370/AM 2½ Dep/Armand Marseille/Germany. 12"--A-B. 30"--C-D. (Gunnel Collection)

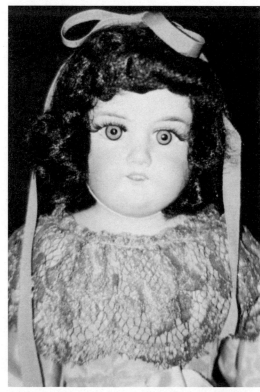

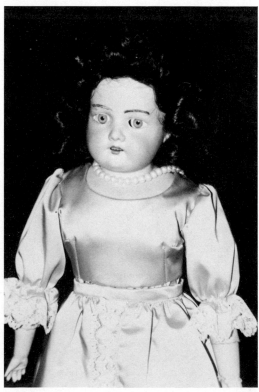

Armand Marseille--22" "Banker's Daughter" Made for Butlers Bros. in 1893. Marks: 370/A.M. 2 Dep/Armand Marseille/Germany. Eyelashes added. 12"--A-B, 30"--C-D. (Gunnel Collection)

Armand Marseille--23" Shoulder plate. Kid body. Inset hair brows. Sleep eyes. Marks: 370/ AM4 Dep/Armand Marseille/Made In Germany. 12"--A-B, 30"--C-D. (Courtesy Kimport Dolls)

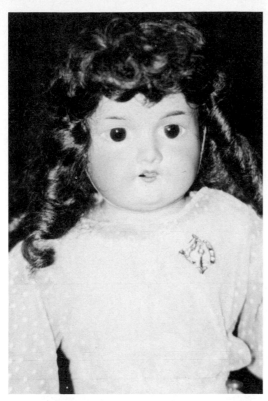

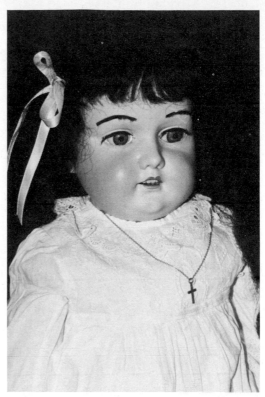

Armand Marseille--25" Shoulder plate/kid. Molded brows. Open mouth. Marks: 370/AM4 Dep/Armand Marseille. 12"--A-B, 30"--C-D. (Gunnel Collection)

Armand Marseille--27" Shoulder plate. Fur eyebrows. Open mouth. Marks: 370/A.M-10-Dep./ Made In Germany. 12"--A-B, 30"--C-D. (Walters Collection)

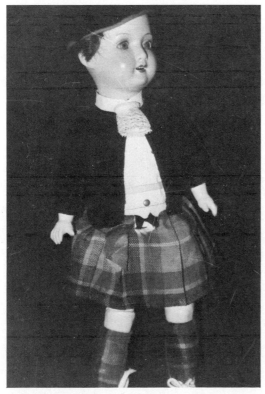

Armand Marseille--11½" Pápier maché body. Wood upper arms and legs. Composition head. Open crown. Blue glass eyes. Open mouth4 teeth. Original. Marks: Armand Marseille/Germany/390/A9/0M. 11½"--A-B.

Armand Marseille--21" Socket head. All original. Marks: A4M/390/Made In Germany. 21"--B-C. (Esler Collection)

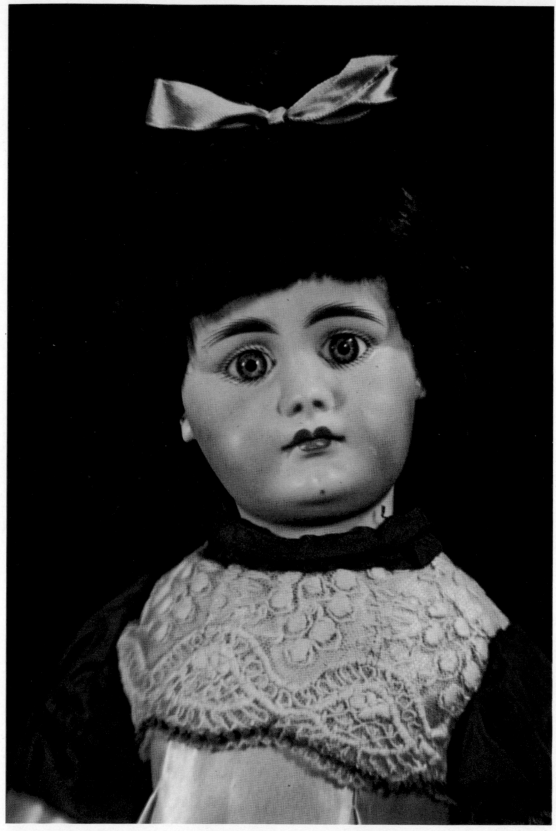

16" Simon & Halbig. Marks: SH 949

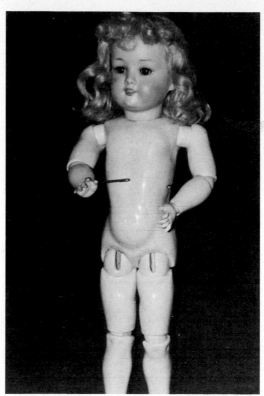

Armand Marseille--18" "Patrice" Socket head. Factory lashes. Excellent pale bisque. Marks: Armand Marseille/390n/germany/A2½M. Made for Berlinbrak in 1914. This was a special order for this one store of 9,000 dolls. The eyes lashes and short "fly a way" eyebrows distinguish this model from other 390n's. 18"--C-D. (Author)

Armand Marseille--18" "Patrice" Shows typical German composition body.

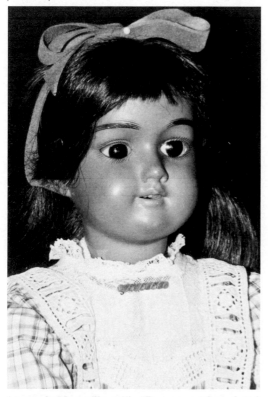

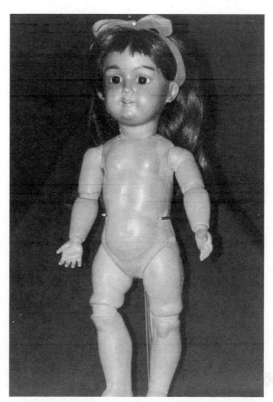

Armand Marseille--16" "Brown socket head. Black sleep eyes. Open mouth/4 teeth. Original clothes. Body incised "39." Marks: Made in Germany/Armand Marseille/390n/D.R.G.M. 246/a/A.2½M. 16"--H-J. (Author)

Armand Marseille--16" Colored body marked 39.

59

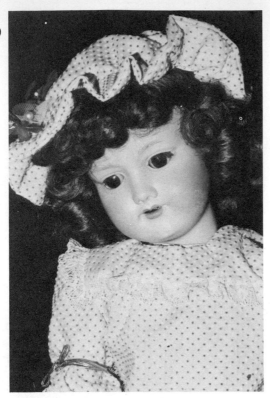

Armand Marseille--22" Socket head. Marks:
Armand Marseille/Germany/390/A5M. 22"--B-C
(Esler Collection)

Armand Marseille--23" A beautiful quality A.M.
390. 23"--C-D. (Penner Collection)

Armand Marseille--23" "My Dearie" for George
Borgfeldt 1908 to 1922. Shoulder plate. Marks:
Armand   Marseille/390n/DRGM/246/1/A.6M.
23"--D-E. (Penner Collection)

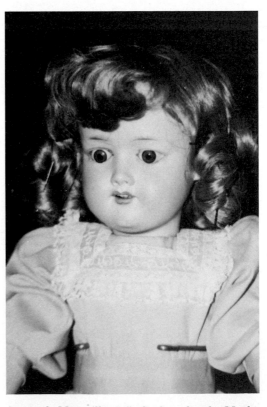

Armand Marseille--24" Socket head. Marks:
Made In Germany/Armand Marseille/390n/
A6½M. 24"--C-D. (Gunnel Collection)

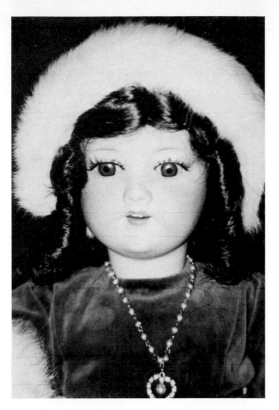

Armand Marseille--24" Socket head. Marks: Armand Marseille/Germany/390/A7½M. Eyelashes have been added. 24"--C-D. (Gunnel Collection)

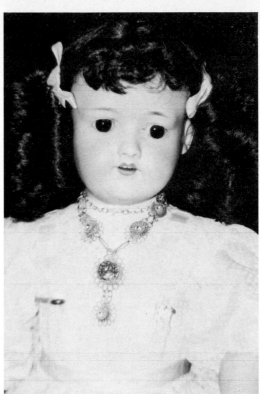

Armand Marseille--24" Socket head. Marks: Armand Marseille/390n/Germany/A6M. 24"--C-D. (Gunnel Collection)

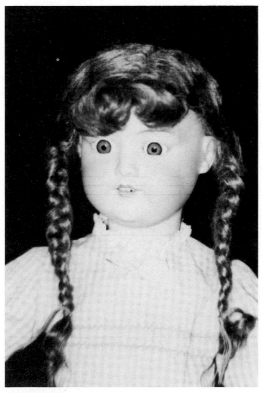

Armand Marseille--26" "My Dearie" Socket head. Made for George Borgfeldt 1908 to 1922. Marks: Made In Germany/Armand Marseille/390n/DRGM 246/7/A10M. This is the first A.M. I have ever seen with pierced ears. 26"--D-E. (Courtesy Ralph's Antique Dolls)

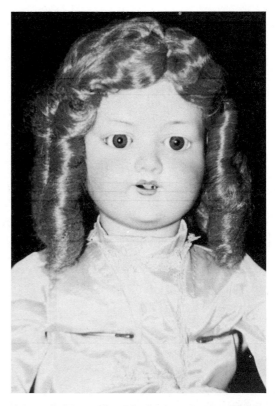

Armand Marseille--27" Socket head. Molded brows. Marks: Armand Marseille/Germany/390n/A11M. 27"--D-E. (Gunnel Collection)

Armand Marseille--7½" Socket head. All original. Open mouth. Marks: Made in Germany/12/0. 7½"--A-B. (Walters Collection)

Armand Marseille--13" Shoulder plate. Open mouth. Marks: Floradora/A.M. 14"--A-B, 26"--C-D. (Gunnel Collection)

Armand Marseille--24" Socket head on papier mache body. Marks: 29/Queen Louise/100/Germany. 12"--A-B, 30"--D-E. (Gunnel Collection)

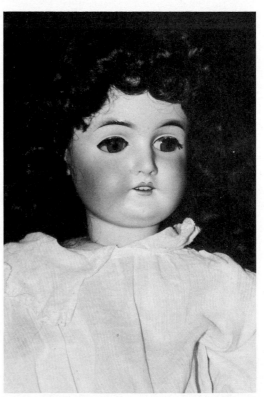

Armand Marseille--25" Socket head. Sleep eyes. Open mouth. Marks: Germany/Queen Louise/10. 12"--A-B, 30"--D-E. (Gunnel Collection)

Armand Marseille--25" Socket head. Open mouth. Marks: Made In Germany/390/A.10M. 25"--D-E. (Gunnel Collection)

Armand Marseille--27" "My Dearie" Socket head. Sleep eyes. Open Mouth. Marks: Made In Germany/Armand Marseille/390n/DRGM246/1. Made for George Borgfeldt 1908 to 1922. 27"--D-E. (Gunnel Collection)

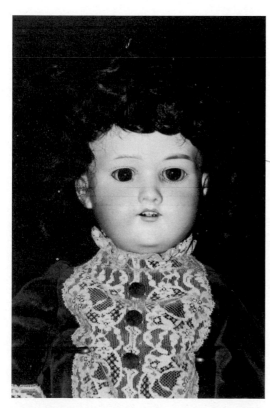

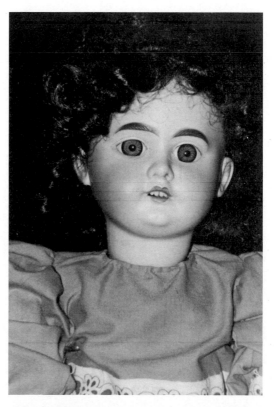

Armand Marseille--27" "My Dearie" Socket head. Spring strung. Open mouth. Marks: Made In Germany/Armand Marseille/390n/DRGM 246/1/A.M. Made for George Borgfeldt 1908 to 1922. 27"--D-E. (Gunnel Collection)

Armand Marseille--20" Socket head. Molded brows. Open mouth. Marks: 1894/A.M. Dep/ Made in Germany/5. 11½"--A-B, 26"--C-D. (Gunnel Collection)

63

Amuso--13" Composition oriental body. Socket head. Original. Marks: Amuso/1006/Germany. 13"--F-H. (Courtesy Kimport Dolls)

Max Oscar Arnold--15½" Shoulder plate. Kid body. Open mouth. Marks: 200/8. ca. 1888. 15½"--B-D. (Walters Collection)

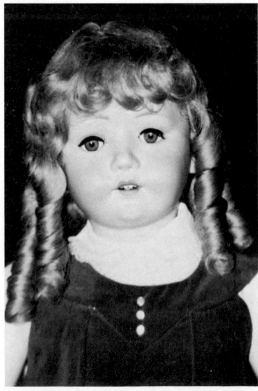

Max Oscar Arnold--33" Socket head. Open mouth. Marks: 🔯 /200/Welsch/ Made In Germany. Made in 1922 for the Welsch Co. 14"--B-D, 33"--D-F. (Courtesy Ralph's Antique Dolls)

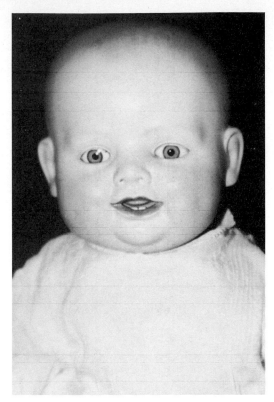

Georgene Averill--13" head cir. Marks: Copr.
By/Georgene Averill/1005/3652/4/Germany.
16"--J-K. (Courtesy Ralph's Antique Dolls)

Georgene Averill--21" "Baby Georgene" Composition head, arms and legs. Blue sleep eyes.
Glued on blonde mohair wig. All fingers curled
under. Marks: Baby Georgene, on head. 21"--
$85.00. (Author)

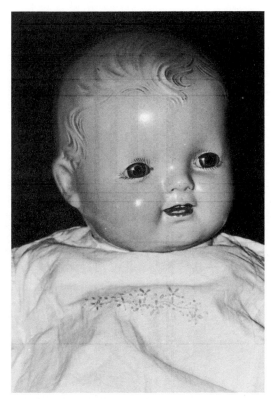

Georgene Averill--22" Composition on cloth
body. Sleep eyes. Open mouth with 2 upper and
lower teeth. Marks: Baby Hendren. 22"--$90.00.
(Walters Collection)

GEORGENE AVERILL

Wife of James Paul Averill and involved in the companies of
Madame Georgene Dolls, Paul Averill Manufacturing Company, Averill Manufacturing Company, Georgene Novelties
and artist, designer for George Borgfeldt as well.

Georgene Averill's first creation was a Dutch boy and was
included in a line of felt dressed character dolls that also
included Indians, cowboys, etc. This was in 1913 and by 1915
they were using the trade name of Madame Hendren. By
1917 Mrs. Averill had designed American babies and little
girls under the trade name of "Lyf-Lyk" and in 1918 they
patented the Madame Hendren walking "Mama Doll," one of
the first American Mama dolls...by 1925 Georgene Averill
was designing many dolls for George Borgfeldt.

"Madame Hendren" was a line of dolls manufactured by
the Averill Manufacturing Co. (U.S.) and Brophey Doll Co.
(Canada)

65

Bahr & Proschild--10" Socket head. Toddler.
Marks: 〘GP〙 /585/3/0/Made In/Germany. 10"
Toddler--E-G. (Minter Collection)

BAHR & PROSCHILD

Bahr & Proschild had a porcelain factory located in Germany, at Ohrdruf, Thur. The first records of the company were in 1871 and their first dolls were china heads, then into bisque. They also made bathing children. They generally use symbols that look like crossed swords: ⚔ , a heart 〘GP〙 or the word "Buporit" and by 1910 had also started making celluloid doll heads and parts.

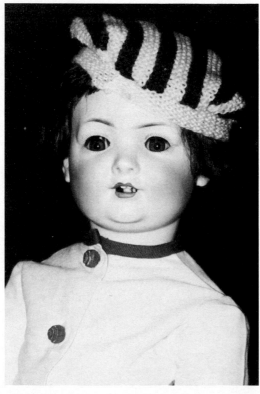

Bahr & Proschild--24" Socket head. Sleep eyes/ lashes. Open mouth/2 teeth. Made for Gimbel Brs. Marks: 〘GP〙 /585/G. 24"--G-1. (Minter Collection)

Bahr & Proschild--10" Socket head toddler. Open/closed mouth. Marks: 〘GP〙 /585/G. 10" Toddler--E-G. (Courtesy Ralph's Antique Dolls)

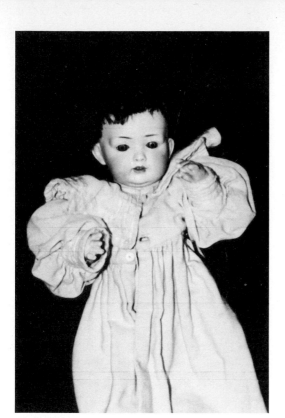

Bahr & Proschild--13" Sleep eyes. Open mouth. Marks: 604/5. 10" Baby--D-F. (Courtesy Kimport Dolls)

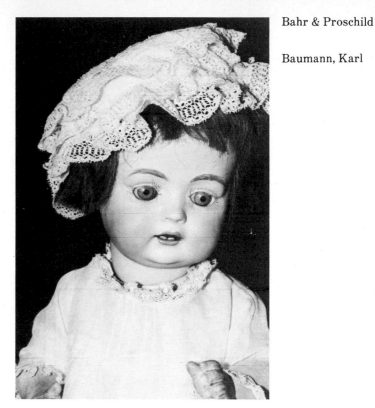

Bahr & Proschild--12" Socket head. Sleep eyes. Open mouth/2 lower teeth. ca. 1911. Marks: ※ /624/4. 12"--D-F. (Clasby Collection)

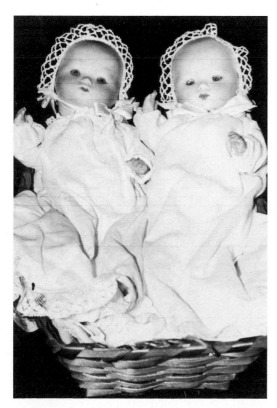

Karl Baumann--9" Bisque head with sleep eyes. Composition baby bodies. Marks: KB-7½. Factory in Uberlingen, Germany. (1920-1926). 9"--B-C each. (Minter Collection)

BELTON

(1842-46), Belton, (1847-52), Belton & Jumeau (1856-57) Widow Belton. These are the dates listed with the use of the name Belton, and it is known that Belton & Jumeau received Honorable Mention at the 1844 Paris Exposition, although this was for the clothing rather than the doll.

The Belton story begins in 1842 and ends in 1857 as F. Pottier is named successor to the Widow Belton's business. We have mystery at the beginning and the end, as we have no information as to who F. Pottier was, this added to the mystery of the middle where we have no information and it all adds up to nothing!

I am listing here any and all information I can find. It will be hazy, as all information concerning Belton is hazy.

First we will describe a "Belton" doll: Beltons have a concave area at the top of their heads, that are solid (no crown slice) with 2 holes for stringing (with wig attached to stringing material) or 3 holes with the wig attached by a plug in the third hole.

From 1842-66 when Jumeau and Belton were making dolls together, they worked in two areas, dolls with bisque (china) heads with kid bodies and bisque heads with wood turned bodies and crude arms and legs. The faces looked more like the later Jumeaus with heavy brows, open/closed full lips. The 1847-1855 period, when Jumeau was no longer with Belton, the dolls took on the "look" of the times: almost white bisque like the Jules Steiners of that same period. They have open/closed mouths but with more space between and this area is painted white. During the time that F. Pottier ran the company, from 1856 to 1857, it is hard to tell if the dolls changed or looked the same. Beltons are not marked and only have a mold size number.

When Belton & Jumeau operated together in Paris, their address was 14 rue Salle au Comte.

"Dome heads" or "bald heads" are different and most are of German origin. Of the German "Belton" types, a fine example would be the Simon & Halbig 950. It is a fair assumption that all Belton heads were actually manufactured in Germany.

Belton--11½" Excellent quality bisque. Open/closed mouth. Lathe turned, inside and out wood body. Pápier maché arms and legs with pin throughs with wood dowels. Set eyes. Ears pierced into head. Painted on orange hose with 5 strap black boots. Original clothes. Marks: 3. G-I. (Author)

Belton--Top of 11½" Belton head. The two small red marks on front of the crown are the artist's marks left from "Cleaning" her brush.

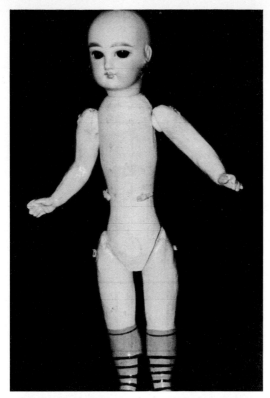

Belton--Body and limbs of 11½" Belton. Painted on shoes and hose.

Belton--21" Socket head with open/closed mouth. Ears pierced into head. Saucer crown/2 stringing holes. Marks: 14, on head. J-K. (Author)

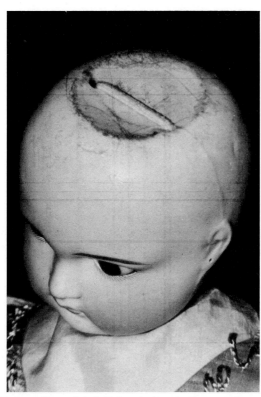

Belton--Top of 21" Belton's head. Ears pierced into head.

CHARLES M. BERGMANN

Charles M. Bergmann was a German by birth and came to the United States and ended up as a cowboy in the 1870's West doing things that cowboys did as well as fighting Indians. He returned to Germany in 1877 and started to work in a doll factory at Waltershausen, Thur, and from there to other doll factories. When he had gained the experience he needed he opened his own factory in 1889, the same year that he took out a French patent for the movement of a doll's head (a mechanism). His business had grown to include a factory at both Waltershausen and Friedrichroda by the year 1909. He made dolls on a ball jointed composition body as well as kid, with heads of bisque. These bisque heads were not made by him but such companies as Armand Marseille, Simon&Halbig, Kestner and others.

Marks on Bergmann dolls very often carry the full name of C.M. Bergmann but at times will have the name or initials of the head maker along with his initials, C.M.B.

The most famous of the Bergmann dolls are: 1897, his "Cinderella Baby" and "Columbia" in 1904.

Carles M. Bergmann--24" Socket head. Open mouth. Marks: Made In Germany/CM Bergmann/II. 24"--C-D. (Gunnel Collection)

Bester Doll--The Bester Doll Manufacturing Co. operated for three years, from 1919 through 1921. The factory and offices were located in Bloomfield and Newark, N.J.

Bester Doll Company--24" Socket head. Painted bisque type material. Open mouth. ca. 1918. Marks: Bester Doll/Co./Bloomfield/U.S.A. 24"--B-C. (Courtesy Kimport Dolls)

BOUDOIR DOLLS

The early 1920's Boudoir dolls were of the lady type and were large, but proportioned, and fashioned after the then-popular movie stars. Faces were in the "vamp" (for vampire) style. Some were of good quality and had less paint than the poorer ones. The doll was elaborate and had ruffles of satin and lace, some having human hair wigs and real eyelashes, some also having key wind Swiss music boxes embedded in their backs. The Boudoir of this period was frilly, ruffled with satin spreads and throw pillows so these dolls fit right in as a beautifier. These first Boudoir Dolls were imported from Paris and some had removable clothes and could be sewn for.

By the mid-20's there were American Manufacturers who started making the Boudoir doll. Among these were, Unique Novelty, Sterling Doll Co., American Stuffed Novelty Co., Fred K. Braiting, Chas. Bloom, Inc., Gerling Toy Co., and many of these were called "Flapper" dolls.

Not all Boudoir dolls were expensive, nor even well made. The cheapest had composition heads and shoulderplates made in 2 pieces and either joined or the front half was glued onto a cloth head. Most all had the heavy painted features of the "Vamp." The rest of the dolls were cloth or some had lower arms and legs of composition or celluloid. If there was hair or bonnets, in most cases these were just stapled onto the head.

Of the expensive Boudoir Dolls of the 20's, they were done more to a classic beauty. Often the faces were painted onto stiffened, shaped cloth like buckram. Hair is better and cloth fingers are individually sewn.

The market for both Flapper and good quality Boudoir dolls faded in the early 1930's. The Flapper doll had cloth bodies with very long legs and was not in proportion like most Boudoir dolls were. They were in imitation of the 1920's Flapper girls, a copy of the movies in caricature. The Flappers had very thin limbs and came both dressed and undressed. The vogue was to dress them to your own taste. There were specials run such as the George and Martha Washingtons for the George Washington Bicentennial in 1932. Flappers do not seem to ever carry a manufacturer's mark, so it is nearly impossible to say who made them.

Lenci did have a Flapper doll, shown in 1929, and was better proportioned than the ususal Flapper doll.

The most unique of American Flapper type dolls was the "Lindy" (Charles Lindbergh) doll by Regal Doll Mfg. Co. in 1929. It has long legs but Regal claims it to be the "flyer in one of his more jovial moods."

To sum up we have this: the finest quality, well proportioned dolls are called Boudoir Dolls. The long legged (and armed), rather poor quality dolls are called Flapper Dolls and both are rightly referred to as Bed Dolls.

Boudoir--27" with muslin main body with flannel over "jacket" upper body and arms. Stitched so elbows are jointed. Stockinet over flannel lower arms. All excelsior filled. Buchram molded face mask. Blue eyeshadow. Real hair lashes. Painted brown eyes. Full human hair wig. Silk and velvet clothes. Fancy high heel shoes with pointed toes. Key wind music box in back. Tag: France. $45.00. (Author)

Boudoir--29" Silk buckram face mask. Hair lashes. Full wig. High heel shoes. Composition arms and cloth legs. Original. $35.00. (Penner Collection)

71

Boudoir Dolls--25" Lenci Boudoir lady. Original. $100.00. (Courtesy Kimport Dolls)

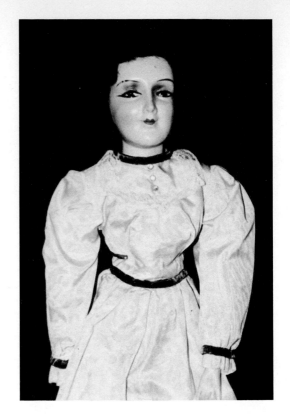

Boudoir Dolls--23" Composition of the 1920's. Painted eyes/lashes. $32.00. (Courtesy Kimport Dolls)

Boudoir Dolls--32" Composition shoulder plate, arms and legs. Very heavy painted face. Marks: none. $35.00. (Courtesy Kimport Dolls)

Boudoir Dolls--32" Máche, composition and cloth bed doll. Original. $35.00. (Courtesy Kimport Dolls)

Boudoir Dolls--27" Cloth stuffed with cotton. Very high heel shoes. Original. Beautiful molded gutta percha hands. Marks: Patented June 2, 1925/No. 1540384/Chas. Bloom Inc. New York. Charles Bloom patented this doll by: "putting a layer of cotton sheeting over 2 layers of buckram and pressing between dies. Head in 2 parts. Features painted on. $55.00. (Author)

BRU

The obvious founders of this company were Leon Casimir Bru and his wife and between 1867 and 1869, took out several French Patents, including "The Surprise Doll," a double faced doll, (Madame Bru patented another in 1872, made of wood/metal and containing a multi-disc music box) a crying doll, and in 1869 they patented a new doll body made with ball joints and included joints at wrists, ankles and waist, all of papier mache and white kid, straight and jointed limbed dolls and worked in rubber, porcelain, "hardened paste," and had carved wood joints.

Casimir Bru, Jeune (Junior) started the company Bru Jne & Cie (Bru Junior & Co.) about 1873 as he is listed on several patents between 1873 and 1882. These patents included a jointed rubber doll (1878) which was built over a wire frame, a nursing doll (Bébé Teteur 1879), a kid bodied doll (1879), the movements of eyelids (eyelids would move while the eyes would remain stationary 1882), and one interesting note...in 1882 Bru & Jumeau held a patent for a boat that was mechanical.

Advertisements for Bru Jne & Cie between 1873 and 1883 show dolls in carved wood (hands and feet), dolls with music boxes, dolls in "ordinary wood" with simple joints, rubber dolls, dolls in kid with arms and hands in jointed wood, 2 faced dolls (1 awake and 1 asleep), kid body dolls with rubber heads, mechanical talking dolls (1879) and the eating Bebe Gourmand (1881).

As for exhibits at International Shows, Bru Jne & Cie dolls were exhibited in Paris in 1878 (Silver Medal) and in 1880 at Melbourne (Silver Medal). Bru dolls did not take (apparently) any gold medals until the time of H. Chevrot.

H. Chevrot took over the Bru firm in 1883 but kept the Bru name. He took out a patent the same year for a kid body doll with a system of joints manipulated from the interior of the doll. From 1883 to 1889 he continued making dolls with newer patented joints, Bebe Teteur (nursing), Bebe Gourmand (eating) and the new Bébé Le Dormeur (sleeping

by means of eyelids). The factory at Montreuil-Sous-Bois was where the bisque heads were made. In a H. Chevrot's 1885 ad, it states "The words Bébé Bru can be examined on each Bebe (chest label). All the gold medals won by the Bru firm was under Chevrot's ownership. 1885, Paris, Antwerp. 1886, Liverpool, Paris. 1887 LeHavre, Toulouse. 1888, Barcelona, Melbourne, Paris and two silver medals: 1889 at Paris and 1893 at Chicago. So it might be said the "Golden Years" for Bru were from 1883 to 1889 and under the leadership of one H. Chevrot.

From 1890 to 1899 the Bru firm moved into the hands of Paul Eugene Girard who continued to patent new ideas like the combined movement of the eyes and eyelids (standard sleep eyes), a walking and talking doll that had a key wind mechanism and was called Bébé Petit Pas, a Mama-Papa doll with expanding chest (1892), kissing dolls that threw kisses as a string was pulled (1885), and a doll who threw kisses by leg movement and also walked and talked, this one patented by Paul Girard's son, Eugene Fredrick Girard in 1897, dolls with hollow wooden bodies, composition heads, natural eyelashes. And as late as 1892, they were making India rubber dolls and still making the Bébé Teteur in 1898.

After 1899 the Bru firm evolved into part of the Societe Francaise de Fabrication de Bébés et Jouets (S.F.B.J.).

The clothes of the majority of Bru dolls were outstanding in workmanship and quality of materials.

As to marks on Bru dolls, this may not be so but stands to reason that the very first Brus were marked ⌒ ⊙ or just ⚇ , usually over the shoulder plate. Then for the ten years of Casimir Bru, Junior (1887-1883) the dolls were marked Bru Jne and Bru Jne R. After passing on to H. Chevrot in 1883, when the greatest number of Bru dolls were manufactured, they were marked with the Bru Jne R but also had a label "Bébé Bru, etc" on their bodies.

The majority of Bru dolls are of excellent quality, but some of "lesser" quality are seen also.

Bru--Bébé Teteur was patented in 1879. The head holds a curved metal rod with a rubber ball below it. A key extends through a small hole out the back of the head and as it is wound the ball compresses, drawing liquid from the baby bottle into the doll's mouth, then as the key is wound again, the liquid is forced back into the bottle. Advertised as "The darling Bébé Le Teteur that sucks all by herself." Patented by Casimir Bru Junior.

Bru--20" "Bébé Teteur" Open mouth/nurser. Composition jointed body with jointed wrists. Marks: Bru Jne/8, on head. Bébé Bru/No. 8, on shoulder plate. Pin: Bébé. Bottle: Bébé Teteur. All original. 20"-Y-Z-Original. (Minter Collection)

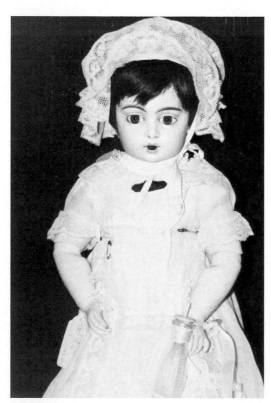

Bru--20" "Bébé Teteur" Shows bottle marked: Bébé Teteur. (Minter Collection)

Bru--19" "Bébé Teteur" Both this nursing doll's head and kid body was patented by Casimir Bru Junior, in 1879. Full kid body with bisque lower arms. Marks: Deposé on front of shoulder plate. Bru Jne/5T/Bru, on head. Open mouth/nurser. Wired formed upper arms. 19"--W-X-Original. (Gregg Collection)

Bru--18" Socket head. Closed mouth. Marks: Bru Jne R. 18"--W-X. (Courtesy Ralph's Antique Dolls)

Bru--18" Socket head on bisque shoulder plate. Closed mouth. Kid body with bisque lower arms. Marks: 11, on head. Bru Jne R, on shoulder plate. 18"--W-X. (Courtesy Kimport Dolls)

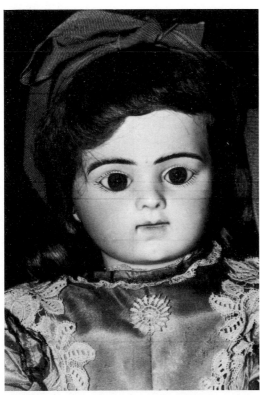

Bru--19" Socket head. Mechanical. Although we can see the mechanism through a cut out in the back we are unable to tell what she did. Closed mouth. Marks: Bru Jne 8. 19"--V-W. (Courtesy Kimport Dolls)

Bru--27" Socket head. Marks: Bru Jne R. Closed mouth. 27"--W-X. (Courtesy Ralph's Antique Dolls)

Bru--14" All kid body. Bisque jointed head and shoulder plate. Pierced ears. Marks: Bru Jne R/5 on head. Bru Jne, over shoulder. 14"--V-W. (Author)

Bru--Full length of 14" Bru R.

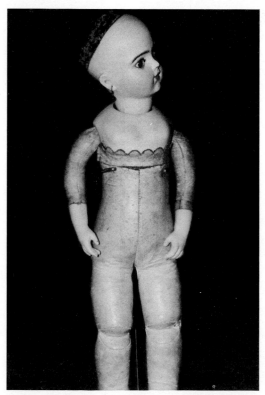

Bru--Show body of 14" Bru R. Stitched toes. Wired arms. Outlined nails. Kid body patented by Casimir Bru, Junior in 1879.

Bru--21" Socket head. Pierced ears. Original clothes. Open mouth. Jointed wrists. Marks: Bru Jne R/9. 21"--U-V This quality of bisque only. (Author)

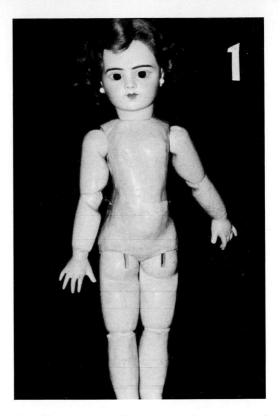

Bru--22" Socket head. Open mouth. 22"--S-T.
(Courtesy Ralph's Antique Dolls)

Bru--Shows composition body on the open mouth
Bru. Marks: "8" incised on bottom of each foot.

George Bruchlos--26" Socket head. Open mouth.
Marks: Germany/GB Body: Eisfeld... George
Bruchlos operated in Eisfeld, Thur from 1883
through 1929. 26"--C-D. (Gunnel Collection)

BUSCHOW & BECK

In 1894, A. Vischer & Company established the trademark in the U.S. for metal head dolls, of "Minerva" and this same trademark in Germany was by Buschow & Beck, not only for metal heads but for celluloid also. This type of metal head was actually patented by Joseph Schon, in 1886.

In 1901 these heads were sheet brass and by 1907, Butler Bros. (distributor) was advertising a combination celluloid, washable enamel coating for them. In 1912 there was a "weeping" Minerva that cried real tears and in 1913 came with washable enamel and flexible sheet metal that could be adjusted to fit any body.

The paint often chipped off these dolls and a completely original is fairly difficult to find.

The "Minerva" mark is a helmet:

Minerva--17" Blonde tin head with leather body and original clothes. Marks: Minerva, on front. Germany, on back. 17"--$55.00. (Penner Collection)

Minerva--13" All celluloid with set blue glass eyes/lashes. Molded blonde hair. Fully jointed. All original. Marks: a helmet/Minerva/Germany/4. 13"--$115.00. (Penner Collection)

Buschow & Beck--17" Metal head with stone bisque forearms. Marks: Germany 4, on back of shoulder plate. Minervia, around a helmet on front of shoulder plate. Body stamped: Made In Germany. 17"--$55.00. (Clasby Collection)

Buschow & Beck--12" Metal head. Cloth body.
All original. Celluloid hands. Marks: Helmet, on
back. 12"--$45.00. (Clasby Collection)

Buschow & Beck--16" Minerva tin head. 16"--
$75.00. (Walters Collection)

Cameo--3½" Kewpie Huggers. Bride wears
original veil and flowers. Groom has painted on
tux jacket and crepe paper top hat. All original.
Half of paper heart label still exists on back.
These were used to top a wedding cake in 1915.
$150.00. (Maish Collection)

Cameo--13" Chalkware Kewie. Movable arms.
On self black base. 13"--$22.00. (Maish
Collection)

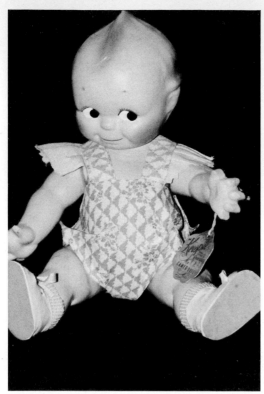

Cameo--13" "Kewpie" All composition. Fully jointed. Original. 13"--$65.00. (Penner Collection)

Cameo--Cloth bodied Kewpie. Composition head and hands. $95.00. (Clasby Collection)

Cameo--11" Kewpie. Composition with jointed shoulders. 11"--$55.00. (Maish Collection)

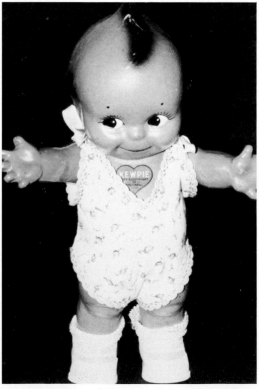

Cameo--11" Colored Kewpie. Jointed shoulders only. 11"--$85.00. (Clasby Collection)

Cartoon Characters--4" Mr. Peanut. Bisque. Marks: Symbol/Made In Japan. $25.00. (Maish Collection)

Cartoon Characters--9½" Mutt and 5½" Jeff. Some sort of modeling compound that lies between chalkware and bisque. Marks: Seals embedded in bases: Sold by Mark Hampton Co Inc. Marbridge Bldg. Ny City. Reg. 1911 Copyrights. 1909-1910 By H.C. Fisher. $50.00 each. (Maish Collection)

Cartoon Characters--2½" Mickey McGuire. Bisque. Has tiny hole in mouth to hold fiber cigar. Marks: Mickey McGuire/Copyright By/ Fontaine Fox Germany. $35.00. (Maish Collection)

Cartoon Characters--2½ Herby. All bisque. This one's head is in one piece with body. It also comes with a nodding head. Marks: Herby #C82 Japan. $25.00. (Maish Collection)

Cartoon Characters--2½" Baby Tarzan and Mother Kala Gorilla. All bisque. Marks: Faint first two digits, last two 55. $25.00. (Maish Collection)

Cartoon Characters--8½ Papier Mache shoulder head. Cloth body. Sewn on shoes. Marks: Annie, printed on back. Origin unknown. Pre. 1935. $22.00. (Maish Collection)

82

Cartoon Characters--3¼" Betty Boop Drummer and violinist. Marks: Betty Boop/Made in Japan/Fleischer Studios. $25.00-$30.00 each. (Maish Collection)

Cartoon Characters--5" Mickey Mouse. Bisque with left arm stationary and right arm movable by elastic running across inside of body, emerging at left hip. Scarce. $40.00 (Maish Collection)

China--5" Black haired China. 5"--$30.00. (Gunnel Collection)

China--7¼" China of 1870's. Holds tiny little "Frozen Charlotte." All original. 7¼"--$125.00. (Courtesy Kimport Dolls)

China--9" Black haired China. Very old note attached to underskirt: "Given to Emma Loucks on Christmas 1866. Mrs. DeWitt Lowe dressed it." Flat feet. 9"--$180.00. (Gunnel Collection)

China--10" Molded blonde high piled hair. Child with painted eyes. 10"--$200.00. (Courtesy Kimport Dolls)

China--13½"--Rare black hairdo with molded flowers and pierced ears. Germany. 13½"--$200.00. (Courtesy Kimport Dolls)

China--13½" Turned head "low brow." No sew holes, with muslin upper body (long waisted) and kid lower body with muslin lower legs. "Jointed" hips and knees. Spoon hands marked "2." 13½"--$40.00.

China--14" Black hair China. 14"--$42.50. (Gunnel Collection)

China--14½" Flat top with white part. Marks: Germany. 14½"--$125.00.

China--16" "low brow" blonde with slightly turned head and partly exposed ears. Marks: Germany. 16"--$60.00. (Penner Collection)

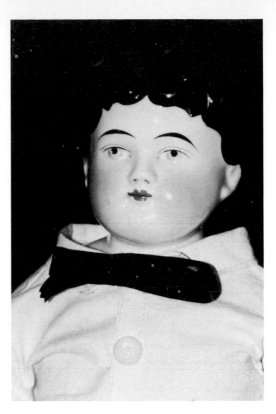

China--16½" Black hair China with ears exposed. 16½"--$200.00. (Walters Collection)

China--16½" Blonde with brush strokes of red with center part. 16½"--$85.00. (Clasby Collection)

China--17" Blonde china. Marks: 3, on back shoulder plate. 17"--$85.00. (Gunnel Collection)

China--17" Blonde with center part. Marks: 3, on back. 17"--$85.00. (Clasby Collection)

China--17½" Blonde china with an off center part. 17½"--$225.00. (Courtesy Kimport Dolls)

China--17½" Black hair China. Flat top with white part. Double row of curls in back. 17½"--$145.00. (Walters Collection)

China--18" Pink luster, black hair china with center part and 13 sausage curls. Marks: Germany. 18"--$325.00. (Penner Collection)

China--18" Blonde china with extremely pale blue eyes. Marks: Germany. 18"--$95.00. (Gunnel Collection)

China--19" Blonde China with bangs. Called "Highland Mary" by collectors. 19"--$325.00. (Walters Collection)

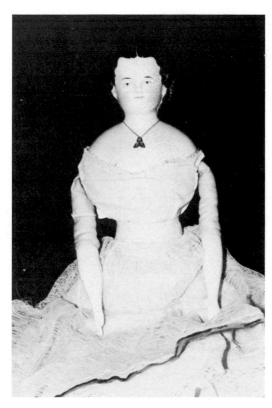

China--20" So called "Adelina Patti." This name, as many other names for dolls is inaccurate but must be referred to as collectors have accepted it. A rare black hairdo China. 20"--$425.00. (Courtesy Kimport Dolls)

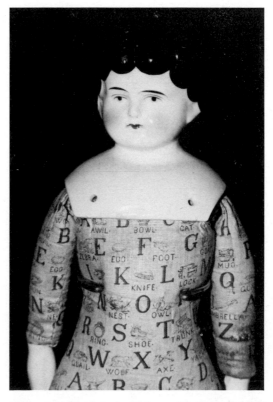

China--20" Black hair China with turned head and primer body. 20"--$115.00. (Walters Collection)

91

China--20" Black hair China name doll "Marion" (on front). Marked on back: Patent App'd For/ Germany. 20"--$95.00. (Walters Collection)

China--20½" Black hair China. 20½"--$185.00. (Walters Collection)

China--21" Flat smooth top with white center-part. 3 large curls and 7 sausage curls. Deep shoulder plate with 3 sew holes, front and back. 21"--$200.00.

China--21" Black hair China boy. Cloth body with sewn on leather boots. 21"--$200.00. (Courtesy Kimport Dolls)

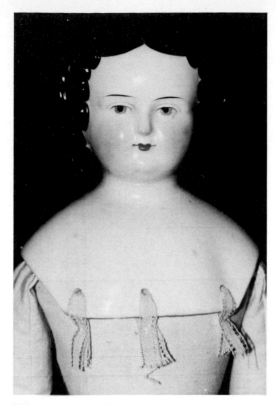

China--21" Black hair lady China. 3 sew holes. 1870's. Marks: f , inside back shoulder. 21"--$250.00. (Walters Collection)

China--21" Early pink luster. ca. 1830's. 21"--$1,000.00. (Courtesy Kimport Dolls)

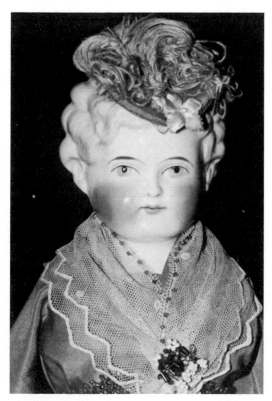

China--21" Center part blonde. Full ears show. 21"--$325.00.

China--21½" China of the 1860's. 21½"--$165.00. (Courtesy Kimport Dolls)

China--22" Black hair. 23 curls. 22"--$95.00. (Gunnel Collection)

China--22" Blonde with very short hair in back. Marks: H. 22"--$195.00. (Gunnel Collection)

China--22" Blonde China with two set in jewels on necklace. ca. 1900. Germany. 22"--$295.00. (Courtesy Kimport Dolls)

China--22½" Black hair with center part. Marks: 6. 22½"--$200.00. (Gunnel Collection)

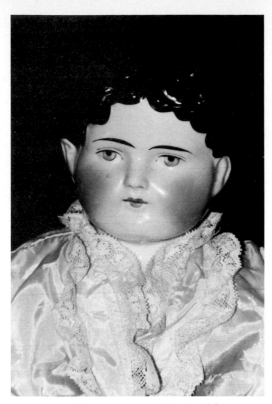

China--23" Black hair China that is either a boy or a girl. Exposed ears. 23"--$250.00. (Walters Collection)

China--23" Blonde China of 1895. Marks: Germany. 23"--$125.00. (Courtesy Kimport Dolls)

China--23" Blonde child of the 1860's. Leather arms and feet. 23"--$275.00. (Courtesy Kimport Dolls)

China--24" Black hair China with bangs and brush strokes. May be a Currier and Ives doll. 24"--$325.00. (Walters Collection)

China--25½" Pink tint china of 1860. Cloth/kid body. 25½"--$300.00. (Courtesy Kimport Dolls)

China--26" Flat top China of 1870. 26"--$200.00. (Courtesy Kimport Dolls)

China--26" Flat top China of 1865. Germany. 26"--$200.00. (Courtesy Kimport Dolls)

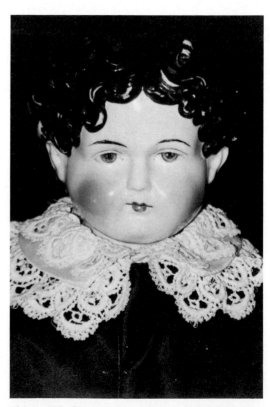

China--29" Black hair China. Exposed ears. Molded eyelids. 29"--$350.00. (Walters Collection)

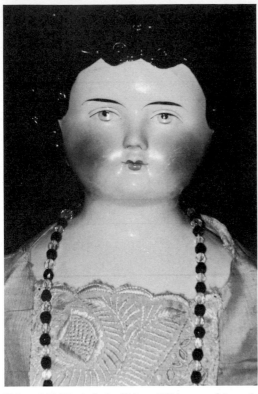

China--30" Black hair China. Ribbon and bow in front of hair. Molded eyelids. "Dolly Madison" type. 30"--$425.00. (Walters Collection)

DANEL & CIE

Danel & Cie--Danel & Cie was in business from 1889 to 1895, in Paris. They registered, in France, "Paris Bébé" with a picture of the Eiffel Tower (1889). In 1891 they registered "Bébé Francais." Jumeau registered "Bébé Francais" in 1896, so may have controlled this company by then.

Danel & Cie--23" Socket head. Closed mouth. Marks: Paris Bébé/Tête Deposeé/18H/10. 23"--M-O. (Courtesy Ralph's Antique Dolls)

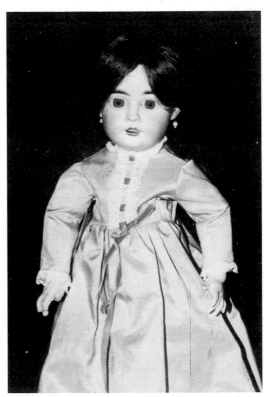

Danel & Cie--17" Socket head. Open mouth. Marks: 4, on head. A/Paris Bébé/Deposé, on body. ca. 1889. 17"--J-K. (Courtesy Kimport Dolls)

97

E. DENAMUR

E. Denamur--Denamur of Paris made dolls from 1857 to 1898. After 1875 his business was known as "Le Maision de Bambin" (The House of Bambin) and made "Le Bambin Bébé."

E. Denamur--15" Socket head. Closed mouth. Marks: E.6D./Depose. 15"--L-N. (Author)

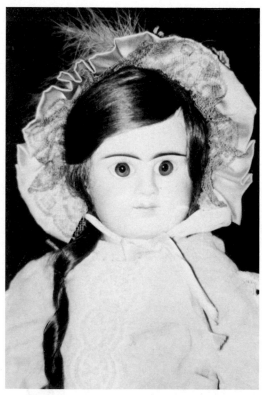

E. Denamur--20" Socket head. Closed mouth. Marks: E9D. 20"--L-N. (Courtesy Ralph's Antique Dolls)

E. Denamur--14" Socket head. Closed mouth. Marks: E.14D. 14"--L-N. (Minter Collection)

E. Denamur--20" Socket head. Open mouth/4 molded teeth. **Marks:** E.9D./Depose. 20"--J-L. (Penner Collection)

The Dressel firm was founded in 1700, but up to 1863 not much is known about them except they made wood and papier mache toys. The main thing is that Otto Dressel, Sr. along with his sons, Otto Junior and Cuno, were listed as doll makers in 1873. They used the initials E D (with reversed E) and, in 1875, registered the "Holz-Masse" in Germany. Their marks have been found on dolls of heads of wax, papier mache, bisque and composition. They purchased bisque heads from any porcelain factories, such as Armand Marseille, Simon & Halbig, etc. As for composition, right near the turn of the century, they used composition to make such dolls as portraits of President McKinley, Admiral Sampson and Admiral Dewey. These were 15½."

Cuno and Otto Dressel (C.O.D.) began using the "Jutta" trademark in 1906 and, in 1909, registered "Bambina" and were making dolls with kid bodies. By 1911, they were also making celluloid heads. In 1914 much of their factory at Sonneberg burned, but they rebuilt and re-opened in 1915. Besides the doll factory there were 2 toy factories, one at Nurnberg and the other at Grunhainichen.

Sample marks of the Cuno and Otto Dressel Comany are:

Dressel

"Holz Masse"

C & O
Dressel

Cuno & Otto Dressel--13" Socket head on adult body. Closed mouth. **Marks:** C.O.D./Germany/2. 13"--F-H. (Courtesy Ralph's Antique Dolls)

Cuno & Otto Dressel--21" Shoulder plate. Kid body. Open mouth. **Marks:** 1896/C.O.D.4Dep./ X. 21"--B-D. (Walters Collection)

Cuno & Otto Dressel--18" Shoulder plate. Kid body. Open mouth. Marks: C.O.D./93-9 Dep. 18"--B-C. (Walters Collection)

Cuno & Otto Dressel--26" Shoulder plate. Molded brows. Marks: Germany/Holz-Masse. 26"--C-D. (Courtesy Ralph's Antique Dolls)

Cuno & Otto Dressel--14" Toddler with wiggle tongue. Sleep eyes/lashes. Marks: Otto Dressel/Germany/5½. 14"--D-E. (Minter Collection)

Cuno & Otto Dressel--13" Shoulder plate with bisque lower arms. Open mouth/4 teeth. Original clothes. Marks: 1410/Germany. 13"--A-B. (Maish Collection)

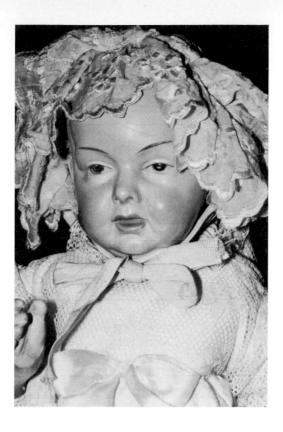

Eisenmann & Co.--13" Painted bisque socket head. Intaglio eyes. Open/closed mouth. Marks: Einco/7½/Germany. Joseph Eisenmann & Co. made dolls in Furth, Bavaria. This doll ca. 1914. 13"--D-E. (Courtesy Kimport Dolls)

EFFANBEE

This company was started in 1910 by Bernard E. Fleischaker and Hugo Baum. In 1947, Effanbee was bought by Noma (maker of Christmas decorations) and sold back to Bernie Baum, Perry Epstein and Morris Lutz. In 1971 the company was sold once more.

Effanbee's first dolls (1910) were of concrete type composition and were advertised as unbreakable. As their dolls improved, their business grew and by 1920 had two factories.

In 1912 their doll line included Baby Dainty, Little Walter, Johnny Tu-Face and Miss Coquette (formally called Naughty Marietta). In 1913 they introduced the Betty Bounce line and began using the trademark EFFandBEE.

From 1913 through 1920, their dolls included Pajama Baby, Baby Grumpy, Baby Huggins, Jumbo Infant, Baby Grumpy, Jr., Uncle Sam, Columbia, Mary Jane, Dolly Dumpling, Riding Hood Bud, Valentine Bud, Baby Bright Eyes, and a line of Mama dolls.

About 1920 Lenox Pottery made bisque doll heads for Effanbee. These are considered rare by collectors.

During the 1920's Effanbee re-introduced Baby Grumpy, and added dolls such as, Salvation Army Lass, Margie, a Mama doll who said Papa, Honeybunch, Beach Baby, Nancy Ann, Mary Ann, Betty Lee, Alice Lee, Barbara Lee, Baby Catherine, Tiny Tads, Marilee, Bubbles, Dolly Bubbles, Pat-O-Pat.

In 1922 Effanbee trademark was "They Walk and They Talk" and in 1933, "They Walk, They Talk, They Sleep." A button with the Effanbee name was pinned to the dress of every doll. It was also in 1923 that they began using the heart-shaped pendant, "The Doll With The Golden Heart."

In 1925 the Effanbee Patsy era began and moved into the 1930's with the DyDee Baby doll. As you can see the Effanbee Company produced many, many dolls and because their quality was so good many remain today.

Effanbee--30" "Mae Starr" Composition one piece shoulder plate and head. Composition limbs. Cloth body. Red human hair wig over molded hair. Sleep pale brown eyes. Record player center back. Wind lever on side. Marks: Mae/Starr/Doll. Original. 1928. 30"--$110.00.

Effanbee--Full length of 30" "Mae Starr" to show fat legs.

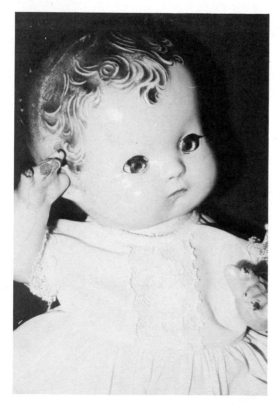

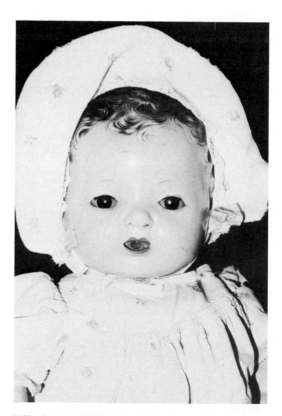

Effanbee--10½" "Patsy Baby" All composition with molded hair. Blue sleep eyes. Marks: Effanbee/Patsy Baby, head and body. 1932. $40.00.

Effanbee--14" "Dy Dee Baby" All rubber body, arms and legs. Composition head looks like hard plastic. Brown sleep eyes. Open mouth/nurser. Marks: Eff-An-Bee/Dy-Dee Baby/3 US Patents/ 1 England/2 France/1 Germany, on back. 6, on head. 1933. $27.50. (Westbrook Collection)

Effanbee--11" "Patsy Jr." All composition with light brown painted molded hair. Molded hair ribbon. Painted brown eyes. Marks: Effanbee/ Patsy Jr., on back. 1930. $40.00. (Maish Collection)

Effanbee--5" "Wee Patsy" All composition with molded painted hair and features. Painted on shoes and socks. Marks: Effanbee/Wee Patsy, on back. Considered extremely hard to find. 1930. $85.00. (Maish Collection)

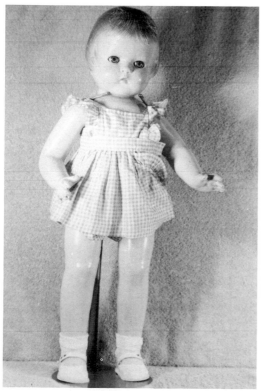

Effanbee--22" "Patsy Lou" All composition with red/brown molded hair. Green sleep eyes. "This is my own (Maish) childhood doll and originally wore a yellow organdy dress and bonnet trimmed with tangerine ribbons." Considered a rare size. $75.00. (Maish Collection)

Effanbee--17" Composition head and gauntlet arms. Cloth body and legs. Gray tin sleep eyes. Closed mouth. Molded hair under mohair wig. Wig is set into an open crown. Marks: Large Script "Effanbee" on shoulder plate. ca. 1915. $50.00. (Maish Collection)

103

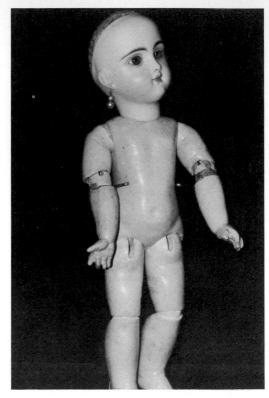

Ferte--15" Socket head. Composition and wood. Cork plate. Set paperweight eyes. Very short upper arms. Crude hands with unjointed wrists. Very deep crown slice. Pierced ears. Closed mouth. Marks: B.6.F. ca. 1875. 15"--N-P. (Author)

Ferte--Body on 15" marked: B.6F.

Fleischmann & Blodel--21" All pápier maché body with pin/wired arms and legs. Open mouth/6 molded teeth. Marks: Eden Bébé/ Paris/9/Deposé. 21"--J-K. (Author)

FLEISCHMANN & BLODEL

This company began with a factory in Fürth, 1873, and also had a branch in Paris. They made, exported and distributed dolls and obtained patents on such items as new joints for dolls (French Patents) in 1890. In 1892, a French patent for an unbreakable doll and English and German patents for a walking doll, whose head turned as it walked. In 1894, patents for moving eyelids, walking dolls, a doll that threw kisses and talked when a button was pressed. These were all French patents and, the same year, they took out a German patent for a kiss throwing and talking doll. Also in 1895, a German patent for a moving doll. They became assignees of a patent by Claude Jospeh Simonot of Paris for a walking doll whose head turned as it walked.

In 1890 they registered in France "Eden Bébé" and as a trademark (in Germany) in 1896. "Eden Puppee" was registered (in Germany) in 1891, "Bébé Triomphe" in France, in 1898.

Fleischmann & Blödel were one of the first members of the Société Française de Fabrication de Bébés et Jouets (S.F.B.J.), in 1899. In fact, Fleischmann was head of S.F.B.J. as World War I began, but since he was an alien in France, his property was sequestered.

Fleischmann & Blodel--Full length to show clothes on 21" Eden Bébé.

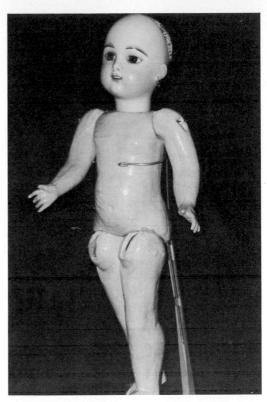

Fleischmann & Blodel--Shows body shot of 21" Eden Bébé. This doll does not appear to have ever been restrung, so the doll may have come from the factory with her legs on the wrong side.

Fleischmann & Blodel--20" Socket head. Open mouth. Marks: Eden Bébé/Paris/8. 20"--J-K. (Courtesy Ralph's Antique Dolls)

Fleischmann & Blodel--20" Socket head. Open mouth. Marks: Eden Bébé/Paris/9/Depose. 20"--J-K. (Gunnel Collection)

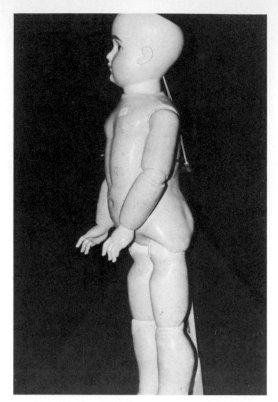

Fouquet & Douville--26" Composition/wood body. Unpierced ears. Dark red line through lips. French sleep paperweight type eyes. Just the very top of the head sliced to allow for mechanism. Flirty, unsleeping eyes. Marks: 103/16/X. 4 brush strokes along crown. 26"--K-M. (Author)

Fouquet & Douville--Shows body of 26" flirty eyed doll. Small breasts and very delicate, posed fingers.

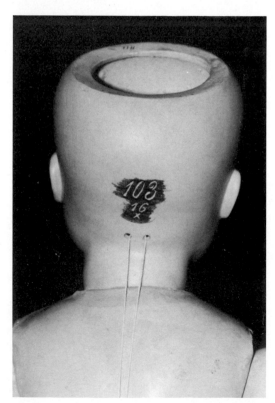

Fouquet & Douville--Marks on 26" flirty eyed doll. Show pulls that operate eyes.

FROZEN CHARLOTTE

I thought it might be interesting to relate the ballad of 1865
about "Young Charlotte." It is not known which came first,
the ballad or the doll.

Young Charlotte

Young Charlotte lived by the mountain side,
  in a wild and lonely spot;
No dwelling there for three miles around,
  except her father's cot;
And yet on many a Winter's night
  young swains would gather there,
For her father kept a social board,
  and she was very fair.

Her father liked to see her dressed
  as fine as a city belle,
For she was the only child he had
  and he loved his daughter well;
It was New Year's Eve, the sun had set,
  why looks her anxious eye
So long from the frosty window forth,
  as merry sleighs pass by.

At the village inn, fifteen miles off
  there's a merry ball tonight;
The piercing air is as cold as death,
  but her heart is warm and light;
But ah! how laughs her beaming eye
  as a well known voice she hears.
And dashing up to the cottage door
  young Charles and sleigh appears.

"O daughter dear," her mother said,
  "this blanket round you fold,
For it is a dreadful night abroad
  and you'll get your death of cold"
"Nay, mother, nay," fair Charlotte said,
  and she laughed like a gypsy queen,
"To ride in blankets muffled up I
  can never be seen."
"My silken cloak is quite enough,
  it is lined throughout, you know;
Besides I have a silken scarf which
  around my neck I throw."
Her gloves were on, her bonnet tied,
  She jumped into the sleigh
and away they ride by the mountain side
  and o'er the hills away.
There is life in the sounds of the merry bells
  as o'er the hills they go;
What a creaking noise the runners make
  As they bite the frozen snow;
With muffled faces silently,
  o'er five long miles they pass,
When Charles with these frozen words
  the silence broke at last;

"Such a night as this I never saw,
  the reins I scarce can hold."
When Charlotte, shivering faintly said,
  "I am exceedingly cold."
He cracked his whip and urged his team
  more swiftly than before,
Until five other dreary miles in silence
  were passed o'er.
"O see," said Charles, "how fast the
  frost is gathering on my brow."
When Charlotte in a feeble voice said,
  "I am growing warmer now."
And on they ride through the frosty air
  and the glittering cold starlight
Until at last the village inn and ball
  room are in sight.

They reached the inn and Charles jumped
  out and held his arms to her;
"Why sit you like a monument without
  the power to stir?"
He called her once, he called her twice,
  she answered not a word;
He called her name again,
  but still she never stirred.

He took her hand in his, O God!
  'twas cold and hard as stone,
He tore the mantle from her brow and
  on her the cold stars shone;
And then into the lighted hall
  her lifeless form he bore,
For Charlotte was a frozen corpse and
  words spoke nevermore.

He sat himself down by her side and
  the bitter tears did flow,
And he said "My young intended bride,
  I never more shall know."
He threw his arms around her neck
  and kissed her marble brow,
And his thoughts went back to where she said,
  "I'm growing warmer now."

He bore her out into the sleigh
  and with her he drove home,
And when he reached the cottage door,
  O how her parents mourned;
They mourned the loss of their daughter dear
  while Charles mourned o'er their gloom,
Until with grief his heart did break,
  and they slumber in one tomb...

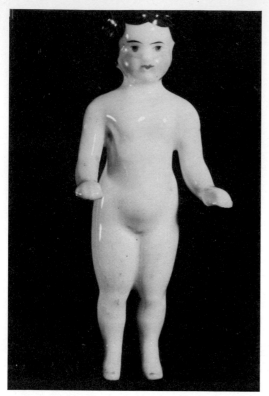

Frozen Charlotte--5" Marks: 100, on back. 5"--A-C. (Gunnel Collection)

Frozen Charlotte--6" Blonde. 6"--B-C. (Courtesy Kimport Dolls)

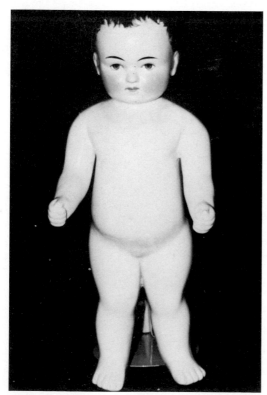

Frozen Charlotte--15½" "Frozen Charlie." Flesh tint to face and neck area, rest white. 15½"--F-G. (Courtesy Kimport Dolls)

FULPHER POTTERY COMPANY

The Fulpher Pottery Company of Flemington, New Jersey, began in 1805 but only produced a line of doll heads for the short years between 1918 and 1921, inclusive and at no other time.

The heads were originally developed for the Horsman Doll Company. Harold Bowie, Benjamin Goldenberg, both from Horsman, helped in the production and worked closely with Mr. J. Martin Stangl, the head Ceramic Engineer at Fulpher Pottery.

The heads were made of all-American materials and are considered choice items for all collectors of Americana.

Some have celluloid/metal sleep eyes (patented by Samuel Marcus in 1918), but these may have been put into the heads by the companies who bought the heads without eyes. Dolls assembled at Fulpher Pottery had either glass blown eyes or the heavy solid white glass, with glass iris and pupil inserts. A few have molded hair and intaglio eyes. Some were made for other companies besides Horsman, such as Amberg Dolls and Colonial Doll Co.

It should be noted that Fulpher also made all bisque "Kewpies" in 1920 and all bisque "Peterkin" in 1919.

Sample Fulpher marks:

F
U
L
P
H
E
R

Made in U.S.A.

Amberg Dolls
The World Standard

Made In U.S.A
HORSMAN
Doll
19 © 10

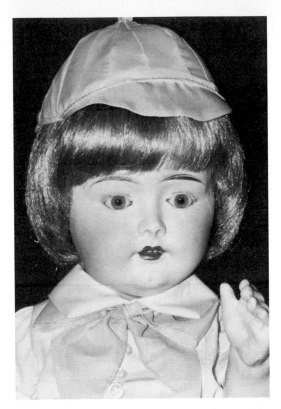

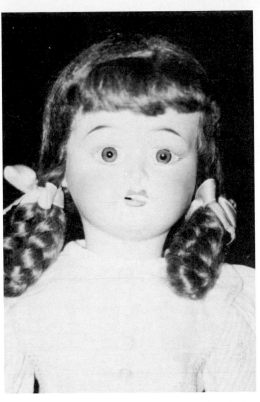

Fulpher--15" Head circumference. Composition baby body. Marks: Vertical Fulpher, in square/ Made in/USA/2AA. 15"--D-F. (Penner Collection)

Fulpher--19" Socket head. Open mouth. Marks: Fulpher, in square/Made In/U.S.A./70. ca. 1917. 19"--C-D. (Courtesy Ralph's Antique Dolls)

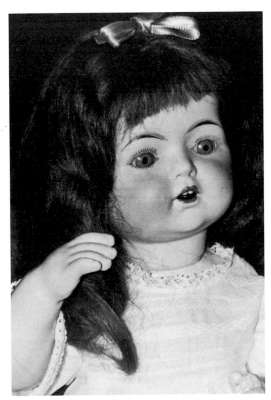

Fulpher Pottery--18" Socket head. Open mouth. Marks: ⊕ /Made In U.S.A./13. 18"--D-F. (Walters Collection)

Fulpher Pottery--17" Socket head. Open mouth. Set eyes. Marks: ⊕ . Made in 1918. 17"--B-C. (Courtesy Kimport Dolls)

109

Fy--13" Pouty. On toddler body and also seen on a baby body. Sleep eyes. Excellent quality bisque. Marks: Fy/Nippon/301. 13"--E-F. (Author)

Fy--20" Socket head, set in shoulder plate. Open mouth. Marks: Fy 9/Nippon/402. 20"--B-C. (Penner Collection)

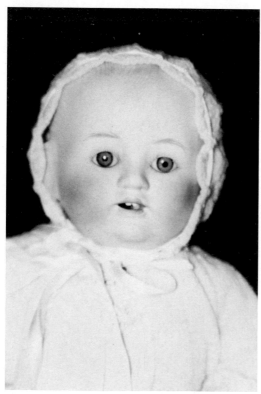

Fy--10½" head cir. Open mouth. Sleep eyes. Marks: Fy/20/8/676018/Nippon. 10½"--A-B. (Courtesy Ralph's Antique Dolls.)

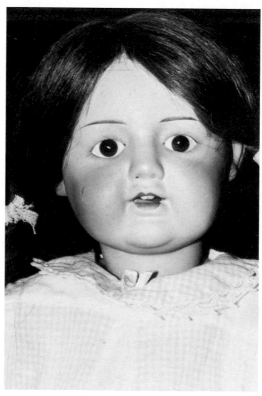

Fy--18" Socket head. Open mouth/2 upper teeth. Marks: Fy/No. 70018/Nippon/004. 18"--B-C. (Clasby Collection)

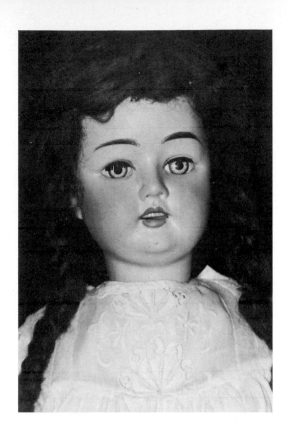

GANS & SEYFARTH

Gans & Seyfarth--20" Socket head. Tin sleep eyes. ca. 1924. Marks: Gans *d* Seyfarth. This company operated from 1909 through the early 1930's. They used both their full company name and also "G.S." 20"--C-D. (Gunnel Collection)

FERNAND GAULTIER

Fernand Gaultier--Little is known about this company except its initials F.G. There are records to the medals won and atest to the quality of the dolls/clothes. In 1878, Paris (silver), 1880 Brussels (bronze), 1883 Amsterdam (silver), 1884 Nice (silver), 1885 Antwerp (silver), 1889 Paris (silver) and 1900 Paris (bronze).

Fernand Gaultier--21" Wood arms and legs. Composition body with flaired hips. Papier mache hands and feet. Amber brown set paperweight eyes. Pierced ears. Closed mouth. Original clothes. Shoes marked: ALa/Providence/74 Rue/Rivoli. Head: F.G., in scroll/8. 21"--M-O. (Author)

111

Fernand Gaultier--Full length of original clothes
(except hose) of 21" F.G.

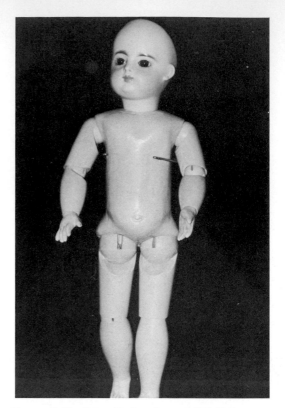

Fernand Gaultier--Body view of 21" F.G.

Fernand Gaultier--Back view of body of 21" F.G.

Fernand Gaultier--Shoe on the right from 21"
F.G. Marked: A La Providence/74 Rue Rivoli.
Shoe on left from doll marked #8-1009.

Fernand Gaultier--25" Socket head with "portrait" sized eyes and closed mouth. Marks: 10/F.G., in scroll. 25"--N-Q. (Minter Collection)

Fernand Gaultier--29" Socket head. Closed mouth. Marks: F.G., in scroll. 29"--S-T. (Minter Collection)

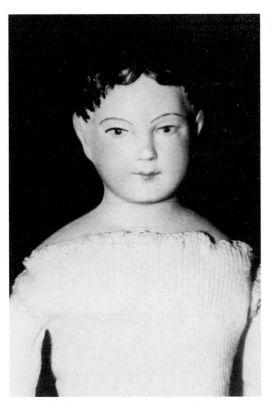

Fernand Gaultier--18" Socket head. Closed mouth child. Marks: F.G., in scroll/7. 18"--L-N. (Penner Collection)

Fernand Gaultier--9" Cloth body. Bisque head, arms and lower legs. Closed mouth. Molded man's hair. Flat feet. Marks: 2/0 on one side and F.G. on other side of shoulder plate. 9"--D-F. (Courtesy Kimport Dolls)

113

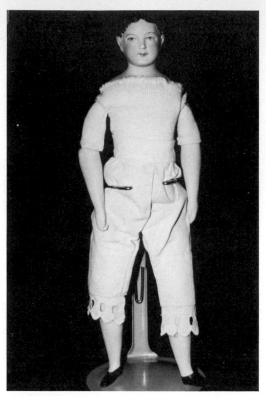

Fernand Gaultier--Shows full length view of 9" F.G. boy.

Fernand Gaultier--11" Swivel head on bisque shoulder plate. Marks: F.G. 11"--G-I. (Courtesy Ralph's Antique Dolls)

Fernand Gaultier--20" Socket head. Closed mouth. Marks: F.G., in a scroll. 20"--L-N. (Courtesy Ralph's Antique Dolls)

Fernand Gaultier--16" Socket head. Straight wrists. Closed mouth. FG, in a scroll. 16"--L-N. (Courtesy Kimport Dolls)

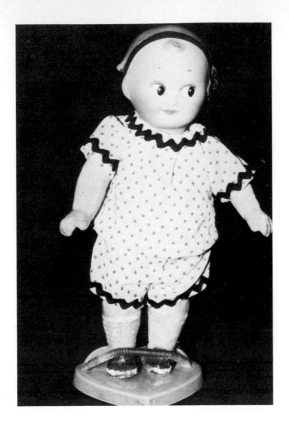

William Goebel--6½" Painted eyes. Pápier maché body. Painted on hose and red shoes. Molded blonde with red molded ribbon. Jointed hips and shoulders. William Goebel is the son of Franz Dellev Goebel and has used this mark since 1879. Marks: ⤳   12/0-Germany. 6½"--B-C. (Clasby Collection)

L. Greiner--16½" Greiner. Molded hair. Painted eyes. Marks: Greiner's Patent Doll Heads Pat. Mar. 30, '58. 16½"--E-F. (Courtesy Kimport Dolls)

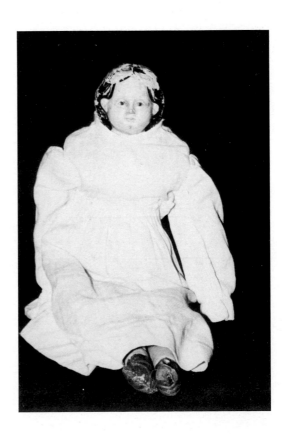

HALF DOLLS

"Half Dolls" of china or bisque (most have sew holes in bases) were not always meant to be atop a pin cushion. They were used on items such as: small lamps, candy boxes, powder boxes, clothes brushes, perfume bottles, etc.

Most date, in the U.S., from about 1900 and some really fine examples were made after 1925. The majority seem to have been made in Germany but only a few carry a maker's mark. One of the finest in quality that was marked was made by the Dressel, Kister & Company of Germany, whose mark is: ⊕ The William Goebel porcelain factory marked their also: ⊻

Collectors seem to want the Half Dolls that have the arms molded away from the body and also included in "very desirable" are molded curls, jointed arms, bald heads, molded flowers, children or men, holding fans, mirrors, books, letters, cups, or anything else.

A great many Half Dolls came from Japan but, generally, are of lesser quality than the German ones.

Half Doll--2½" China. Beautifully made with arms extended. Marks: Germany 5882. ca. 1920. $25.00. (Maish Collection)

Half Doll--3" China. Painting of features very good. Marks: Germany. ca. 1900-1920. $35.00. (Maish Collection)

Half Doll--3½" China. One arm extended. Marks: Germany 8033. ca. 1920. $30.00. (Maish Collection)

Half Doll--4½" China. Exceptional quality. Both arms away from body. Marks: Germany 3889. Pre-1900. $40.00. (Maish Collection)

Half Doll--2½" China doll on pincushion base. The green dotted bodice is repeated on the green dotted georgette skirt. Original. 1925-35. $12.00-$15.00. (Maish Collection)

Half Doll--4½" China Broom. Nice quality porcelain and features. Japan. 1925. $12.00. (Maish Collection)

Half Doll--2" China. Mass produced, cheaply made. Japan. 1925-1935. $2.50. (Maish Collection)

Half Doll--14" Lamp doll. Bisque half doll on metal stand that is a lamp. Marks: △ , on back. $35.00. (Gunnel Collection)

Half Dolls--3½" Marks: 5581/Germany. $15.00. (Clasby Collection)

Half Dolls--2½" Bald head. Original wig. Marks: Germany. $40.00. (Clasby Collection)

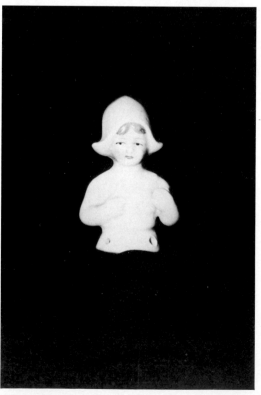

Half Dolls--2½" Child pincushion doll. Marks: Germany. $60.00. (Clasby Collection)

Half Dolls--4" Marks: Made In/Japan. $8.00.
(Gunnel Collection)

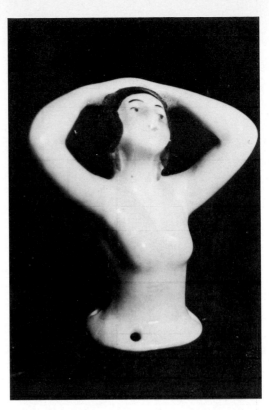

Half Dolls--2" Marks: Germany. $35.00. (Gunnel
Collection)

Half Doll--9" Whist broom half doll. Marks:
8031/Germany. $25.00. (Gunnel Collection)

Half Doll--3½" Marks: Japan. $18.00. (Gunnel
Collection)

Half Doll--3½" Marks: Japan. $15.00. (Gunnel Collection)

Half Doll--3" Turned head. Marks: Germany/ 14753. $40.00. (Gunnel Collection)

Half Doll--3" Molded hair band. Marks: Germany. $35.00. (Gunnel Collection)

Half Doll--3½" Turned head with orange curly hair. Marks: none. $35.00. (Gunnel Collection)

HEINRICH HANDWERCK

This company began in 1876, in Gotha, which was near
Waltershausen, Thur. They made dolls and doll bodies.
Many of their heads were made by Simon & Halbig and
other companies.

As early as 1891 Heinrich Handwerck had registered an 8
point star as a trademark and had registered, in Germany,
such dolls as "Bébé Cosmopolite" (1895), Bébé Re'clame"
(1898) and "Bébé Superior" (1913). The 1913 "Bebe
Superior" was actually made by Kammer & Reinhardt as
they bought the Handwerck Factory, at the death of Heinrich, in 1902 but continued to use the Handwerck
trademarks.

In 1897 Heinrich Handwerck patented in Germany, a ball
jointed doll (#100297) and some of the dolls bodies are so
marked.

Some of the distributors for Handwerck dolls were
Nerlich & Co., George Borgfeldt, B. Illfelder, Foulds &
Freure, Davis & Voetsch and were being sold as late as 1927.

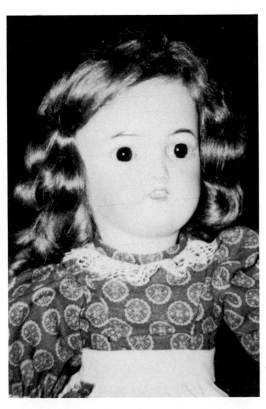

Heinrich Handwerck--14" Shoulder plate. Open
mouth/4 teeth. Original deep red Caracul wig.
Marks: HcH/12/0/H. 14"--B-C. (Clasby Collection)

Heinrich Handwerck--15" Socket head. Open
mouth. Marks: Heinrich Handwerck/Simon &
Halbig/Germany. Head by S&H, body and sold
by H. Handwerck. 15"--B-C. (Courtesy Ralph's
Antique Dolls)

121

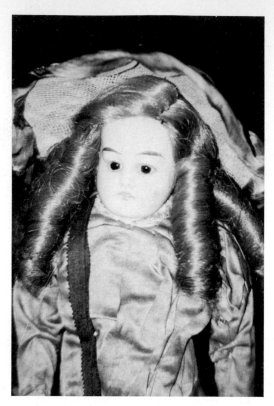

Heinrich Handwerck--15" Shoulder plate.
Original. Marks: ✦ /HCH9/0H. 15"--B-C.
(Minter Collection)

Heinrich Handwerck--16" Socket head. Marks:
Heinrich Handwerck/Simon-Halbig/Germany/
0½. 16"--B-D. (Penner Collection)

Heinrich Handwerck--17" Shoulder plate. Kid
body. Open mouth. Marks: HcH5/0H/ ∞ .
17"--B-D. (Walters Collection)

Heinrich Handwerck--18" Socket head. Open
mouth. Pierced ears. Sleep eyes/lashes. Marks:
Germany/Heinrich Handwerck/Simon Halbig.
18"--B-D. (Courtesy Kimport Dolls)

Heinrich Handwerck--26" Shoulder plate.
Marks: Made In Germany/horseshoe/HCH.9H.
26"--D-F. (Minter Collection)

Heinrich Handwerck--28" Socket head. Marks:
Germany/Handwerck/Halbig/6½.   28"--E-G.
(Minter Collection)

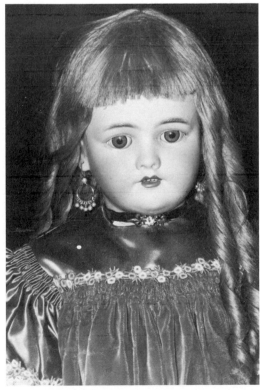

Heinrich Handwerck--30" Sleep eyes. Pierced
ears. Socket head. Open mouth. Marks: Hein-
rich/Handwerck/Simon & Halbig/6. On body, 6.
30"--F-H. (Clasby Collection)

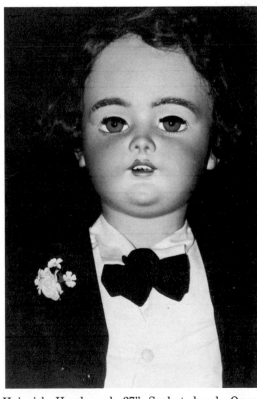

Heinrich Handwerck--37" Socket head. Open
mouth. Marks: Heinrich Handwerck/Simon
Halbig. 37"--H-I. (Courtesy Kimport Dolls)

125

MAX HANDWERCK

Max Handwerck entered the doll field "late" for antique dolls...1900. His factory was at Waltershausen, Thur. In 1901 he registered his trademark of Bebe Elite and, in 1913, Cornouloid (Celluloid) Dolls and Madame Butterfly.

The Bebe Elite heads were made by the William Goebel firm.

The Max Handwerck bodies of 1913 were made following his American and German patents: they were hollow and constructed of paper/cloth. They were made by uniting two halves of thin material with staples at the overlapping edges. This inner body was covered by a slightly larger outer body that was united to the inner one by bonding. The outside body was kept together by flanges, which were trimmed.

As for the marks on his dolls, the full name "Max Handwerck" generally was incised.

Max Handwerck--20" Socket head. Open mouth. Marks: $\frac{1}{0}$. ca. 1910. 20"--B-C.

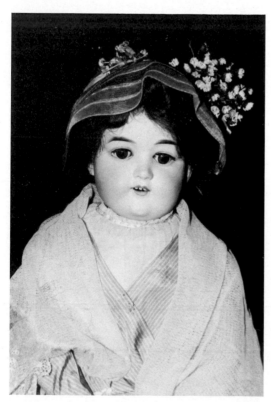

Max Handwerck--22" Socket head. Open mouth. Sleep eyes/lashes. Marks: M.H./6½. 22"--B-C. (Courtesy Kimport Dolls)

Max Handwerck--23" Open mouth. Socket head. Marks: $\frac{h}{2}$. 23"--C-D. (Courtesy Kimport Dolls)

Max Handwerck--24" Socket head. Open mouth. Marks:)–(. 24"--C-D. (Courtesy Kimport Dolls)

Max Handwerck--29" Socket head. Sleep eyes. Open mouth. Marks: Max Handwerck/Germany/4½. 29"--E-F. (Clasby Collection)

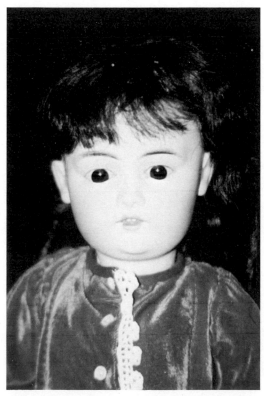

ERNST HEUBACH OF KOPPELSDORF

This porcelain factory had its beginning in 1887 at Koppelsdorf, Thur. and by 1895 were employing over 200 workers. Ernst Heubach was the brother-in-law of Armand Marseille and it must be assumed they used each other's facilities.

Typical Ernst Heubach mold marks: the initials "EH," Heubach-Koppelsdorf

Robert Hiller & Co.--21" Socket head. Open mouth. Marks: RH, in a circle with an overlapped picture (incised) of a swan. ca. 1895. The Hiller Company operated at Breslau, Silesia. 21"--C-D. (Courtesy Ralph's Antique Dolls)

Ernst Heubach Of Koppelsdorf--14" Shoulder plate. Marks: Germany/275-18/Heubach Koppelsdorf. 14"--A-B. (Gunnel Collection)

Ernst Heubach Of Koppelsdorf--15" Kid body with bisque lower arms. Open mouth. Marks: Made In Germany/A Horseshoe/1900 6/0. 15"--A-B. (Minter Collection)

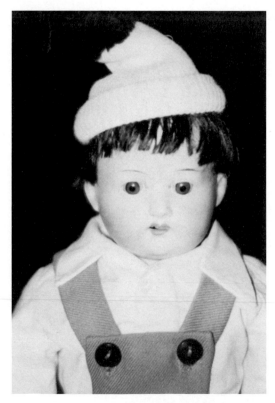

Ernest Heubach Of Koppelsdorf--15" Shoulder plate. Marks: Germany/275 9/0/Heubach Koppelsdorf. 15"--A-B. (Gunnel Collection)

Ernst Heubach--18" Shoulder plate. Kid body. Open mouth. Marks: 3095. 18"--C-D. (Walters Collection)

Ernst Heubach--15" Socket head. Lady doll with slim shaped legs. Marks: 🐎 1900-3/0. 15"--B-C. (Walters Collection)

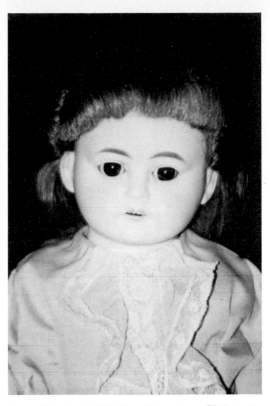

Ernst Heubach--22" Shoulder plate. Kid body. Open mouth. Marks: 🐎 /1901-1. 22"--C-D. (Courtesy Ralph's Antique Dolls)

Ernst Heubach--14" Socket head. Open mouth. Marks: 340/Dep./V.. which is raised rather than incised. Head was made for H & A Van Raalte in London, in 1890. 14"--B-C. (Courtesy Kimport Dolls)

Ernst Heubach--16" Socket head. Sleep eyes. Open mouth. Marks: Heubach/250.4/0/Koppels-dorf. 16"--B-C. (Gunnel Collection)

129

Ernst Heubach of Koppelsdorf--16" Socket head. Marks: Heubach/250 3/0/Koppelsdorf/Germany. 16"--B-C. (Gunnel Collection)

Ernst Heubach Of Koppelsdorf--18" Socket head. Marks: Heubach/250 3/0/Koppelsdorf. 18"--C-D. (Gunnel Collection)

Ernst Heubach Of Koppelsdorf--24" Socket head. Very wide spread fingers. Marks: Heubach/250.4/Koppelsdorf/Germany. ca. 1900. 24"--C-D. (Gunnel Collection)

Ernst Heubach--24" Socket head. Pierced ears. Open mouth. Marks: Dep/1900.6. 24"--C-D. (Walters Collection)

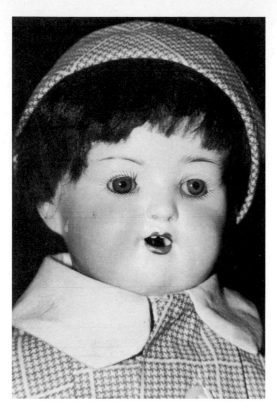

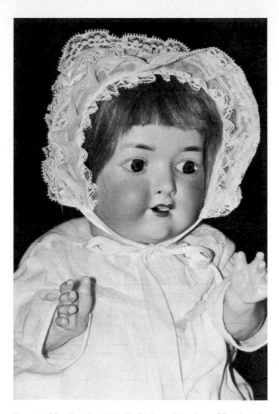

Ernst Heubach--14" Socket head. Open mouth/2 upper teeth. Blue sleep eyes. All original. Marks: Heubach Koppelsdorf/321.116/Germany. 14"--B-C. (Courtesy Kimport Dolls)

Ernst Heubach--19½" Baby. Marks: Heubach-Koppelsdorf/320-6/Germany. 19½"--C-D. (Walters Collection)

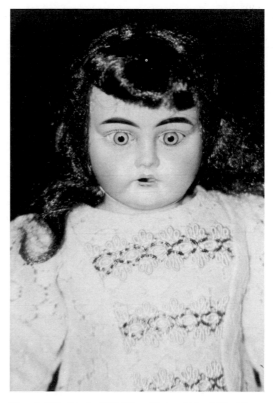

Ernst Heubach Of Koppelsdorf--12" Socket head. Marks: Heubach Koppelsdorf/300 9/0/Germany. 12"--B-C. (Minter Collection)

Ernst Heubach--21" Shoulder plate/kid. Open mouth. Marks: 1900 0½. 21"--B-C. (Gunnel Collection)

GEBRUDER HEUBACH

Gebruder Heubach made dolls from 1863 into the 1930's. Their porcelain factory was in Lichte, Thur and their business address was Sonneberg. They made general type dolls until about 1909 or 1910 when they began to make "character" dolls and babies. Bodies of the Heubach dolls are often of poor quality, but the character heads make up for the lack of quality in the bodies.

The Gebruder Heubach dolls and babies, of the character phase, have every imaginable expression and reflect every mood. They are generally rather small dolls.

The Gebruder Heubach factory produced some of the most fantastic, delightful and beautiful "Piano" babies to be found.

Since the majority of Gebruder Heubachs did have intaglio (painted) eyes and very few sleep eyed dolls, the prices on a sleep eyed Heubach has risen to a pretty high level. This happens when collectors find anything that is rare.

Sample Gebruder Heubach marks are:

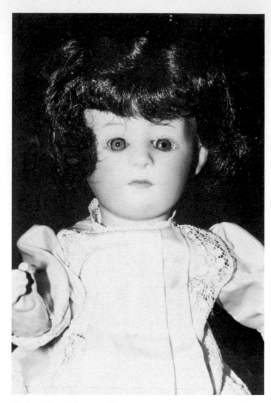

Gebruder Heubach--6" head cir. Socket head with glass eyes. Closed mouth. Marks: 2/0. 6"-- E-G. (Courtesy Ralph's Antique Dolls)

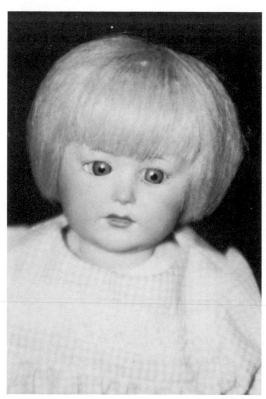

Gebruder Heubach--7½" head Cir. Baby. Socket head. Rare glass eyes. Open crown/wig. Marks: 2 [HEU BACH] 7½"--G-I. (Courtesy Ralph's Antique Dolls)

Gebruder Heubach--8" Socket head. Pápier maché body and limbs. Marks: 3/0 . 8"--J-L. (Courtesy Kimport Dolls)

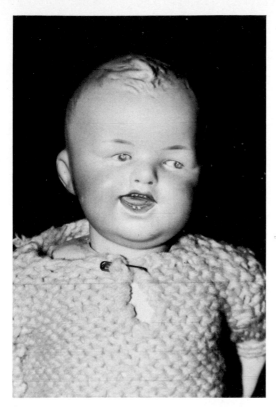

Gebruder Heubach--8" head cir. Open/closed mouth with 2 rows of painted teeth. Marks: 3/31 [HEU BACH] 91/Germany. 8"--H-J. (Courtesy Ralph's Antique Dolls)

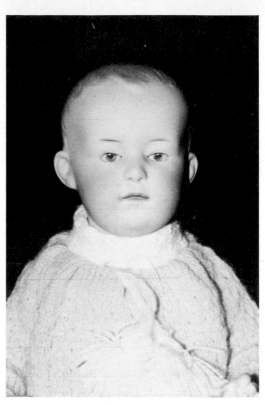

Gebruder Heubach--8½" head Cir. Intaglio eyes. Closed mouth. On baby body. Marks: 4/16, [symbol] 15/Germany. 8½"--C-E. (Courtesy Ralph's Antique Dolls)

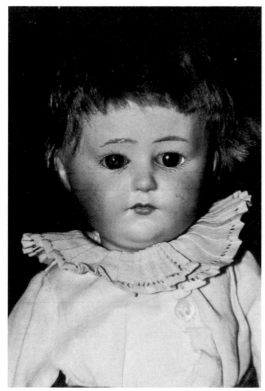

Gebruder Heubach--9½" Socket head. Glass eyes. Closed mouth. Marks: 2/0/ [HEU BACH] . 9½"-- E-G. (Courtesy Kimport Dolls)

Gebruder Heubach--12" Socket head. Glass eyes. Closed mouth. Original. Marks: 3/3420/ [HEU BACH] . 12"--I-K. (Courtesy Kimport Dolls)

133

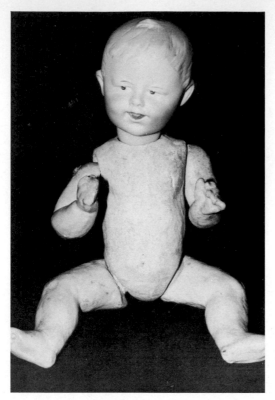

Gebruder Heubach--12" Painted eyes. Open/
closed mouth. Marks: 2 . 12"--E-G.
(Clasby Collection) 19 [HEU BACH] 11
Germany

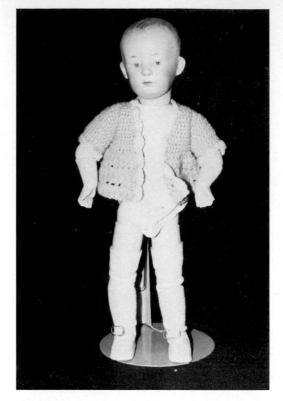

Gebruder Heubach--13" Composition body not of
the toddler type. Straight wrists. Painted eyes.
Closed mouth. Marks: 10 [HEU] 02/3/Germany.
13"--C-E. (Courtesy Kimport Dolls)

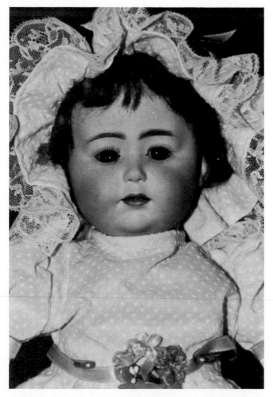

Gebruder Heubach--15" Socket head. Glass eyes.
Closed mouth. Marks: 8429/ [HEU BACH] . 15"--L-N.
(Courtesy Kimport Dolls)

HORSMAN DOLLS COMPANY INC.

The E.I. Horsman company was founded in 1865. Mr. Horsman was a member of an old German toymaking family and he began by importing the finest European doll heads and bodies and putting them together here in the U.S.A.

It was not long before Mr. Horsman began making dolls here in America and his first was "Baby Bisque" known for her beautiful complexion and human hair. Next famous were the Campbell Kids in 1910, molded like the famous children in the Campbell Soup advertisements. Then came the He-Bee-She-Bee's of 1925 and Ella Cinders, also in 1925. Horsman also helped in design and making some Fulpher Pottery Co. heads. They are marked with both names.

Horsman--18" This is the popular "Nippon Baby." Bisque head, round brown eyes, teeth, mohair wig. Jointed composition body. She has a beautiful coloring and a very sweet expression. The doll was made about 1917 and is wearing a baby's Christening dress and bonnet of the times. Marks: No 1 Horsman Nippon in circle on head. 18"--B-C. (Maish Collection)

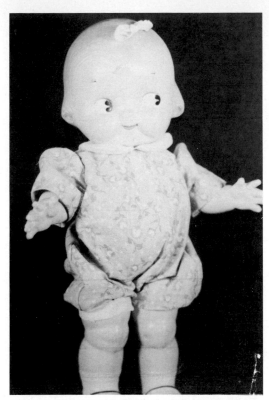

Horsman--12" Campbell Kid. All composition. All jointed. Painted features. 1911-1912. An 11½" almost identical doll was made by American Character in 1925, and a later 12½" was made by Horsman in 1948. One way to differentiate, is that the older one has a glossier, less colorful finish, the 1948 version has rosier cheeks and a matte finish. 12"--$65.00.

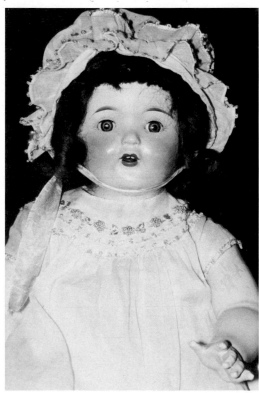

Horsman--23" Composition with cloth body. Open mouth/2 upper teeth. Marks: E.I.H. A.D.C. Tag on dress: Horsman Doll/M'fd In U.S.A. This doll was produced for Horsman by Aetna Doll & Toy Co. 23"--$75.00. (Clasby Collection)

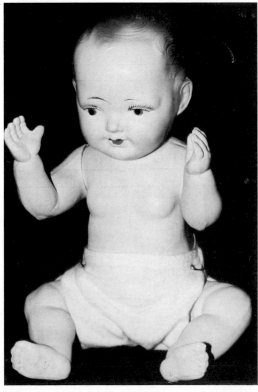

Irokese Trading Corp.--12" All painted celluloid. Molded brown hair. Painted blue eyes. Jointed shoulders and hips that are pin jointed. Marks: Head of Indian. ca. 1921. This company operated by Louis Sametz of Westport, Conn. and was founded in 1918. 12"--$85.00.

Andrew Jergens & Co. 4¼" Soap doll of 1900.
Marks: Andrew Jergens & Co./Cincinnati.
4½"--$22.50. (Courtesy Kimport Dolls)

JULLIEN, JEUNE

Jullien, Jeune (Junior) made Bébés, Soldiers (Zouaves),
Nankeen dolls and had a general line of dolls. He made ordinary and deluxe models, had ladies, brides, peasants, Bébé
with trousseaux, young girls, swimmers, bathers. His dolls
had both swivel and stationary heads, rigid and jointed,
talking dolls, a walking and talking doll in 1895 that had
hollow wood limbs. He made dolls with closed and also open
mouths, as most of the French dollmakers did.

His business ran from 1863 to 1904 and, in 1904, he became
a member of the Société Française de Fabrication de Bébé et
Jouets (S.F.B.J.). It was in 1900 that Jullien, Jeune won a
bronze medal at the Paris Exposition.

Jullien dolls are marked with the name "Jullien" or letters
"J.J."

Jullien--14" Socket head. Open mouth. All original. Marks: Jullien/3, on head. 14"--I-K. (Minter
Collection)

Jullien--13" Socket head. Closed mouth. Marks:
Jullien/2, on head. 13"--K-M. (Courtesy Ralph's
Antique Dolls)

THE HOUSE OF (MAISON) JUMEAU

In the following I will use the French method of writing and would like to preface it with an explanation. "M" before a name stands for "Monsieur" meaning "Mister." "Maison" means "House of."

The first dolls made by a Jumeau were also made with a partner, M. Belton, until 1846 when Pierre François Jumeau "went on his own." His first dolls had bisque heads with the shoulder plates fitted into all kid bodies. At a later date, arms and legs were also of bisque.

The kid bodies were white, pale cream or pink and made with gussets at the elbows, hips and knees, with the stitching between the fingers and toes. On the larger dolls, the fingers and toes were stuffed separately.

Prior to 1862, Jumeau dolls had one piece shoulder plates and, in 1862, Jumeau patented a swivel head. Although it should be noted here that Mademoiselle Calixte Huret had applied for a patent for a swivel head in 1861. All the Jumeaus of this period had closed mouths and all were called "Poupee Parisienne."

Through the last part of the 1860's and the first years of the 1870's Jumeau was making the same kind of dolls but with one important item: he was now making doll heads at a factory located at Montreuil sous-Bois. It is important to note that at the 1873 Exhibition in Vienna, it was said: "M. Jumeau of Paris, the first and most important doll making house, has freed us from our former obligation to have the foreigner (Germany) furnish us with porcelain doll heads. M. Jumeau has established at Montreiul, near Paris, a factory where he makes doll heads of enameled porcelain with the greatest perfection. He has surpassed in beauty the products that we used to buy from Saxony." In reference to the above statement, enameled porcelain generally means a high gloss and could be referring to "china" heads. It could also lead one to believe that both Belton and all "Poupée Parisienne" (fashion) doll heads were made in Germany (Saxony).

At this Vienna Exhibition Jumeau won a gold medal as well as The Medal of Progress. That year the Medal of Cooperation went to four representatives of the Maison P.F. Jumeau: Emile Jumeau, Madame Blanche Pannier, Mademoiselle Elisa Cadet and Oscar Rinders.

It was during this part of the 1870's that the two sons of Pierre François Jumeau, Georges, the elder who was to inherit the factory and Emile, the youngest, tried to persuade their father that it was time for changes. Georges, with patience and ingenuity, obtained small reforms and was leading into major changes when he died. The loss of his eldest son crushed Pierre Jumeau and he lost his desire to work and grew old rapidly. His second son, Emile, who wanted to be an architect, succeeded him.

After Emile Jumeau took over the operation of the business, he created Bébés or children and baby types. Up to this point Jumeau dolls were on kid bodies. At this same period, "unbreakable" bébés appeared in Paris. "Unbreakable" was referring to composition, jointed bodies. It should be pointed out that the full name of Jumeau did not appear on the dolls and that the word "bébé" was used for the first time, in relation to dolls by him. He has been credited with the invention of the Bébé and rightly so. His dolls caused such as stir in France that there were rumors and reports (newspapers and competitors), and articles from papers such as "Figaro" made statements like: "...even though virulent circulars have been written about him, M. Jumeau is and remains the inventor of the "Bébé" which bears his name, and no one else has the right to any claim to it."

It does not appear that Pierre François Jumeau obtained any patents except for a swivel head in 1862, but his son, Emile, took out several. In 1882 Bru and Jumeau took out a patent for a mechanical boat. In 1885 Jumeau took out a patent for eyelids that dropped down over the eyes. In 1886 he got another patent to eliminate the space left when the eyelid was in an open position. Also that year, he got a patent for an unbreakable doll and a patent for sleeping eyes/lashes.

Emile Jumeau registered the trademark "Bébé Jumeau" in 1886 (U.S. in 1888) and the same year: "Bébé Prodige" and in 1896 "Bébé Français."

As to medals at Exhibitions the following are listed: 1844 Paris (Belton & Jumeau) Honorable Mention for doll clothes. 1851 London Gold Medal; 1885 Paris Silver; 1867 Paris Silver; 1873 Vienna Gold; 1876 Philadelphia Gold; 1878 Paris Gold; 1879 Melbourne Gold; 1884 New Orleans Gold; 1885 Antwerp Diploma of Honor; 1885 Paris Gold; and in 1886 names Chevalier de la Legion d'Honneur.

While Buffalo Bill Cody visited Europe in 1887, he purchased a Jumeau doll. This particular model has become known as the "long face" or "Cody" Jumeau. This model was also produced with an open mouth but so far collectors have only referred to the closed mouth version as a "long faced" Jumeau. These dolls have a size number on heads and a marked Jumeau body.

During the 1890's Jumeau turned to quantity and advertisements said (1892) "The Maison Jumeau makes two new models with differences in price of 20 percent and 40 percent, but with the same irreproachable quality remaining and not carrying the Jumeau name.

In 1889 Jumeau joined the Société Française de Fabrication de Bébés et Jouets (S.F.B.J.)

From 1848 to 1866 Jumeau was located on the rue Mauconseil and in 1867 moved to rue Anjou Marais. The Jumeau factory was at Nontruil, Rue de Paris 151. Jumeau had a store on the rue Pastourelle, Paris.

It should be noted that all those red "check" marks and initials around the back of the doll heads or along the top of the crown are nothing but the artist "clearing" her brush before painting the lips, dotting the eyes and nostrils of the Jumeau doll heads.

Sample Jumeau marks: E.J. (incised) Red stamps on heads..blue stamps on bodies:

Deposé	Bébé Jumeau	Jumeau
Tête Jumeau	Diplomé d' Honneur	Medaille d'or
		Paris

Jumeau--9" Pierced ears. Closed mouth. Marks: 1, on head. 9"--L-N. (Minter Collection)

Jumeau--11" Straight wrists. Original. Marks: Deposé/E3J. Closed mouth. 11"--M-O. (Minter Collection)

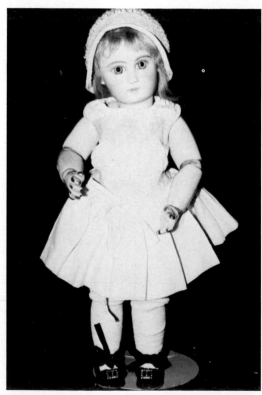

Jumeau--15½" Portrait Jumeau. Closed mouth. Marks: 6, on head. Body stamped "Jumeau." 152"--L-N. (Courtesy Kimport Dolls)

Jumeau--19" "Bébé Dimpolma" Portrait type Jumeau. Closed mouth. Marks: 9X, on head. Bébé Dimpolma/Jumeau/blue stamp on body. Coat and hat original. 19"--P-R. (Minter Collection)

138

Jumeau--20" Portrait Jumeau. Straight wrists. Closed mouth. Applied ears. Marks: Deposé/E.9 J., incised. Body: Jumeau/Medal D'or/Paris. 20"--Q-S. (Penner Collection)

Jumeau--21" Closed mouth. Original clothes. Marks: Depose/Tête Jumeau/BTE S.G.D.G./9. Marked Jumeau body. 21"--M-O. (Minter Collection)

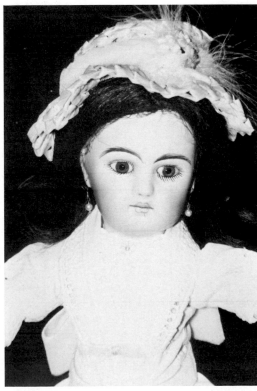

Jumeau--13" Straight wrists. Extremely pale bisque. Closed mouth. Marks: Tête Jumeau/4. 13"--L-N. (Minter Collection)

Jumeau--26" "Cody" or "Long Face Jumeau." Closed mouth. Socket head. Marks: 13, on head. 26"--Y-Z. (Courtesy Ralph's Antique Dolls)

139

Jumeau--29" Long face, or "Cody" Jumeau. Marks: 14, on head. Marked Jumeau body. Unjointed wrists and closed mouth. 29"--Z+. (Minter Collection)

Jumeau--Full face view of 29" "Cody" Jumeau.

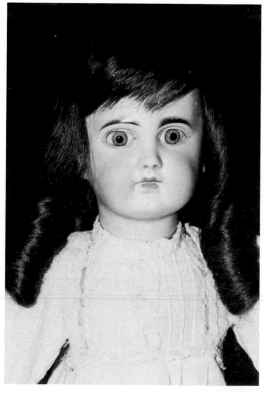

Jumeau--Part profile view of "Cody" Jumeau.

Jumeau--18" Socket head. Closed mouth. "Belton" type. Pierced ears. Kestner head made for Jumeau. Bodies usually marked "Bébé Jumeau." Marks: 137, on head. 18"--I-K.

Jumeau--14" Wood/composition with brown set eyes. Pierced ears. On typical Jumeau unmarked body. Marks: E.J., on head. 14"--M-O. (Author)

Jumeau--Full length view of 14."

Jumeau--19" Marks: Depose/Tête Jumeau/BTE SGDG/8, on head. Original. Marked: Jumeau Body. 19"--M-O. (Minter Collection)

Jumeau--21" Closed mouth. All original. Marks: Depose/Tête Jumeau/8 Body: Bébé Jumeau/ BTE SGDG/Depose. 21"--M-O. (Minter Collection)

141

Jumeau--19" Marks: Depose/Tête Jumeau/BTE S.G.D.G./8H, on head. Jumeau/Medeille D'or/ Paris, blue stamp on body. Dressed by Bessie Greeno. 19"--M-O. (Author)

Jumeau--Full length view of 19."

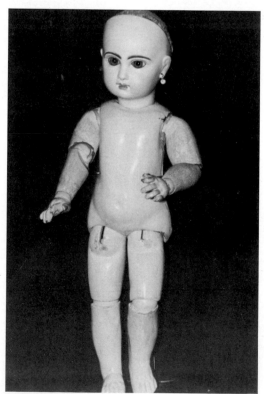

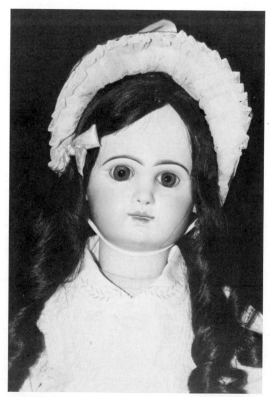

Jumeau--Shows body view of 19." Short upper arms.

Jumeau--24" Marks: Depose/Tête Jumeau/BTE SGDG. Blue stamped Jumeau body. Original. 24"--P-R. (Minter Collection)

Jumeau--26" Socket head. Applied ears. Marks: E.J. Closed mouth. Made during time Emile Jumeau was head of the Jumeau firm. 26"--T-U. (Courtesy Ralph's Antique Dolls)

Jumeau--26" Marks: Depose/Tête Jumeau/BTE SGDG/19/L, on head. Blue stamped marked body. Tag on dress Bebe Jumeau. 26"--Q-S. (Jones Collection)

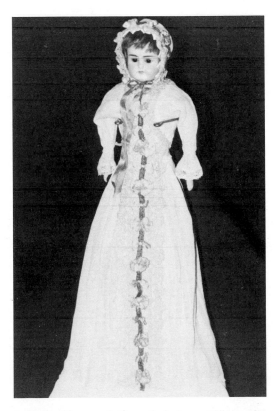

Jumeau--15" Closed dome. Closed mouth with slight smile. Turned shoulder head. Dimple in chin. Kid body. Bisque forearms. Used as a "baby" with very long Christening clothes. Original clothes. Marks: 639 6. Made by J.D. Kestner for Pierre Jumeau in 1874-1877. 12"--C-E, 18"--F-H. (Author)

Jumeau--Shows clothes (baby) on 15" marks: 639 6. Made for Jumeau by Kestner, prior to 1877. 12"--C-E, 18"--F-H. (Author)

143

Jumeau--19" Mechanical Jumeau music box. Key wing. Doll has closed mouth. 19"--X-Y. (Courtesy Kimport Dolls)

Jumeau--22" Socket head. Open mouth. Walker. As she walks, her head turns. Marks: ⊗ 22"--H-J. (Gunnel Collection)

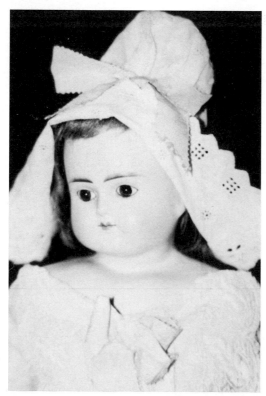

Jumeau--21" Turned shoulder plate. Full solid dome. Paper weight eyes. Marks: 639 #9. Made by J.D. Kestner for Jumeau. Most of these heads were dressed as babies with extremely long christening clothes. 21"--F-H. (Gunnel Collection)

Jumeau--27" Unmarked Jumeau lady. 27"--Q-S. (Courtesy Kimport Dolls)

144

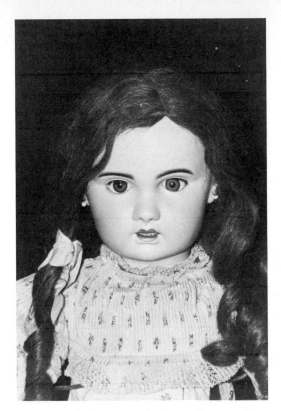

Jumeau--17" All original in original box. Dress is same as shown on box lid. Marks: Tête Jumeau/ 7. Bee marked shoes. 1890. 17"--I-K. (Author)

Jumeau--24" Open mouth. Applied ears. Sleep eyes. Marks: Tête Jumeau with ⑪ incised. Blue stamped body. All original. 24"--I-K. (Minter Collection)

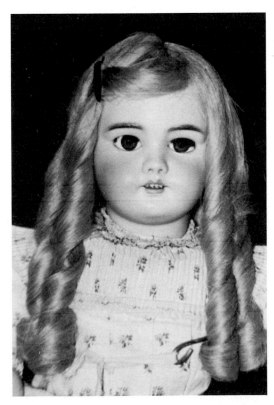

Jumeau--26" "Bébé Parle" Socket head. Lashes. Open mouth. Pull string Mama and Papa talker. Marks: Dep./Tete Jumeau. All original. 26"--I-K. (Gunnel Collection)

Jumeau--32" "Bébé Parle" Pull string talker (Mama-Papa) Sleep eyes/lashes. Open mouth. Original. Marks: Tete Jumeau, on head. 32"--K-M. (Minter Collection)

Jumeau--16½" Socket head. Open mouth. Marks: 1907/6. Made after Jumeau joined S.F.B.J. 16½"--F-G. (Gunnel Collection)

Jumeau--17" Socket head. Set eyes/lashes. Open mouth. Marks: Dep./Tête Jumeau/6. 17"--G-H. (Clasby Collection)

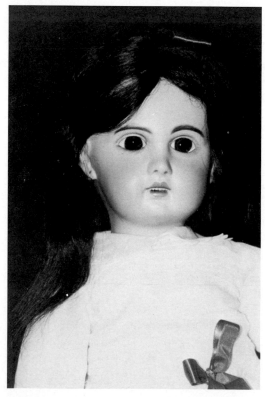

Jumeau--25" Open mouth. Marks: 1907/10. Marked Jumeau body. 25"--I-J. (Minter Collection)

Jumeau--27" Molded brows. Open mouth. Marks: Dep./Tête Jumeau, on head. Bébé Jumeau/Diplome d Honneur, on body. 27"--J-K. (Minter Collection)

Jumeau--23" Open mouth. Marks: Deposé/T5. 32"--J-K. (Gunnel Collection)

Jumeau--37" Socket head. Open mouth. 37"--K-L. (Gunnel Collection)

Jumeau--23" Unmarked Jumeau. Open mouth. Set blue eyes. Marks: 9, very low on neck flange. 23"--H-I.

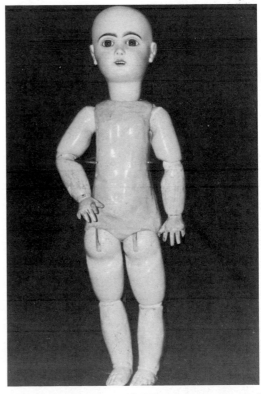

Jumeau--Body view of "Unmarked Jumeau" with typical unmarked Jumeau body.

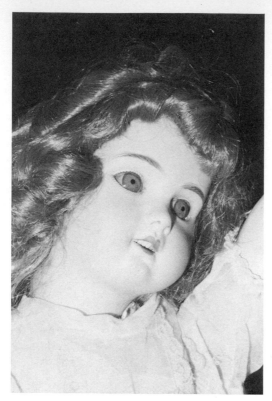

Jumeau--22" "Unmarked Jumeau" Replaced eyes. Molded brows. Marks: 10, on head. 22"--E-F. (Esler Collection)

Jumeau--22" "Unmarked Jumeau" Brown paper weight eyes. Marks: 10, on head. 22"--E-F. (Esler Collection)

Jumeau--13" Celluloid head marked "Jumeau." 13"--A-B. (Penner Collection)

Jumeau--Sovenir fan with advertising, from the Jumeau firm. (Minter Collection)

Jumeau--Back view of Jumeau Souvenir fan.

Jumeau--19½" Portrait swivel head on bisque shoulder plate. Closed mouth. Pierced ears. Portrait fashion, possibly by Jumeau. Marks: none. 19½"--K-M. (Courtesy Kimport Dolls)

Jumeau--14" Portrait with swivel head on bisque shoulder plate. Kid body. Closed mouth. Pierced ears. Marks: Body marked Jumeau. 14"--I-K. (Courtesy Kimport Dolls)

Jumeau--19" "Poupee Parisienne" Referred to by collectors as "Mona Lisa." Bisque swivel head on bisque shoulder plate. Smiling closed mouth. French kid body. Came also on fully articulated wood body. These dolls are marked with letters of the alphabet. To date I have seen "J," "G," "E" and this one is marked "F." (Kid) 19"--L-N. (Courtesy Kimport Dolls)

149

Jumeau--16" "Poupéé Parisienne" Closed mouth. Smiling. Wood body and limbs. Marks: E, on head. These dolls are referred to as "Mona Lisa." (Wood) 16"--P-R. (Courtesy Ralph's Antique Dolls)

KAHL & KOHLE TOY COMPANY

The K & K Toy Company (Kahle & Kohle) made dolls in 1915 including the "Happyfats," "Bye-lo Baby" "Kewpies," and these were distributed by the George Borgfeldt Company. K&K was located in New York City and about 1925 were brought out by the Cameo Doll Company.

They made both sleep eyed and painted eyed dolls of bisque and composition and had a very delightfully "happy" Mama type line of dolls. Many of the bisque heads were made in Germany and imported to be placed on bodies in the New York factory.

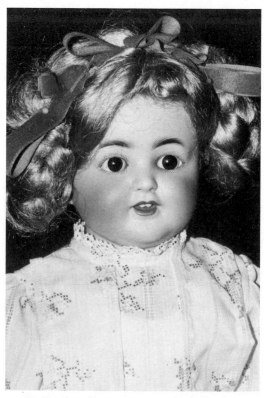

Kolh & Kohle--17" Shoulder plate. Kid body with composition lower arms and muslin lower legs. Beautiful quality bisque. A happy child. Marks: 38/K&K/45/Thuringia. 17"--C-D. (Author)

KAMMER & REINHARDT

Kammer & Reinhardt started in 1886 and ran into the 1930's. They bought the Heinrich Hanwerck factory in 1902 and most of their heads were made by the Simon & Halbig Company. In 1916, Kammer & Reinhardt stock was sold to Bing Works, (Marks: G.B.N., B.W.&Bin) who was one of the largest Germany toy manufacturers and had as many as 4000 employees. They kept Mr. Reinhardt in the capacity of advisor-counsellor and by 1933, 95% of the stock was owned by Eichorn & Sons.

Kammer & Reinhardt have used the trademark of K. Star R since 1895 and "Mein Liebling" (My Darling) and "Majestic Doll" from 1901. It was in 1901 that Ernst Kammer, who was modeler and creator of their dolls died and was replaced by Karl Krauser.

In 1909, Kammer & Reinhardt introduced a line of "Character" dolls such as "Baby" (Mold #100), mistakenly referred to as the "Kaiser" baby. It must be remembered the bent limb baby body was very new and the Kaiser of Germany was born with a slight deformity, the doll came from Germany and so a connection was made somewhere, by someone! The model #101 was a boy, Peter and girl, Marie.

Kammer & Reinhardt said all these dolls were modeled after real children. In 1910 came #107, Carl, #109, Elise, #114, Hans & Gretchen. It wasn't until 1920 that mold #126 was used and it is the most frequently found. Mold # 116 looks suspiciously like the Kestner "Hilda" and 116A has an entirely different look with close set eyes, dimples and an open/closed mouth. They followed this pattern with other mold numbers also, like 117 has a rather closed mouth "pouty" look and 117A has a fantastic "sweet face" look and is considered the most desirable of all the Kammer & Reinhardt "children," the 117N is an open mouth doll. It must be noted that this company made many of their molds in celluloid, with the heads made by the Rheinische Gummi & Celluloid Fabric Co.

I would refer any serious students of collection of Kammer & Reinhardt dolls to Patricia N. Schoonmaker's "Research on Kammer & Reinhardt Dolls"

Sample marks:

K ✡ R

Simon & Halbig

Kammer & Reinhardt--17" Socket head. Marks: K ✡ R/Simon Halbig. 17"--C-D. (Minter Collection)

Kammer & Reinhardt--27" Unjointed shoulder plate. Open mouth. Kid body. Molded brows. Marks: SH/K ✡ R. 27"--D-E. (Courtesy Kimport Dolls)

151

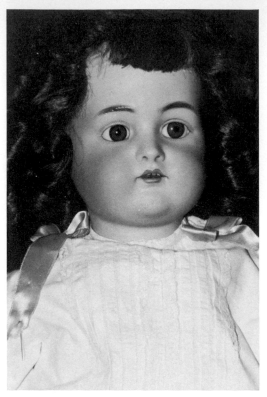

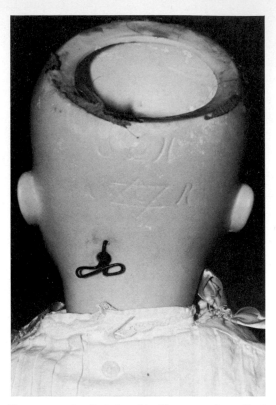

Kammer & Reinhardt--27½" Socket head. Made by Simon & Halbig for Kammer & Reinhardt. Has eye mechanism operated by wire through back of head. Marks: S&H/K ✡ R. 27½"--E-F. (Courtesy Kimport Dolls)

Kammer & Reinhardt--Shows wire that operated the sleep/lock eyes of the patent of Simon & Halbig of 1890.

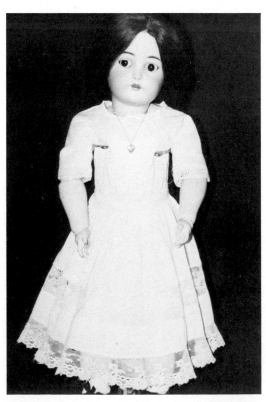

Kammer & Reinhardt--27" Socket head. Open mouth. Marks: X3/400, in red and incised K ✡ R/Simon Halbig/29. 27"--D-E.

Kammer & Reinhardt--25" Socket head. Flirty eyes with tin eyelids. All original. Marks: Simon Halbig/K ✡ R/62. 25"--F-G. (Clasby Collection)

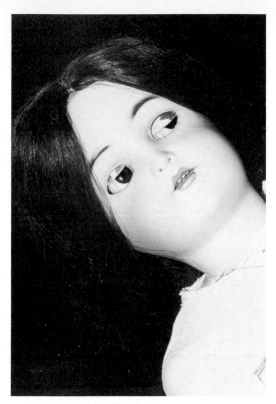

Kammer & Reinhardt--25" Shows tin eyelids that drop down over the flirty (non-sleep) eyes.

Kammer & Reinhardt--23" Socket head. Sleep eyes. Original wig. Marks: 109-12/Germany. Body: Handwerck. Made in Heinrich Handwerck factory after Kammer & Reinhardt bought them out in 1902. 23"--G-H. (Penner Collection)

Kammer & Reinhardt--9" "Hans" (girl: Gretchen) Called "Playmates" by company. Painted eyes. Marks: K ✡ R/114/26. 9"--M-O. (Minter Collection)

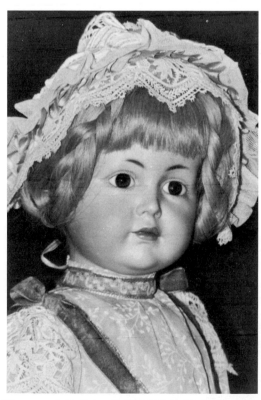

Kammer & Reinhardt--23" "Mein Liebling" (My Darling). Closed mouth. Unpierced ears. Made in 1906 through 1923, after K&R bought Heinrich Hanwerck factory in 1902. Marks: K ✡ R/Simon Halbig/117/A. Body: Heinrich Handwerck/Germany, in red. Dressed by Bessie Greeno. 23"--T-U. (Author)

153

Kammer & Reinhardt--Full length view of 117/A.

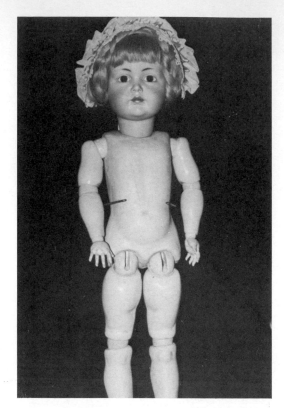

Kammer & Reinhardt--Full body view of 117/A. Body is marked Heinrich Handwerck, in red.

Kammer & Reinhardt--20" Flirty brown eyes/ lashes. Open mouth. Marks: K ✡ R/S & H/117n. 20"--F-G. (Courtesy Kimport Dolls)

Kammer & Reinhardt--18" Socket head. Flirty almond shaped sleep eyes. Hawaiian. Marks: K ✡ R/Simon Halbig/117n. 18"--F-G. (Gunnel Collection)

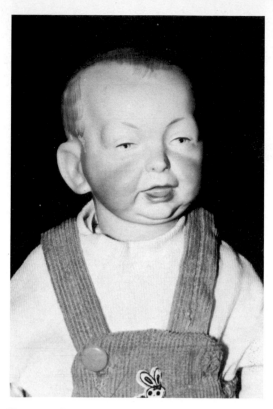

Kammer & Reinhardt--7½" Socket head on fully jointed body. Open mouth/2 teeth. Palms down with separate fingers. Marks: K ✡ R/Simon Halbig/126/Germany. Appears to be original clothes. 7½"--C-D. (Watson Collection)

Kammer & Reinhardt--8" head cir. Painted eyes. Open/closed mouth. Marks: K ✡ R/100. 8"--F-G. (Courtesy Ralph's Antique Dolls)

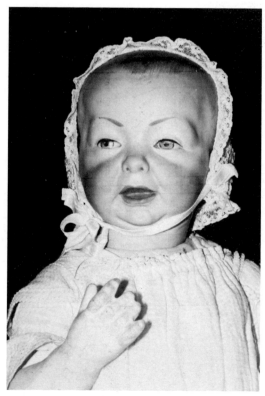

Kammer & Reinhardt--19" Open/closed mouth. Intaglio eyes. Marks: K ✡ R/100. 19"--H-K. (Courtesy Kimport Dolls)

Kammer & Reinhardt--17" Socket head. Movable tongue. Original wig. Marks: K ✡ R/Simon Halbig/116a/42. 17"--K-M. (Clasby Collection)

155

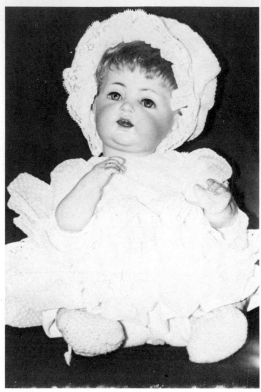

Kammer & Reinhardt--15" Sleep blue
eyes/lashes. Open mouth/2 teeth. Molded
tongue. Dimples. Original wig. Marks: K ✡
R/Simon & Halbig/116/a. 15"--F-G. (Minter
Collection)

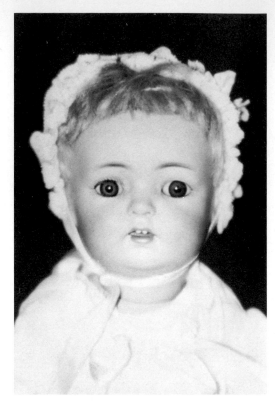

Kammer & Reinhardt--8½" head cir. Open
mouth. Original baby wig. Marks: K ✡ R/
121. ca. 1920. 12"--D-E.

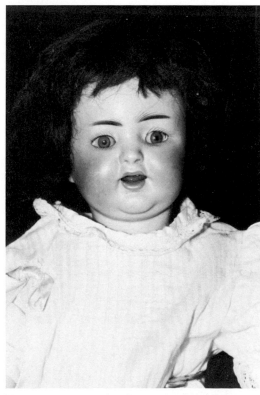

Kammer & Reinhardt--13½" Open mouth/
upper teeth. Sleep eyes. Marks: K ✡ R/Si-
mon Halbig/126. 13½"--F-G.

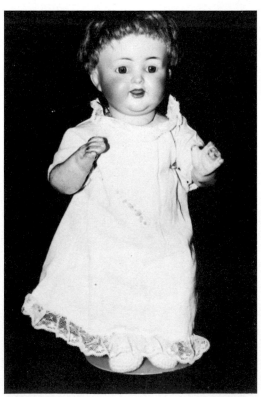

Kammer & Reinhardt--13" Sleep eyes. Open
mouth. Marks: K ✡ R/Simon Halbig/126. ca.
1920. 13"--E-F. (Courtesy Kimport Dolls)

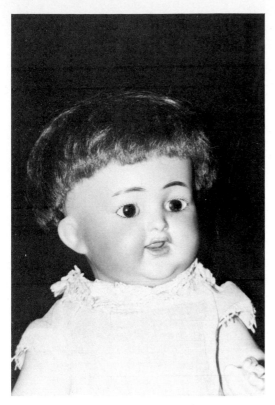

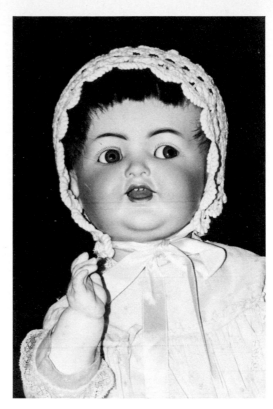

Kammer & Reinhardt--10" Open mouth/2 teeth.
Molded tongue. Original baby wig. Marks:
K ✡ R/Simon Halbig/126. 10"--E-F. (Minter
Collection)

Kammer & Reinhardt--18" Flirty sleep eyes/
painted lashes. Open mouth/2 teeth. Marks: K
✡ R/Simon Halbig/126. ca. 1920. 18"--F-H.
(Minter Collection)

Kammer & Reinhardt--21" Celluloid. Flirty eyes.
Open mouth. Marks: K ✡ R/728/0 Ger-
many/50/5. 21"--C-D. (Courtesy Kimport Dolls)

JOHANNES DANIEL KESTNER

Johannes Daniel Kestner first made buttons and slates of papier mache in a factory at Waltershausen, Thur and when these lines were not successful, he began making doll bodies, using the same lathes. This was in 1804 and, in essence, became the founder of the Waltershausen doll industry and by 1906 employed close to 1000 workers.

The Kestner Company made all kinds of dolls and doll bodies. They made entire dolls (one of the few German companies that did) and as early as 1845, their dolls were on either kid or muslin bodies, or had wooden limbs, and pápier maché heads and by 1860 they had purchases a porcelain factory in Ohrdruf, Thur and were making their own china and bisque heads. They also made wax heads, worked in leather, cardboard and celluloid. By 1893, Kestner Company had several patents but the best known one is for their "Excelsior" bodies, Patent #70685. This is a jointed composition body. In 1895 Kestner Company registered their trademark of a crown/streamers in the U.S. and in Germany in 1896.

The Ladies Home Journal had a series of paper dolls created by Sheila Young called "Lettie Lane" and in 1911 "Lettie Lane" introduced her doll "Daisy." The only way to get the doll was to sell three subscriptions, at least one renewal and two new ones, plus $4.50. The promotion included doll and patterns that followed the paper dolls. In April 1911, "Lettie Lane's Most Beautiful Doll as a Bride," July 1911 "Lettie Lane's Doll in Vacation Clothes," October 1911, "Lettie Lane's Doll in Her Vacation Clothes" and December 1911, "Lettie Lane's Most Beautiful Doll in her Party Clothes."

The first order for the dolls was 5,000 but they were gone in a short time and 2 factories had to be used for a total of 26,000 additional dolls before the close of the offer, in January 1912. The "Lettie Lane" paper doll's "real live doll" "Daisy" was a Kestner 174 and also used was the Kestner 171. As you can see with 31,000 being given out in the U.S. over a period of only 9 months and as late as 1911, that is why the mold #171, especially, is referred to as the Kestner most common mold number.

Kestner was one firm who made "Kewpie" (1913) and in 1914 made their most famous baby "Hilda." The open crowned/wigged dolls are incised "Hilda" were girl babies, the ones with mold numbers, example 1070, but with closed domes and brush stroked hair and not incised with the name "Hilda" were boy babies. Next in line for popularity is Kestner's "snooty" Gibson Girl, with head thrown back as if she had just been offered hamburger instead of steak.

During 1915 the Kestner Company registered two Crown trademarks in Germany, one carries the words "Kronen Puppe" and the other "Crown Doll/Kestner/Germany" and after World War I, in 1924, they made Bye-Lo baby doll heads.

Most Kestner dolls are marked with sizes that include a letter and a number, for example C-7, F-10, D-8 and some carry a mold number along with these, for example 166, 243, 260, 171. Often the J.D.K. is incised also. The most common mold number is 154 and 171.

Kestner--21" Socket head. Open mouth. Made since 1892. Marks: 1 Made in 13/German/129. 21"--D-E. (Gunnel Collection)

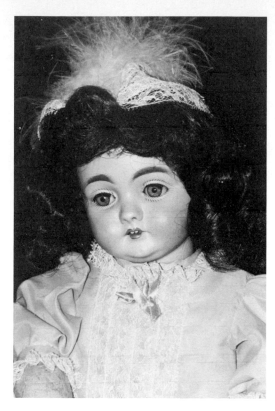

Kestner--19" Socket head character. Open mouth/2 teeth. Marks: H Made In 12/Grmany/ 143. Body:Germany/2. ca. 1892. 14"--D-E, 19"--F-. (Penner Collection)

Kestner--10½" Socket head. Closed mouth. Marks: 145. 10½"--A-B. (Walters Collection)

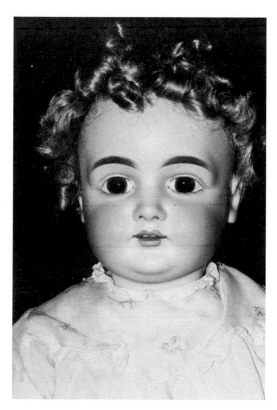

Kestner--25" Toddler. Marks: Made In/M Germany/16/146, incised on head. E5 (or "S")/132, stamped above incised mark. Body marked: Made In Germany. 25"--F-G. (Courtesy Kimport Dolls)

Kestner--25" Turned shoulder plate. Open mouth/4 teeth. Marks: J.D.K./12/147. 25"--D-E. (Gunnel Collection)

159

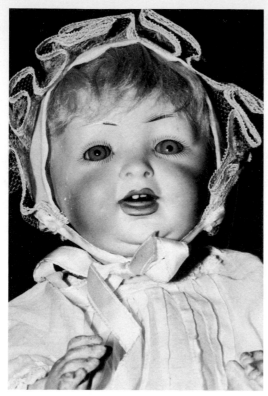

Kestner--12" Sleep eyes. Open mouth/2 upper teeth. Original wig. Marks: Made In Germany/ 152/4. 12"--B-C, 20"--F-G. (Clasby Collection)

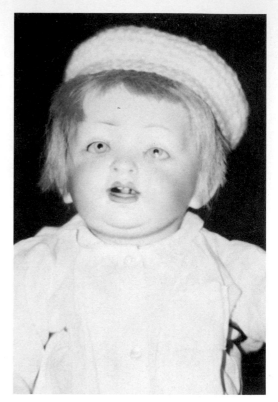

Kestner--12" Pale blue eyes. Open mouth/molded tongue and 2 upper teeth. Marks: 152/4. 12"--B-C, 20"--F-G. (Gunnel Collection)

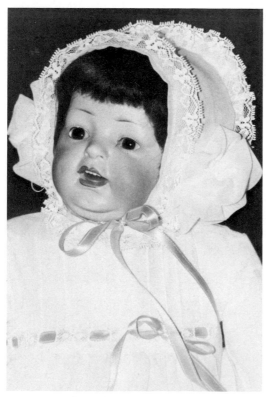

Kestner--20" Open mouth/4 teeth. Molded tongue. Dimples. Marks: 152. ca. 1912. 12"--B-C, 20"--F-G. (Penner Collection)

Kestner--13" Shoulder head. Open mouth. Marks: Dep. 154-1. 12"--A-B, 26"--D-E. (Walters Collection)

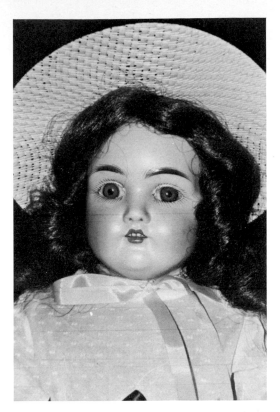

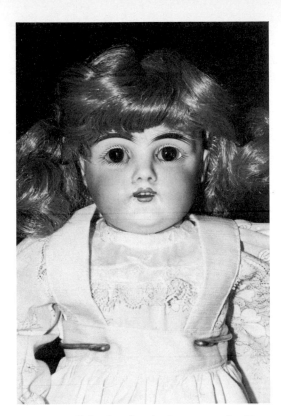

Kestner--17" Shoulder plate. Kid body. Open mouth. Marks; 5¾. 154. Dep./Made In Germany. 12"--A-B, 26"--D-E. (Walters Collection)

Kestner--17" Socket head. Open mouth. Very flat head in back. Marks: DR 154 5½. 12"--A-B, 26"--D-E. (Clasby Collection)

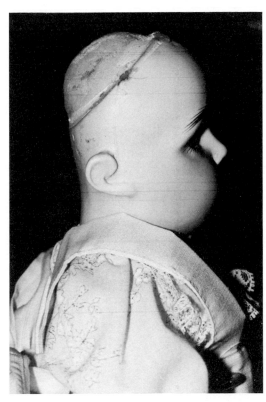

Kestner--17" Marks: DR 154 5½. Shows original plate on very flat head. (Clasby Collection)

Kestner--22" Shoulder plate. Marks: 9 154 D5, on head. Royal Crown seal on front shoulder plate. 12"--A-B, 26"--D-E. (Penner Collection)

161

Kestner--24" "Felice" Shoulder plate. Blue sleep eyes. All original. Given for selling subscriptions to the Youth's Companion. 1888. Marks: G154D1 12"--A-B, 26"--D-E. (Minter Collection)

Kestner--24" Shoulder plate. Open mouth. Marks: 11 Dep 154. ca. 1911. 12"--A-B, 26"--D-E. (Gunnel Collection)

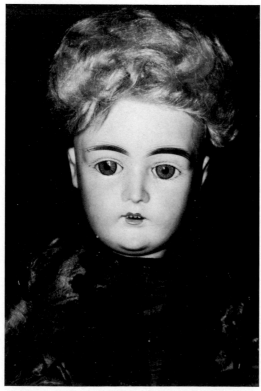

Kestner--17½" Socket head on an adult body. Marks: D Made In 8/Germany/162. 17½"--G-H. (Courtesy Kimport Dolls)

J.D. Kestner--23" Socket head. Marks: Made In/ K Germany 12/162/11. Original Bride costume, and wig. ca. 1910. 12"--A-B, 32"--H-I. (Courtesy Ralph's Antique Dolls)

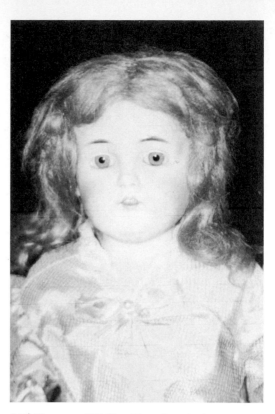

J.D. Kestner--32" Socket head. Unpierced earss. Marks: M½ 16½/164. ca. 1895. 12"--A-B, 32"--F-G. (Courtesy Kimport Dolls)

J.D. Kestner--19" Shoulder plate/kid. Marks: 8/166. ca. 1890. 12"--A-B, 26"--F-G. (Courtesy Ralph's Antique Dolls)

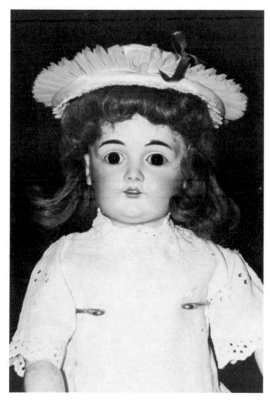

Kestner--25" Socket head. Original. Marks: h½ Made in 12/Germany/167. ca. 1892. 12"--A-B, 26"--F-G. (Minter Collection)

J.D. Kestner--23" Socket head. This mold number has been made since 1892. Marks: Made/in/Germany/F168 10. 12"--A-B, 26"--D-E. (Courtesy Kimport Dolls)

Kestner--23" Socket head. Sleep eyes. Open mouth. Marks: E½ Made in —½/Germany/168/08. Made since 1892. 12"--A-B, 26"--D-E. (Clasby Collection)

Kestner--14" Molded eyebrows. Unpierced ears. Set brown eyes. Marks: B Made in 6/Germany/169. ca. 1892. 14"--I-J, 21"--J-K. (Author)

Kestner--Full length view of 14."

Kestner--Body view of typical German composition/wood ball jointed body. Finger creases outlined only.

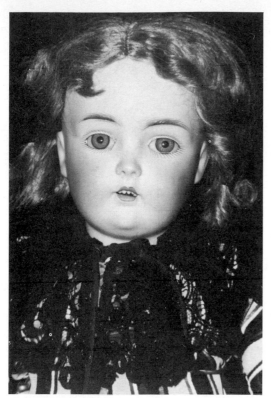

Kestner--22"Socket head. Open mouth. Sleep eyes. Marks: e½ Made In 9½/Germany/171. 12"--A-B, 26"--D-E. (Gunnel Collection)

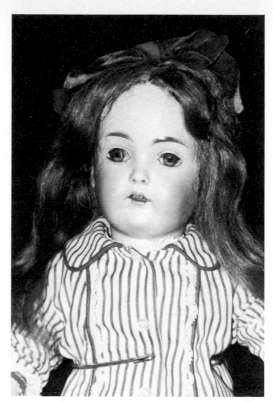

Kestner--18" Pápier maché straight legs and arms. Open mouth/4 teeth. Marks: C½ Made in 7½/Germany/171. 12"--A-B, 26"--D-E. (Minter Collection)

Kestner--24" Molded brows. Open mouth. Made both as socket head and shoulder plate. Marks: K½ Made In 14½/Germany/171. Made since 1892. Used as "Daisy" a Premium Doll for selling subscriptions but not all 171's are "Daisy." 12"--A-B, 26"--D-E. (Gunnel Collection)

Kestner--25" Socket head. Marks: Made In/Germany/171, on head. Body: Excelsior/Germany/ 2. 12"--A-B, 26"--D-E. (Penner Collection)

165

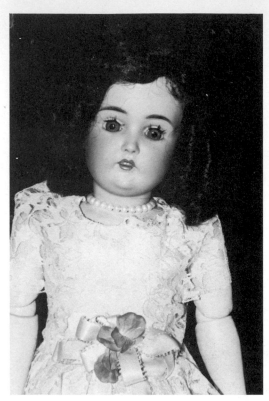

J.D. Kestner--26" Socket head. Marks: K½Made in 14½/Germany/171. Used as "Daisy" in 1911, but this mold number has been made since 1892. 12"--A-B, 26"--D-E. (Courtesy Kimport Dolls)

J.D. Kestner--27" Socket head. Open mouth. This mold number has been made since 1892 and used in 1911 as "Daisy." Marks: 171. 12"--A-B, 26"--D-E. (Courtesy Kimport Dolls)

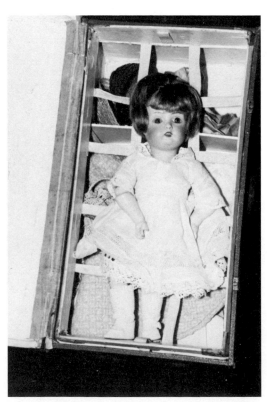

Kestner--10" "Gibson" Shoulder plate. Sleep eyes. All original. Marks: G-O/172/Made In Germany. ca. 1910. 10"--K-L, 13½"--M-N. (Minter Collection)

J.D. Kestner--10" Socket head. Original clothes and trunk. Open mouth. This mold number was used for the original order of 5,000 for the 1911 "Daisy." Refer to company (Kestner) information. Marks: Made In/Germany/174. 10" with trunk--D-E, 10" doll only--C-D, 26"--F-G. (Courtesy Kimport Dolls)

Johannas Daniel Kestner--21" Socket head. Large eyes. Open mouth. Marks: 192. ca. 1890. On a Bébé Schmitt (Maurice & Charles) body. This head was also made for Jumeau (on marked Jumeau body). 21"--H-I. (Gunnel Collection)

J.D. Kestner--21" Socket head. Open mouth. Marks: F½ Made In 10½/Germany/196. Made since 1892. 21"--C-D. (Courtesy Kimport Dolls)

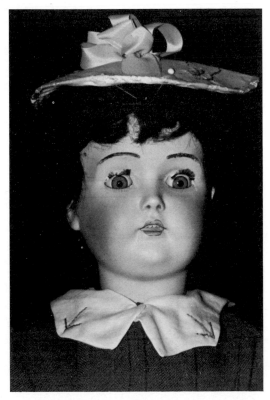

Kestner--23" Socket head. Fur eyebrows. Open mouth. Made in 1891. Marks: Germany/196. 23"--C-D. (Courtesy Kimport Dolls)

Kestner--19" Celluloid. Open mouth. Marks: J.D.K./201/4, on head. On body: Crown and Streamers Label/J.D.K. Germany/½ Cork Stuffed. 19"--C-D. (Walters Collection)

167

J.D. Kestner--12½ Socket head. Sleep eyes. Marks: F Made 10/in/Germany/J.D.K./211. ca. 1912. 12½--D-E. (Courtesy Kimport Dolls)

Kestner--27" Sleep eyes/lashes. Open mouth. Socket head. Marks: k/r Made In Germany/ 14½ JDK/214. 14"--B-C. 27"--F-G. (Minter Collection)

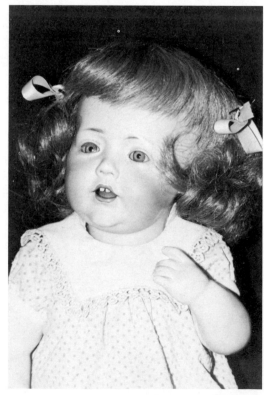

Kestner--14" "Hilda" Open crown/wig. Marks: G Made in Germany 11/245/J.D.K. Jr./1914/Hilda 14"--J-K, 20"--K-l (Minter Collection)

Kestner--15" Socket head toddler. Marks: Made In/Germany/J.D.K./257. 12"--C-D, 20"--G-H. (Gunnel Collection)

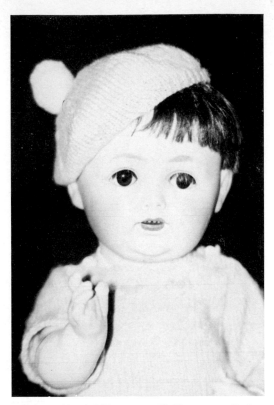

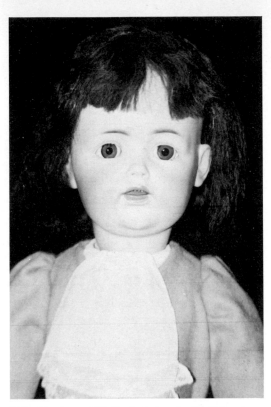

Johannes Daniel Kestner--15" Sleep eyes/lashes Open mouth/4 upper teeth. Marks: Made In Germany/J.D.K./260. 12"--C-D, 20"--G-H. (Gunnel Collection)

J.D. Kestner--28" Socket head. Toddler boy. Open mouth/teeth. Marks: Made In Germany/ J.D.K./260. 12"--C-D, 28--I-J. (Courtesy Ralph's Antique Dolls)

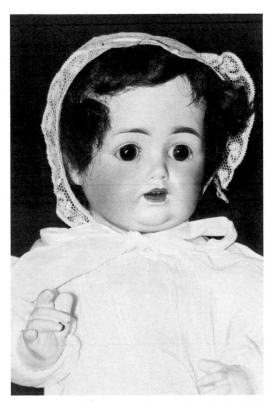

Kestner--16" Open mouth. Marks: JDK/260/ Germany/48. ca. 1912. 12"--C-D, 20"--G-H. (Minter Collection)

Kestner--14" Unjointed shoulder plate. Closed dome. Blue paperweight eyes. In original very long baby dress. Kestner head used by Jumeau firm. (Ref. Shae, Vol. 111, also refer to Jumeau section) Marks: 639 #5. 12"--D-E, 18"--G-H. (Minter Collection)

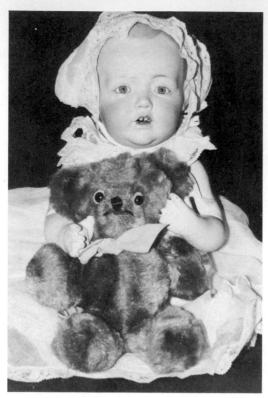

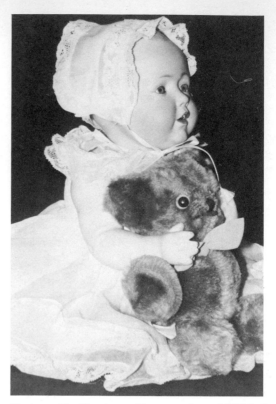

Kestner--14" Boy version of "Hilda" Marks: J.D.K./Ges. Gesch/11 N 1070/Made In Germany. 14"--J-K, 20"--K-L. (Author)

Kestner--Profile view of boy version of "Hilda."

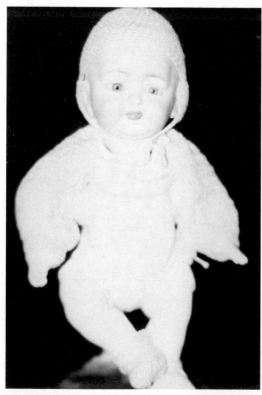

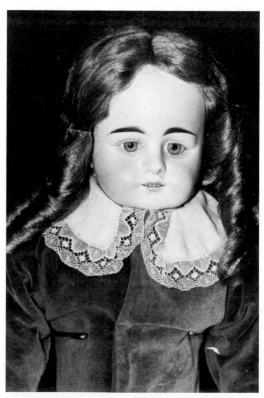

Kestner--8" Sleep eyes. Tremble tongue. Marks: J.D.K.3/Made In Germany. 8"--A-B, 22"--G-H. (Minter Collection)

Kestner--24" Shoulder plate character. Kid body. Character face. Open mouth. Marks: Made In Germany/8. 24"--F-G. (Clasby Collection)

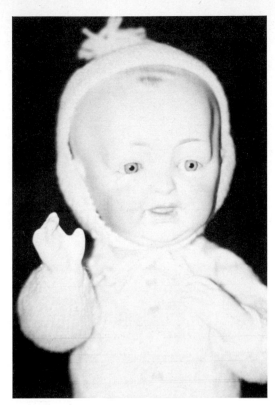

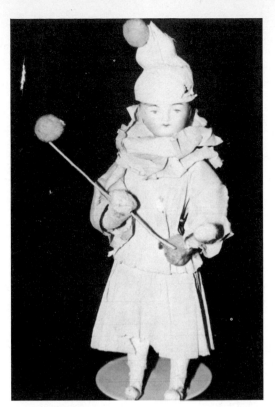

Kestner--11" Head cir. Marks: J.D.K./11/Germany. 8"--A-B, 22"--G-H. (Gunnel Collection)

Kestner--4½" Open crown/wig. Painted eyes. All original. Paper (cardboard) body. Marks: M/12/0. 4½"--$50.00. (Courtesy Kimport Dolls)

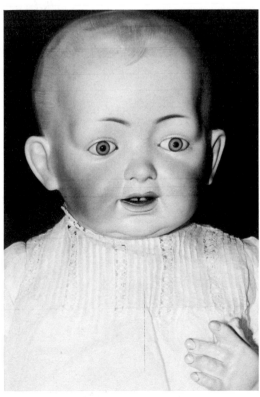

Kestner--22" with 15" head cir. Open mouth/2 upper teeth. Marks: J.D.K./Made in 16 Germany. 8"--A-B, 22"--G-H. (Author)

Kestner--12" Socket head. Black sleep eyes. Open mouth. Marks: C/5/0x. 12"--B-C. (Clasby Collection)

171

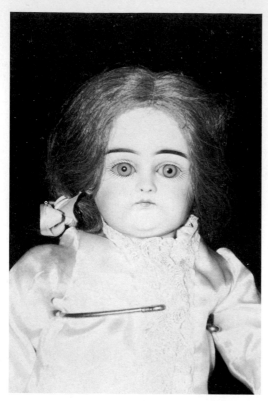

Kestner--15" Sleep eyes. Socket head. Marks: D Made In 8/Germany. 14"--I-J, 21"--J-K. (Minter Collection)

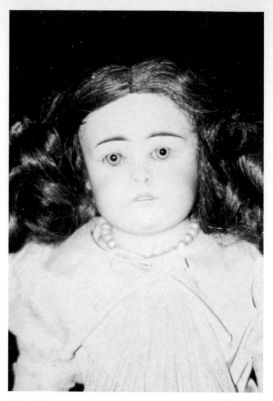

J.D. Kestner--18" Shoulder head/kid. Open/ closed mouth with molded teeth. Character. Marks: ½ Made In Germany H. 18"--E-F. (Courtesy Ralph's Antique Dolls)

Kestner--23" Turned shoulder plate. Sleep eyes. Open mouth. Marks: H½ Made In Germany. 23"--F-G. (Gunnel Collection)

Kestner--27" Turned shoulder plate. Open mouth. Marks: M/Germany. 27"--F-G. (Gunnel Collection)

Kestner--19" Shoulder plate. Open mouth. Marks: B4/0/Made In Germany. Made for discount trade. 1899. 19"--B-C. (Gunnel Collection)

Kestner--23" Socket head. Open mouth. Pápier maché body. Marks: B3. Made for discount trade, 1901. 23"--B-C. (Gunnel Collection)

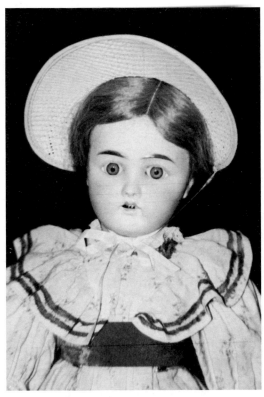

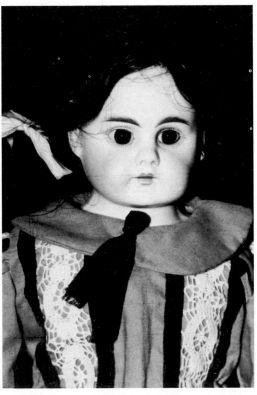

Kestner--22" Socket head. Open mouth. Marks: Germany/B.5. Made for discount trade. 1900. 22"--B-C. (Gunnel Collection)

Kestner--16" Shoulder plate. Character. Open/closed mouth. Pierced ears. Marks: none. 16"--E-F, 20"--F-G (Courtesy Ralph's Antique Dolls)

Kestner--13" Socket head. Closed mouth. Pierced ears. Marks: 3. 13"--G-H, 21"--J-K. (Minter Collection)

Kestner--18" Turned shoulder plate. Open mouth. Marks: G/Made In Germany. 18½"--E-F. (Walters Collection)

Kestner--23" Socket head. Pierced ears. Open mouth. Marks: D4. 14"--B-C, 27"--F-G. (Courtesy Ralph's Antique Dolls)

Kestner--16" Socket head. Open mouth. Marks: C. 14"--C-D, 26"--E-F. (Gunnel Collection)

Kestner--21" Turned shoulder plate. Marks: K/ Made In Germany. 21"--F-G. (Gunnel Collection)

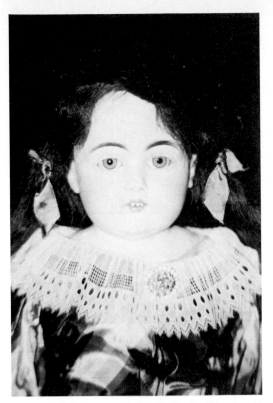

Kestner--21" Shoulder plate/kid. Marks: 11/147. Armand Marseille used 147 on his Floradora dolls and Unis France used 147 mold numbers. This doll does not fit into either. Comparison would lead to Kestner. 14"--A-B, 23"--C-D. (Courtesy Ralph's Antique Dolls)

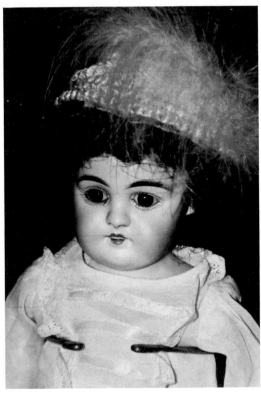

Kestner--15" Shoulder head. Kid body. Open/ closed mouth. Marks: 4/Made In Germany. 14"--D-E, 23"--G-H. (Walters Collection)

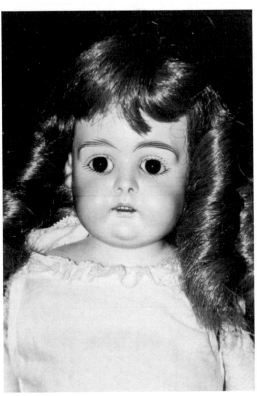

Kestner--17" Shoulder plate character. Open mouth. Marks: 5. Taken from mold #143. 14"--D-E, 19"--F-G. (Walters Collection)

175

KIMPORT...DOLLS FROM THE WHOLE WIDE WORLD

The McKim Studio began in the 1920's and was not concerned with dolls, nor even the thought of dolls. What it was concerned with was a large mail order business dealing in items, such as quilt patterns and allied needlework ideas, all designed and executed by Ruby Short McKim. Her book "101 Patchwork Patterns" is still in print and has sold hundreds of thousands of copies. The McKim Studio was located in Independence, Missouri.

Who is Ruby Short McKim? A fantastic woman who married an equally fantastic man, Arthur McKim. Two creative people who joined into a marriage that allowed freedom of creation to both but also united an idea of a working combination where the talents of each would complement the other.

Ruby Short McKim had for many years been the Art Needlework Editor for Better Homes and Gardens Magazine while her husband, Arthur McKim, was being a success in the advertising field and business management. They both sold widely distributed syndicated newspaper features and articles to major publications.

Just past forty, the McKims who had already had very active business careers decided to close down the successful Art Needlework Company "The McKim Studio" and travel a bit...so, along with two small daughters, Betty and Marilyn, (Kim, the youngest and only son had not been born yet) left for Europe and while there visited the French Colonial Exhibition in Paris. It was there that they bought some interesting native crafted dolls for the girls. After returning to the United States both girls wanted other costume dolls to add to the ones bought in Europe, and the McKims found they couldn't buy them in this country. It was this that caused the spark of adventure and enthusiasm that involved them in a "retirement" project with a tremendous work load, long hours but much fun! The youngest was born and so was the name of the new company: "Kim" for the son (Kim McKim) and "port" for the word "import." Arthur McKim spent every day at the office until his death in 1967 and Ruby Short McKim spent every day there until 1973 and she still edits the house publication "Doll Talk" which is now in its 37th year of publication.

During the 1930's and up to World War II, Kimports specialized in authentic foreign costume dolls, all actually made and dressed in the country they represented, and antique dolls were strictly a side line. The entire world was involved in some way with World War II and imports were impossible to obtain, so the Kimport emphasis was directed at American doll artists and American crafted dolls, plus the antique dolls, which were just beginning to become popular.

As the hobby of collecting dolls increased, so did Kimport. With this growth the staff expanded to include secretaries, stenographers, packers, doll artists, doll repair people... some who are still working for the McKims. One such delightful person is Mrs. Georgie Johnson, bookkeeper and general aide. Another is Bessie Hagan, who conducts the doll repair section and sews costumes for the Presidential Series.

Kim McKim, only son and namesake of the business, joined the Kimport staff in 1951 and for three years worked as stock clerk, packer, errand runner, buyer and manager... "right up through the ranks" to purchase ownership from his parents. With that purchase, Kimports entered a second generation of McKim ownership.

Arthur McKim   Ruby McKim

It was on the day of sale that Arthur McKim told his son, "Kimport is not just a company; it is a way of life." The meaning of this statement was apparent to the young Kim, for he knew the pride felt for "this way of life" which was considered one of the choicest, one of the most educational and often most beautiful of all hobbies...doll collecting. Kim carried this idea structure and pattern of thought right into business with him and so takes pride in maintaining one of the oldest and largest mail order firms, in the United States, dealing exclusively to doll collectors.

Kimports are proud, not only of their backgrounds, their beginnings and their "todays," but also of the pioneer business ideas that are now standard practices in the doll world. Items such as full guarantee of satisfaction or complete refund, free budget terms, and especially the "want list" system, with no obligation to buy.

Right now there are over 30,000 specific "wants" from almost as many doll collectors on file at Kimports. As dolls arrive from buying sources in Europe or from collections purchased, names are taken from the "want" list, in order, and they are offered choice, often extremely rare, dolls on a first opportunity basis. And here a few words about the "boys in the back room!" These two, Dennis and Mark, are really the most important and valuable people in relation to the collector, for they are the packers who see that the doll arrives at its destination in perfect condition.

Kim McKim at his desk on a cold winter's day.

The Kimport business is primarily mail order though they do have private doll showings around the country each year. They visit various major populated areas and invite all their customers or any collectors who may be interested.

Antique dolls obtained greater emphasis during the second growth stage of the 1960's, but Kimport has always and still does handle the choicest imported foreign costume dolls; a field that is beginning to grow again as interest has been renewed into "traditions." They also handle American Doll Artists Dolls, portrait dolls, related items, such as, doll stands, books and even have all the original quilt patterns from the old "McKim Studio."

The McKim children number seven and pictured here are two that seem to be destined to carry on the traditions and ideals of Kimport: Laurie and Chris, two delightfully young, energetic and business-like people who have found that Kimport Dolls From the Whole Wide World, Is "a way of life."

Laurie

Chris

Lynn McKim

Kim McKim

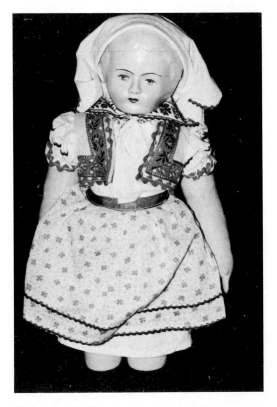

Kimport--12" Czechoslovakia. $6.50

Kimport--12" Hungarian boy. ca. 1939. $5.00.

Kimport--10" Cuban lady. ca. 1940. $8.95.

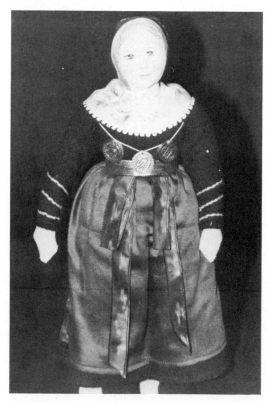

Kimport--10" Danish portrait by Karen Steen. 1936. $75.00.

Kimport--10" Bali Stick dolls. ca. 1940. $12.00.

Kimport--13" Yugoslavia. ca. 1939. $7.50.

Kimport--13" Hindu Prince. ca. 1940. $10.00.

Kimport--13" Mexico. $7.95.

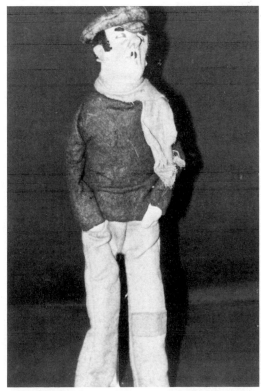

Kimport--12" German made cloth caricature of London's White Chapel District. $35.00.

Kimport--12" German made cloth caricature of London's White Chapel District. $35.00.

Kimport--13" Mexico. 1945. $18.50.

Kimport--12" Yugoslavia. ca. 1939. $12.50.

Kimport--7" Dutch Guiana Gutta Percha. $10.00 each.

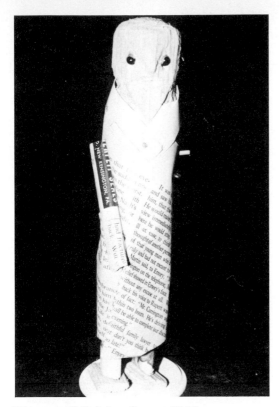

Kimport--5" Belgian Congo. $7.95.

Kimport--14" West Indies doll of Orris root. $6.50.

Kimport--11" Anna of Cleves and King Henry VIII. by Saroff. Anna--$25.00, King--$37.50.

Kimport--10" Poland. 1950. $4.50.

181

Kimport--9" Voodoo Queen. $25.00.

Kimport--7" Croatia. $5.75.

Kimport--9" Bermuda Banana leaf doll. $3.75.

Kimport--7" Korea. $5.95.

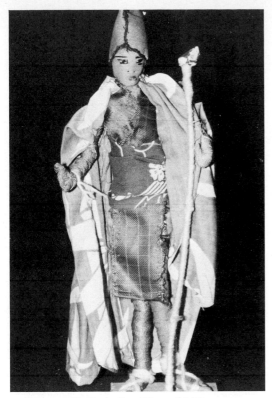

Kimport--10" Hawaiian King. $6.50.

Kimport--8" Singapore Traffic Cop. 1939. $10.00.

Kimport--11" Queen Victoria. $25.00.

Kimport--8" Aran East. ca. 1939. $17.50.

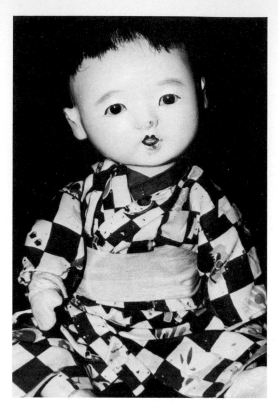

Kimport--6" Chile woman. $8.95.

Kimport--12" Japan. ca. Pre World War II. $27.50.

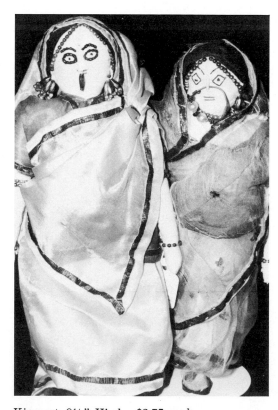

Kimport--12" Hungarian nursing mother. $35.00.

Kimport--8½" Hindu. $3.75 each.

Kimport--8" Ceylon-Kandy Prince and Princess. ca. 1941. $10.00 each.

Kimport--12" Nassau Policeman. $12.50.

Kimport--9" French-India-China man of 1937. $15.00.

Kimport--14" Persia. 1937. $30.00.

Kimport--10½" Philipians Lady. ca. 1939.
$12.50.

Kimport--16" Peruvian Ceremonial Doll. $17.00.

Kimport--11" Korea. 1963. $7.50.

Kimport--5" Egyptian Tomb "doll." $35.00.

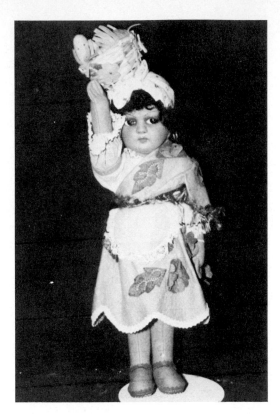

Kimport--13" "Rosa of Brazil." All felt. ca. 1939. $12.50. (Kimport)

Kimport--8½" Philipines Bride. Pink cloth body, upper arms and legs. Excelsior stuffed. Composition shoulder plate head. Inset glass eyes. Composition lower arms and legs. Molded heeled shoes painted red. Original. ca. 1939. $35.00.

Kimport--12" Wool dust filled cloth body. Pink stockinette arms and legs. Glued on wooden shoes. Stitched fingers with separate thumb. Composition head with painted brown hair. Painted blue eyes. $18.00.

Kimport--4" Cloth body. Wire arms and legs. Glued on hemp hair. Painted blue eyes. Wire holds head. Original. $6.00.

KLEY & HAHN

From 1895 to 1902, Kley & Hahn made bisque heads and bathing dolls at a porcelain factory in Ohrdruf, Thur and from 1902 until 1929, made entire dolls for themselves including "leather" dolls. It was in 1902 when they registered the trademark "Walkure" and, by 1910, had registered "Meine Einzige" (My Only One), in a 6 pointed star and, in 1913, "Cellunova" (celluloid) for dolls and doll heads.

There are some excellent examples of the fineness of the Kley & Hahn artists and, as with all doll companies, a few examples of cheapness. Some of the most elusive and beautiful German closed mouth dolls came from the Kley & Hahn factory, examples are mold numbers 143, 169, 220, 520, 526, 549, etc.

Noted for "fly away" eyebrows, separately feathered strokes that seem to fly onto the forehead; although none of the examples shown in this book have these eyebrows. Many Heubach Koppelsdorf and other's eyebrows are painted this way also.

Sample marks:

K & H

KH
Walkure

Kley & Hahn--23" Socket head. Registered in 1902. Marks: 250/KH/Walkure/3¼/Germany. 18"--C-D, 27"--E-F. (Minter Collection)

Kley & Hahn--24" Socket head. Marks: Walkure/Germany. 18"--C-D, 27"--E-F. (Gunnel Collection)

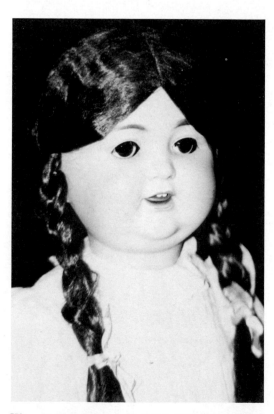

Kley & Hahn--28" Socket head. Toddler. Open mouth. Marks: M680/70/K&H/Made In Germany. 14"--D-E, 28"--G-H.

Edmund Knoch--19½" Shoulder plate. Open mouth. Marks: ⊗ /HcH H. Head made by Heinrich Handwerck. Edmund Knoch operated at Monchroden, Thur from 1896 to 1937. After 1937 the factory was used to make mattresses. 19½"--C-D. (Courtesy Kimport Dolls)

Gebruder Knoch--12" Socket head. Open mouth. Marks: ✕ /Made In Germany/201 15/0/Dep 12"--A-B. (Walters Collection)

Gebruder Knoch--13" Socket head. Open mouth. Marks: 199/2/0. 13"--B-C. (Gunnel Collection)

Gebruder Krauss--18" Socket head. Molded brows. Open mouth. Marks: 26/GBR165K/2/ Germany. The Krauss Brothers were in operation from 1863 to 1921, in Germany and they had Gottschalk as a distributor in Paris. 18"--B-C. (Gunnel Collection)

189

LANÉÉ

Lanéé--Lanee of Paris (1882-1895) had a factory in Montreuil-sous-Bois, located near Paris, along with a great many other doll makers. He specialized in men dolls and made relatively few girl dolls. He used the initials ".B.L." and "D.L." along with the "Montruil."

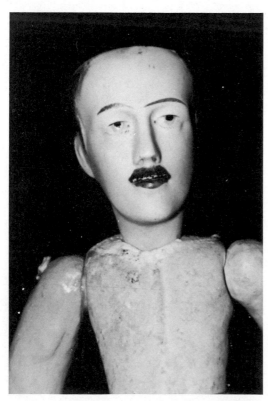

Lanéé--13" Character. Bisque head. Pápier maché body. Marks: Montriul/France/L. Maker unknown. 13"--I-J. (Courtesy Kimport Dolls)

Lanéé--7" Socket head. Composition and maché body and limbs. Marks: Montriul/France/DL. 7"--B-C. (Walters Collection)

A. LANTERNIER & CIE

This is one of the porcelain factories located at Limoges, France and started business in 1855 making decorated porcelain. The company was under the direction of A. Lanternier, Jr. who had been instructed in the pottery business at Wedgewood, in England.

The dolls' heads, coming from this company, usually bear names such as "Lorraine," "Favorite," "La Georgienne," etc.

Sample marks:

Fabrication
Francaise

AL & Cie
Limoges

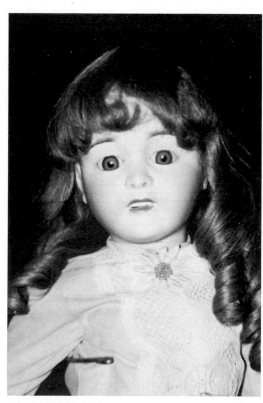

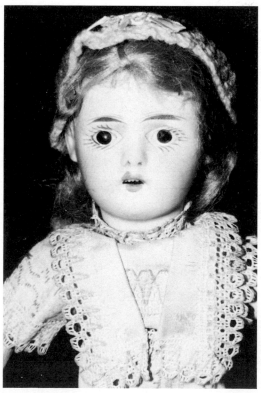

A. Lanternier & Cie--26" Socket head. Called "Laughing Limoge" by collectors. Marks: Fabrication/Francaise, in square/Favorite/ N08/Ed. Tasson/Al & Cis/Limoges. 14"--A-B, 26"--G-H. (Gunnel Collection)

H. LeConte & Co. 12½" Socket head. Pápier maché body and limbs. Original clothes. Marks: ⚓ /5/2/0. 12½"--A-B. (Courtesy Kimport Dolls)

191

LENCI

Lenci--The pet name of Elena Konig di Scavini, wife of doll maker Enrico Scavini was "Lenci." Lenci dolls were made in 1920 through the 1940's. They are felt and usually have felt clothes. There were little children to grand ladies, with everything in between. The dolls bear a cloth tag stating "Lenci/Made In Italy."

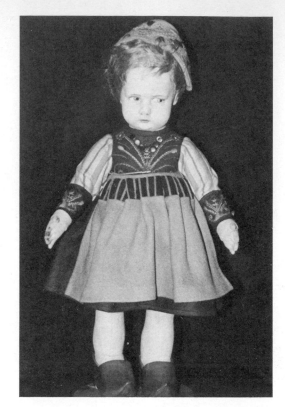

Lenci--17" Felt with painted features. All original. 17"--$115.00. (Minter Collection)

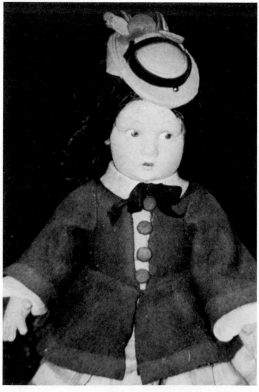

Lenci--14" All felt. 14"--$95.00. (Gunnel Collection)

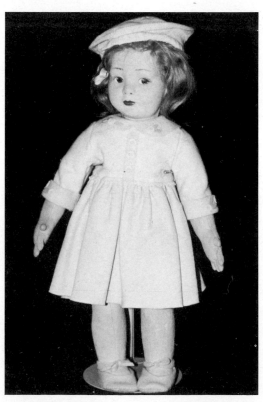

Lenci--21" Felt with painted features. All original. 21"--$165.00. (Minter Collection)

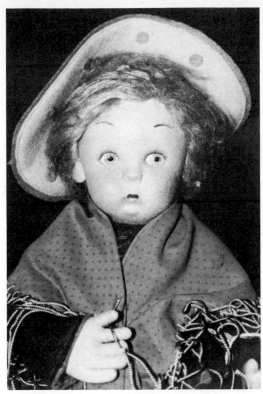

Lenci--11" Felt. All original. Pre-World War II. 11"--$75.00. (Courtesy Kimport Dolls)

Limbach was a porcelain factory near Alsbach, Thur and established by Macheleidt in 1761 and passed into the hands of Gotthelf Greiner in 1772.

It is not known when they began to make bisque dolls. It is known that they showed dolls in Chicago in 1893, and in 1919 registered in Germany the trademark of "Limbach Puppen."

The Greiner family owned seven porcelain factories and acquired the following, besides Limbach, from the Macheleidts: Wallendorf: Under the patronage of Prince of Schwarzburg in 1762 (established) passed to Greiners in 1770. Grossbreitenbach: 1783. Rauenstein: established 1760, to Greiners in 1783. Gera: 1779, first copied Chinese and then made German wares. Ilmenau: 1786. Closter Veilsdorf: 1789.

Some sample porcelain and pottery marks:

— Limbach
— Wallendorf
— Gera

Sample of doll marks: (Limbach Factory)

Wally
Willy
Lilly

Limbach Porzellanfabrik--22" "Wally" Socket head. Open mouth. Marks: Wally 5, high on crown. ☘ /Limbach/Made In Germany. 22"--C-D. (Courtesy Ralph's Antique Dolls)

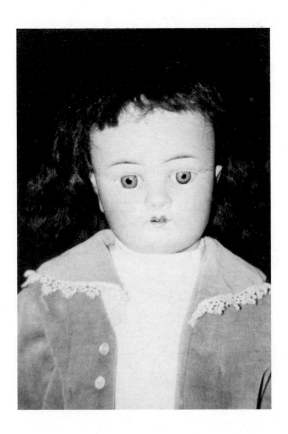

Manufacturer Unknown--26" "Lacquer Head" of
the 1820's. 3 "Puff" hairdo. On wood body/limbs.
26"--$975.00. (Courtesy Kimport Dolls)

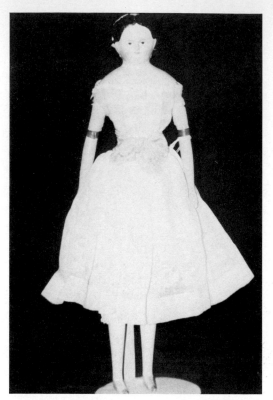

Manufacturer Unknown--16" Lacquer head. Kid
body with wood limbs. ca. 1830. 16"--$350.00.
(Courtesy Kimport Dolls)

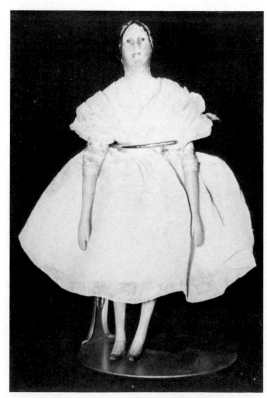

Manufacturer Unknown--6" "Milliners Model" or
rightly called "Lacquer head." Jointed with
wood lower arms and legs. 6"--$165.00. (Minter
Collection)

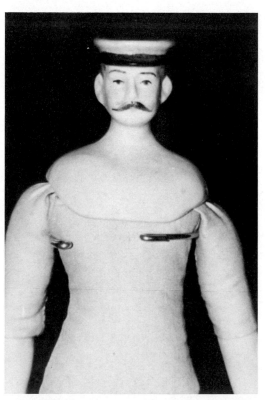

Manufacturer Unknown--9" Bisque shoulder
plate. Molded on hat and mustache. Cloth body
with bisque forearms and lower legs. Marks:
none. 9"--$175.00. (Courtesy Kimport Dolls)

Manufacturer Unknown--8" Shoulder plate/kid. A Fashion doll. All original. Painted eyes. 8"--E-F. (Minter Collection)

Manufacturer Unknown--16" Music Box doll. Set eyes/lashes. Open mouth. Pierced ears. Doll just stands on a key wind music box. Marks: Dep. 16"--N-O. (Minter Collection)

Manufacturer Unknown--8" "Needleworker" Bisque shoulder head, bisque arms and feet. Sits on a powderbox. All original. ca. 1850. Marks: Henry a la Pensee Paris, label on bottom of the box. This is a store in Paris that handled this doll. 8"--$245.00. (Minter Collection)

Manufacturer Unknown--12" French Fisherwoman. Terra Cotta limbs. Original. Marks: 13-17, on back. 12"--$225.00. (Courtesy Kimport Dolls)

195

Manufacturer Unknown--9½" "Fisherwoman" All original. Blonde molded hair. Painted blue eyes. 9½"--$200.00. (Minter Collection)

Manufacturer Unknown--12" Metal head. Painted features. All cloth stuffed with cotton and sawdust. All original powder blue crepe dress and bonnet. Marks: Germany, on head. 12"--$35.00. (Maish Collection)

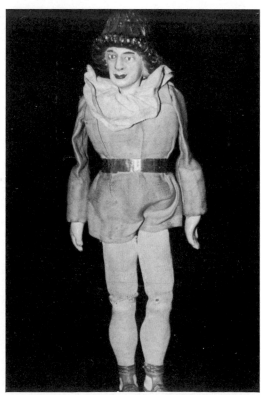

Manufacturer Unknown--9" All metal marionette. All original. Marks: none. 9"--$87.50. (Courtesy Kimport Dolls)

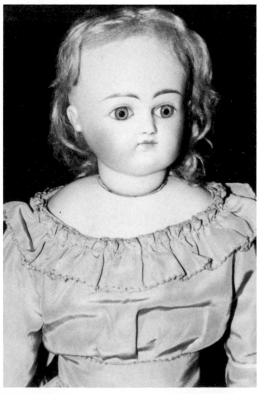

Manufacturer Unknown--16" Swivel neck with kid inset into bisque shoulder plate. Fashion type kid body. Closed mouth. Marks: 5, on head. 16"--I-K. (Courtesy Ralph's Antique Dolls)

Manufacturer Unknown--18" Wood bodied fashion with jointed ankles. Marks: 4, high on head. 18"--T-U. (Courtesy Kimport Dolls)

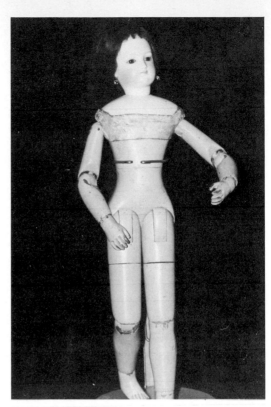

Shows wood body on fashion.

Manufacturer Unknown--18" Turned shoulder plate. Kid body. Open mouth. Marks: H. 18"--E-F. (Walters Collection)

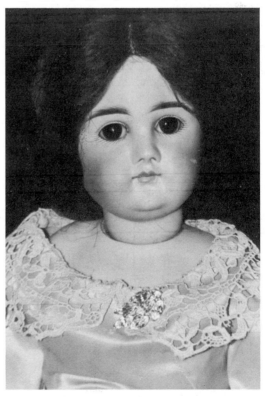

Manufacturer Unknown--21" Swivel head on bisque shoulder plate. Closed mouth. Marks: 8, on head. 21"--J-K. (Gunnel Collection)

197

Manufacturer Unknown--19" Extremely thin
poured bisque head. Short composition torso.
Long wood legs and arms, with composition
lower arms with unjointed wrists. Very protruding stomach. Brown set paperweight eyes.
Open mouth. "High" forehead. All original
clothes, minus top coat. Marks: 1009 No. 8/Dep.
19"--H-I. (Author)

Manufacturer Unknown--Shows original clothes
on 19" doll. Minus top coat.

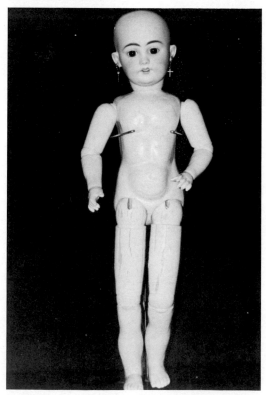

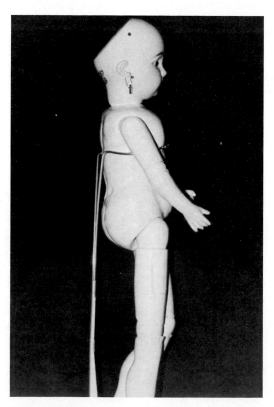

Manufacturer Unknown--Shows front view of
19" doll.

Manufacturer Unknown--Shows side view of 19"
doll.

Manufacturer Unknown--5½" Socket head. Open mouth. Sleep eyes. Jointed neck, shoulders and hips. Painted on shoes and socks. Marks: none. 5½"--B-C. (Gunnel Collection)

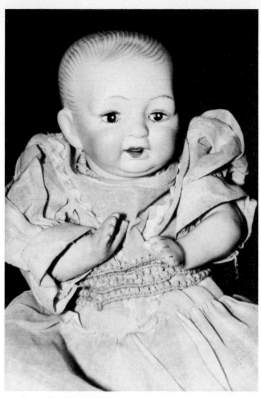

Manufacturer Unknown--6" Baby with brush stroke hair. Open mouth. Painted teeth and eyes. Marks: 3-4-10. 6"--$50.00.

Manufacturer Unknown--6" Bisque head on composition body. Jointed neck, shoulders and hips. Yellow glass eyes. All original. Marks: ⬦. 6"--$32.50. (Courtesy Kimport Dolls)

Manufacturer Unknown--7½" Bisque heads. Glass eyes/closed mouths. Solid dome heads with curly mohair wigs. Composition bodies with pegged joints. Painted knee socks with red line and black slippers. All original Ivory linen suits with coral trim. Little metal anchors on caps. Marks: 39-18, in script. 7½"--C-D pair. (Maish Collection)

199

Manufacturer Unknown--7½" Bisque head. Brown sleep eyes. Open mouth/4 teeth. Mohair Dutch bob. Composition body, arms and legs. Painted brown shoes/white socks. All original. Marks: Germany 12/0. 7½"--A-B. (Maish Collection)

Manufacturer Unknown--8" Shoulder plate. Head unmarked except Germany/18/0. Body marked Kestner. 8"--$65.00. (Walters Collection)

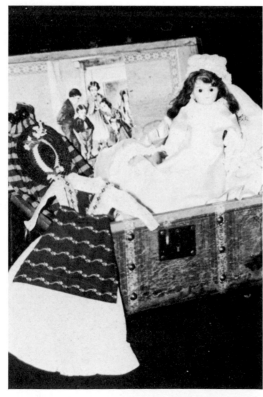

Manufacturer Unknown--9" Shoulder plate. Closed mouth. Kid body. Original clothes and trunk. Marks: 5½/0. 9"--Doll and Trunk--K-L. (Courtesy Kimport Dolls)

Manufacturer Unknown--10" Socket head. Open mouth. Marks: 4/886. 10"--B-C. (Walters Collection)

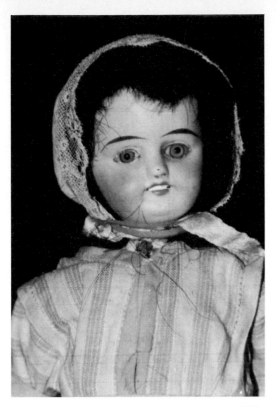

Manufacturer Unknown--10" Socket head. Open mouth. Original. Marks: E. 10"--A-B. (Courtesy Kimport Dolls)

Manufacturer Unknown--10½" Socket head. Open/closed mouth. Marks: none. 10½"--G-H. (Courtesy Kimport Dolls)

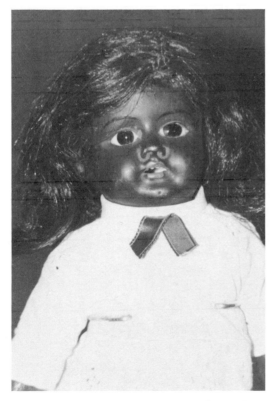

Manufacturer Unknown--11" Socket head. Open mouth. Papier mache body and limbs. Marks: 12/0. 11"--D-E. (Courtesy Kimport Dolls)

Manufacturer Unknown--11½" Russian bisque of 1930 using an old German mold. All original. Marks: 𝟝𝔰 . 11½"--A-B. (Courtesy Kimport Dolls)

Manufacturer Unknown--13½" Belton type. 3 holes/2 for stringing. Fully closed mouth. Marks: S/4, on head. 12"--D-E, 18"--G-H. (Minter Collection)

Manufacturer Unknown--14" Socket head. Open mouth/4 teeth. Marks: 3/0, along with incised, unreadable marks. 14"--C-D. (Penner Collection)

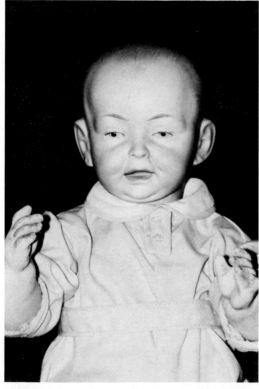

Manufacturer Unknown--15" Molded brush stroke hair. Painted blue eyes. Open/closed mouth. Marks: 2/Germany. 15"--D-E. (Minter Collection)

Manufacturer Unknown--16" Socket head. Pierced ears. Original mohair wig. Marks: ⌐ / 2X. 16"--D-E. (Gunnel Collection)

Manufacturer Unknown--16" Turned shoulder plate. Open mouth. **Marks:** 1897 1½0. 16"--D-E. (Gunnel Collection)

Manufacturer Unknown--16" Shoulder plate. Pierced ears. Closed mouth. Marks: 302/3. 12"--D-E, 18"--G-H. (Gunnel Collection)

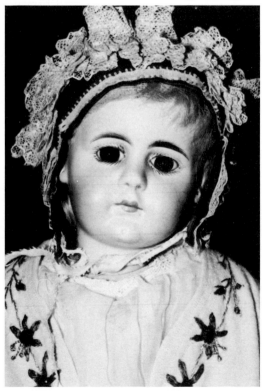

Manufacturer Unknown--16" Swivel head on bisque shoulder plate. Kid body. Closed mouth. Pierced ears. Marks: 3226, on head. 16½"--I-J. (Courtesy Kimport Dolls)

Manufacturer Unknown--16½" baby. Marks: BG (or 86)/ ✕ /Nippon. 16½"--B-C. (Walters Collection)

203

Manufacturer Unknown--17" Shoulder head/kid. Marks: 2015 ⚓ 1. Made for Louis Wolf and sons. ca. 1890. Original. Armand Marseille used this mold number for "Queen Louise," which was handled by Louis Wolf, but a comparison study does not lead to A.M. 17"--B-C.

Manufacturer Unknown--17" Shoulder plate/ kid. Open mouth. Marks: 6/Made In Germany. 17"--B-C. (Gunnel Collection)

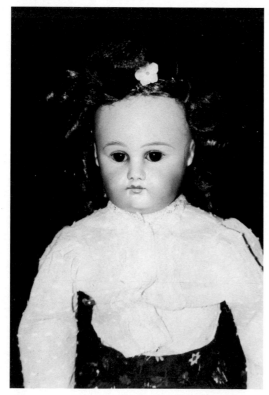

Manufacturer Unknown--17" Socket head. Closed mouth. Marks: 6, on head. 17"-G-H. (Minter Collection)

Manufacturer Unknown--17" Socket head. Closed mouth. Inset paperweight eyes. 17"--G-H. (Courtesy Kimport Dolls)

Manufacturer Unknown--17" Turned shoulder/
kid. Open mouth. Marks: 6 Frederica/Made In
Germany. 17"--C-D. (Courtesy Ralph's Antique
Dolls)

Manufacturer Unknown--20" Shoulder plate.
Open mouth. Kid body. Unpierced ears. Marks:
7. 20"--C-D. (Courtesy Kimport Dolls)

Manufacturer Unknown--20" Shoulder plate.
Closed mouth. Belton type. Marks: none. 12"--
D-E, 20"--H-I. (Gunnel Collection)

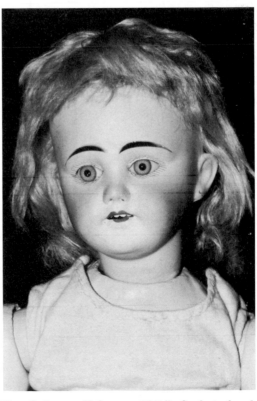

Manufacturer Unknown--20¼" Socket head.
Unjointed wrists. French body. Open mouth.
Paperweight eyes. Marks: none. 20"--G-H.
(Courtesy Kimport Dolls)

205

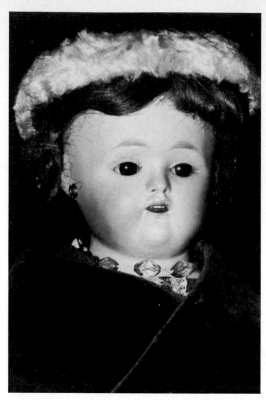

Manufacturer Unknown--21" Shoulder plate. Unpierced ears. Earrings are glued on. Open mouth. Sleep eyes. Marks: ✕✕ /Nippon. 21"--B-C. (Gunnel Collection)

Manufacturer Unknown--21" Turned shoulder head/kid. Marks: none. Hat has a veil that is over the face. 21"--C-D. (Courtesy Ralph's Antique Dolls)

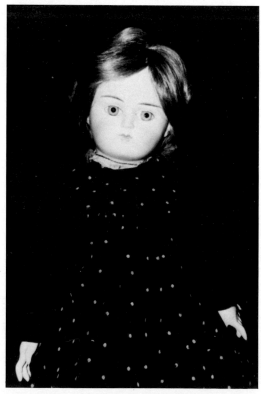

Manufacturer Unknown--21" Socket head. Open/closed mouth. Marks: none. 21"--I-J. (Courtesy Kimport Dolls)

Manufacturer Unknown--21" Turned shoulder plate. Open mouth. Marks: N, in script. 12"--B-C, 26"--F-G. (Gunnel Collection)

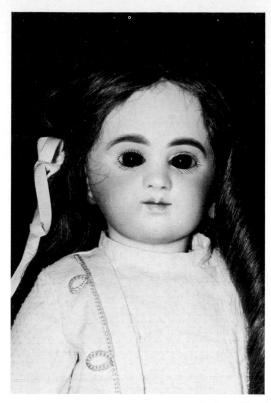

Manufacturer Unknown--21" Socket head.
Closed mouth. Marks: 8, on head. 21"--L-M.
(Courtesy Ralph's Antique Dolls)

Manufacturer Unknown--22" Socket head. Open
mouth. Marks: ♀ B. 3/Something I can't
read. 22"--C-D. (Gunnel Collection)

Manufacturer Unknown--23½" Socket head.
Unpierced ears. Open mouth. Made for the
George Borgfeldt Company. Marks: Germany/
GB. 23½"--B-C. (Courtesy Kimport Dolls)

Manufacturer Unknown--24" Socket head. Open
mouth. Marks: Dep/11. 24"--E-F. (Gunnel
Collection)

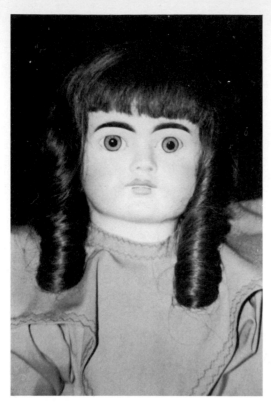

Manufacturer Unknown--25" Socket head. Open/closed mouth. Marks: none. 25"--H-J. (Courtesy Ralph's Antique Dolls)

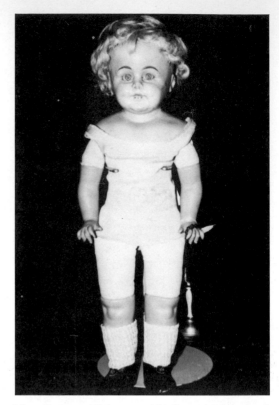

Manufacturer Unknown--14" Composition shoulder plate, arms and legs. Sleep eyes. Open mouth/molded teeth. Open crown. Undershirt is stamped "The Munsing Underwear Co." Cloth body. Old baby rattler attached to ribbon. 14"--$165.00. (Courtesy Kimport Dolls)

Manufacturer Unknown--15½" Composition head. Sleep eyes. Kammer & Reinhardt body. Marks:3 $\frac{33}{4}$. 15½"--$50.00. (Courtesy Kimport Dolls)

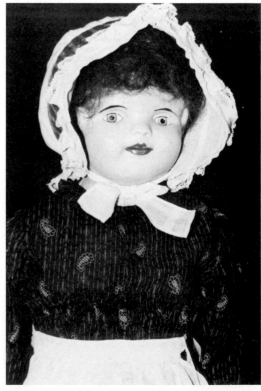

Manufacturer Unknown--25½" Composition with painted eyes. Bright red mohair over molded hair. Marks: none. 25½"--$65.00. (Courtesy Kimport Dolls)

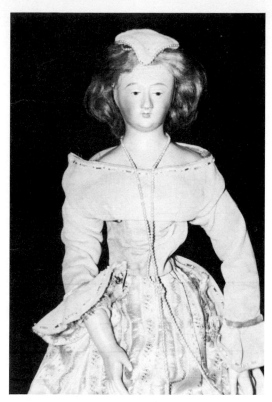

Manufacturer Unknown--22" Early French composition portrait of the 1830's. 22"--$495.00. (Courtesy Kimport Dolls)

Manufacturer Unknown--15½" German composition of the 1880's. Inset eyes. Closed mouth. 15½"--$175.00. (Courtesy Kimport Dolls)

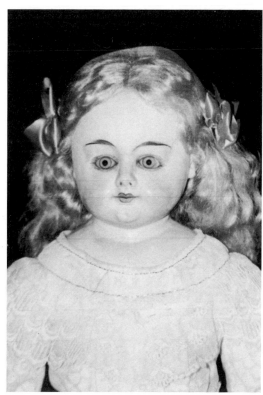

Manufacturer Unknown--33" German composition of 1885. Closed mouth. Glass eyes. Cloth body. 33"--$200.00. (Courtesy Kimport Dolls)

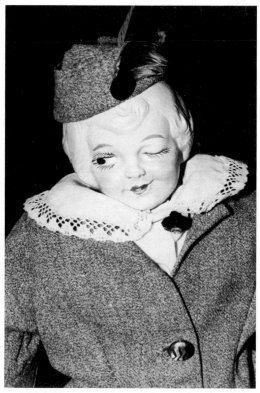

Manufacturer Unknown--14" Composition shoulder plate on cloth body. Character. Marks: none. 14"--$90.00 (Clasby Collection)

Manufacturer Unknown--6½" All composition with painted features. One is "frozen," the other has jointed shoulders. Painted bathing suits date the dolls to 1930-35. $15.00 each. (Maish Collection)

Manufacturer Unknown--6½" All composition with jointed shoulders. Painted hair, shoes and socks. ca. 1930. $12.00 . $15.00. (Maish Collection)

Manufacturer Unknown--6" All composition baby. Jointed neck, shoulders and hips. Molded and painted on shoes and socks. Marks: none. 6"--$27.50. (Gunnel Collection)

Manufacturer Unknown--11" Celluloid with cloth body. Painted eyes. Marks: American/head of Indian. 11"--$47.50. (Clasby Collection)

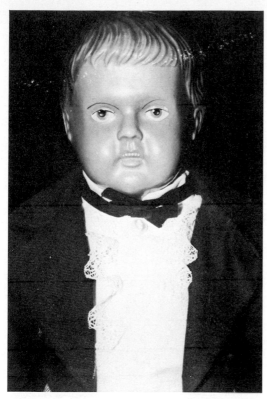

Manufacturer Unknown--15" Celluloid head with painted eyes. Open/closed mouth with molded and painted teeth. Excelsior filled body. Marks: Made In U.S.A., on back. 15"--$67.50. (Clasby Collection)

Manufacturer Unknown--6" Celluloid. Jointed shoulders only. Marks: Made In Japan. 6"-- $22.00. (Courtesy Kimport Dolls)

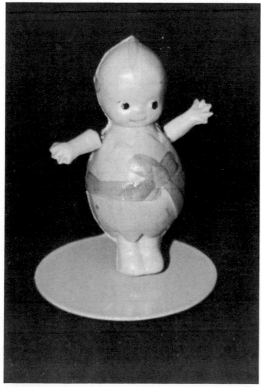

Manufacturer Unknown--2½" Celluloid. Jointed shoulders only. Marks: Made In Japan. 2½"-- $35.00. (Courtesy Kimport Dolls)

Manufacturer Unknown--3" Celluloid Preacher. Jointed arms only. Marks: Made In Japan. 3"--$30.00. (Courtesy Kimport Dolls)

211

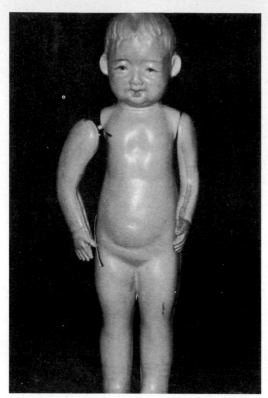

Manufacturer Unknown--5" Celluloid. Jointed at shoulders only. Marks: ⚘ /Made In Japan. 5"--$18.00. (Gunnel Collection)

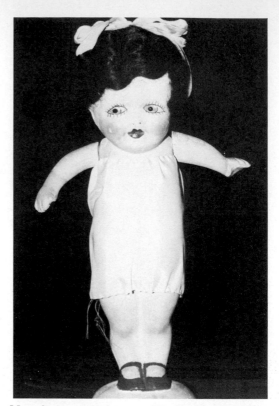

Manufacturer Unknown--13" Chalk jointed at shoulders only. Original mohair wig. Heart shaped paper sticker label on stomach (unreadable). 13"--$22.00. (Clasby Collection)

Manufacturer Unknown--12" All chalk. Jointed arms only. Painted eyes. Original bright red mohair wig. Wings high on back of neck. 12"--$27.00. (Clasby Collection)

Manufacturer Unknown--7" Mechanical clown. All original. Bisque head walker. Open mouth. Glass eyes. Feet are made of lead. Marks: none. 7"--$400.00. (Gunnel Collection)

212

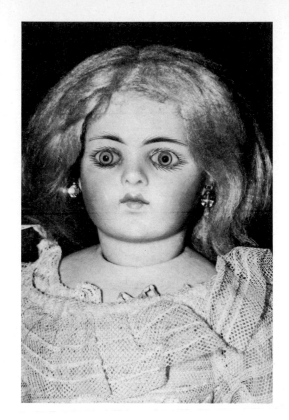

Manufacturer Unknown--15" Socket head on bisque shoulder plate. Closed mouth. Pierced ears. Paperweight eyes. Kid body with stitched toes. May be original clothes and wig. This bisque looks poor but is not, the doll is just very dirty. Marks: G.K./34.23. I do not think this doll or others with the GK and 4 numbers with a dot in the middle are Gebruder Krauss, Gebruder Kuhnlenz or Gebruder Knoch. More study must be made. 15"--I-J. (Courtesy Kimport Dolls)

Manufacturer Unknown--7½" Ivory Chinese Doctor Doll. Ladies were too bashful to undress before the doctors so had their maids take these dolls to the doctors and point to the area where their mistresses hurt. This one is rather late as the feet are full size instead of being bound and very small. 7½"--$110.00. (Gunnel Collection)

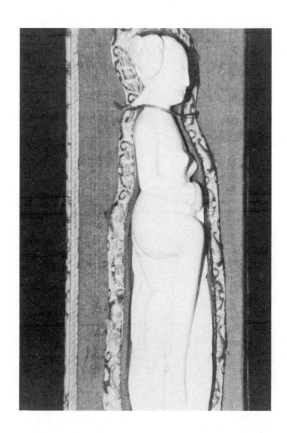

MORIMURA BROTHERS

Morimura Brothers was the name of a very large Japanese Import Firm and they operated from 1915 to 1922 (Doll section). In 1922, after World War I, their import section that handled dolls was taken over by Langfelder, Homma & Hayward, Inc.

In 1915, a Hikozo Araki of Brooklyn, N.Y., took out a design patent for "Queue San Baby" and it was assigned to Morimura Brothers to be made in Japan, but they were only sold in the U.S.

At the outbreak of World War I in Germany, the German Doll and Toy companies converted to wartime operations and Japan stepped into the toy picture very clearly. There were many obstacles for Japan to overcome in making dolls but soon they had and the quality of their dolls not only improved but many are excellent.

German dolls reappeared on the U.S. scene by 1922 and the Morimura Brothers stopped handling dolls at the same time.

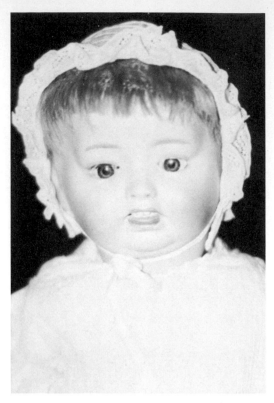

Morimura Brothers--13" Open mouth/4 upper teeth. Molded tongue. Marks: 2 ⊕ /Japan/5. ca. 1918. 13"--A-B. (Gunnel Collection)

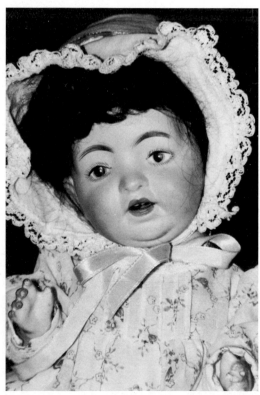

Morimura Brothers--11" baby. Painted blue eyes. Composition body. Marks: ⊕ /Japan. 11"--A-B. (Walters Collection)

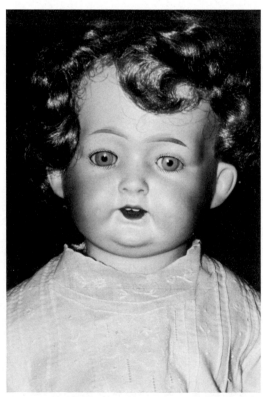

Morimura Brothers--19" Open mouth/2 upper teeth. Dimples. Marks: 22/ ⊕ /Japan. 19"-- C-D. (Courtesy Kimport Dolls)

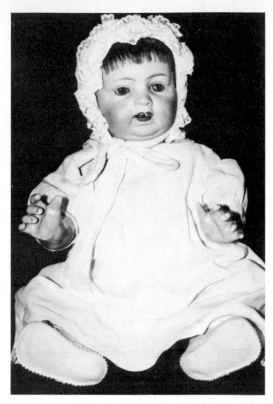

Morimura Brothers--20" Sleep eyes. Open mouth/2 upper teeth. Dimples. Marks: ⊕ / Japan. 20"--C-D. (Courtesy Kimport Dolls)

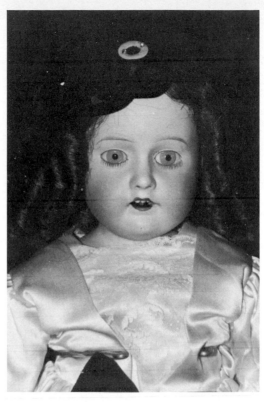

Morimura Brothers--22" Socket head. Lashes painted below eyes only. Open mouth. Marks: 5/ ⊕ /Japan. 22"--C-D. (Gunnel Collection)

Morimura Brothers--23" Socket head. Open mouth. ca. 1917. Marks: ⊕ /Japan/7. 23"--C-D. (Courtesy Kimport Dolls)

Morimura Brothers--24" Socket head. Open mouth. Marks: 1/ ⊕ /Japan/68. 24"--C-D. (Walters Collection)

Müller & Strassburger--14" Maché shoulder head. Painted eyes. Molded blonde hair. Cloth body, kid hands. Stripped sewn on stocking and shoes. Marks: Label: M&S/Superior/2015, in square. 14"--F-G. (Minter Collection)

PÁPIER MACHÉ

Most so called "pápier maché" parts on dolls were actually laminated paper and not pápier maché at all. Laminated paper doll heads/parts are several thicknesses of molded paper that has been bonded (glued) together or pressed after being glued.

Pápier maché is a type of composition in that it was a plastic (meaning moldable) material from paper pulp, wood and rag fibers, containing paste, oil or glue. Flour and/or clay, sand is added for stiffness. The hardness of pápier maché depends on the amount of glue that is added.

Some of the earliest dolls were pápier maché, ca. 1540, and as early as 1810 were being mass produced, by molds.

In 1858 Ludwig Greiner patented heads containing paper, whiting, rye flour, glue and reinforced with muslin and linen. About 1870, pápier maché was used on jointed dolls.

In French, pápier maché means "chewed paper."

Pápier Maché--29" Called a "Pre-Greiner," meaning made prior to 1840. German, with glass eyes. Excelsior/hair filled body. Composition type arms. Sewn on oil cloth type feet. 29"--$365.00. (Minter Collection)

Pápier Maché--42" Eggshell-Maché head, hands and feet. Maché body. Set in eyes, pierced nostrils. Cotton kimona. Marks: Japan, paper label on foot. 4½"--$25.00. (Maish Collection)

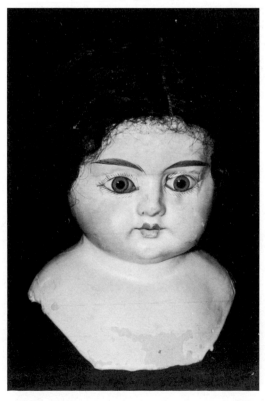

Pápier Maché--5" head only. Has sticker across side of face: Made in France. Bald head painted black. Head only--$35.00. (Courtesy Kimport Dolls)

Pápier Maché--5" Head of pápier maché. 5"--$35.00. (Walters Collection)

217

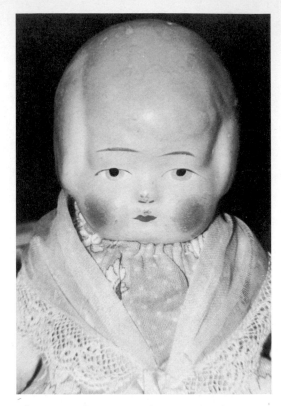

Pápier Maché--6½" All painted pápier maché. Molded bust. Jointed shoulders and hips. ca. 1890's. Marks: none. 6½"--$125.00. (Courtesy Kimport Dolls)

Pápier Maché--6½" All pápier maché. Came in a wicker basket. Jointed hips and shoulders. Marks: Germany, on back. 6½"--$35.00. (Penner Collection)

Pápier Maché--7" Santas. Cotton beards, paper clothes. Marks: Made in Germany. 1920. 7"--$15.00. (Maish Collection)

Pápier Maché--9½" Santa. Pápier maché. (Molded-pressed cardboard) ca. 1920. 9½"--$35.00. (Maish Collection)

16" Rabery & Delphieu. Marks: R.O.D. ("O" is size number)

Pápier Maché--10½" German pápier maché shoulder plate. Jointed shoulders and hips. Painted eyes. 10½"--$65.00. (Courtesy Kimport Dolls)

Pápier Maché--11" pápier maché head. Open crown. Painted brown eyes. Cloth body with stitched fingers. Marks: $\mathcal{F}$ /0/S. 11"--$65.00. (Walters Collection)

Pápier Maché--13½" pápier maché head. Cloth body. Original felt clothes. Marks: none. 13½"--$165.00. (Courtesy Kimport Dolls)

Pápier Maché--14" Twins. All original. 14"--$300.00 pair. (Walters Collection)

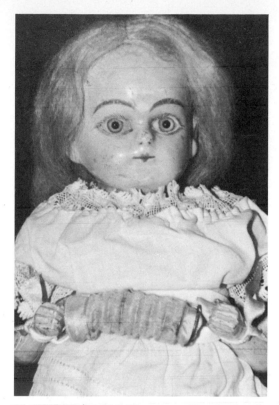

Pápier Maché--14½" Glass eyes. Wooden hands, maché overlay composition head. Squeeze type cloth body. As you squeeze her body, she plays the Consitina, also has cord through top of head and if pulled, she plays. 14½"--$495.00. (Courtesy Kimport Dolls)

Pápier Maché--17½" Thin maché shoulder head from Sicily. Inset porcelain eyes. Molded on sandles. Dates as early as the Sixteenth Century. 17½"--$1000.00. (Courtesy Kimport Dolls)

Pápier Maché--20" Blonde molded hair pápier maché of the 1880's. 20"--$185.00. (Courtesy Kimport Dolls)

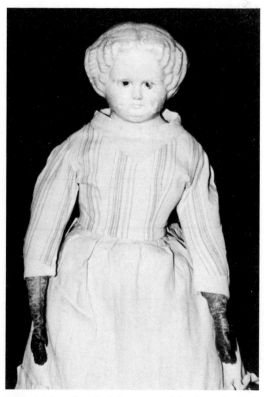

Pápier Maché--24" Pápier maché of 1870 with blonde molded hair. Painted eyes. Cloth and leather body and limbs. 24"--$225.00. (Courtesy Kimport Dolls)

14" Boy version "Hilda" by Kestner. Marks: JDK N. 1070/Ges. Gesch. 11/Made In Germany

14" Marks: E.J., on head. Jumeau marked body.

Parian--"Parian" is an untinted bisque but has an "ivory" finish, a smooth almost transparent depth to it. It is not only smooth but almost silky to the touch. White Bisque dolls are often referred to as Parian but are not.

Parian--12½" Mechanical walker. Pierced ears. Decorated shoulder front. Key to operate shows on front of dress. Dolls is a "Parian." 12½"--$595.00. (Courtesy Kimport)

Parian--14" Blonde. Could be boy or girl. Marks: Germany. 14"--$125.00. (Gunnel Collection)

Parian--14" Parian of 1870. Germany. 14"--$175.00. (Courtesy Kimport Dolls)

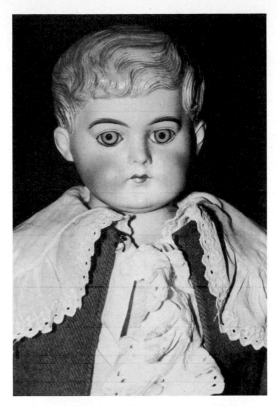

Parian--17" Parian with glass eyes. Side part boy's hair do. 17"--$435.00. (Courtesy Ralph's Antique Dolls)

Parian--17½" Parian with molded band across hair. Pierced ears. 17½"--$325.00. (Courtesy Kimport Dolls)

Parian--18" Parian. All of ears are exposed. Pierced ears. Molded clothes top and ribbon. 18"--$425.00.

Parian--22" A pressed head with molded on head with molded on head band and ribbons. 22"--$475.00. (Courtesy Ralph's Antique Dolls)

21" Composition Gesland body. Marks: F.G., in scroll

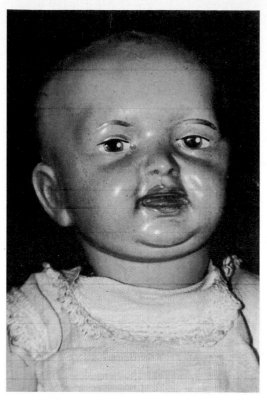

Parian--24½" Pink Parian "Dolly Madison" with molded upper and lower lids. Made at Grosbreitenbach by Macheleidt. Marks: 8 24½"--$650.00. (Courtesy Kimport Dolls)

Parson Jackson--10" "Biskoline" is the trademark material used by Parson-Jackson for their dolls. Marks: A picture of a stork/Trademark/ Parson Jackson Co/Cleveland, Ohio. ca. 1910. 10"--$150.00. (Courtesy Kimport Dolls)

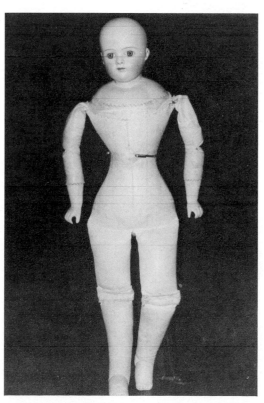

Laurent Marie René Péan--19" Lady, not a fashion doll. Kid body, with wire in kid arms. Stitched toes. Very high forehead with deep cut slice. Blue set paperweight eyes. Unpierced ears. Deep chest mold. Marks: PF. Old clothes. 19"--J-K. (Author)

Laurent Marie René Péan--Shows body of 19" Lady doll. Wire in kid arms.

227

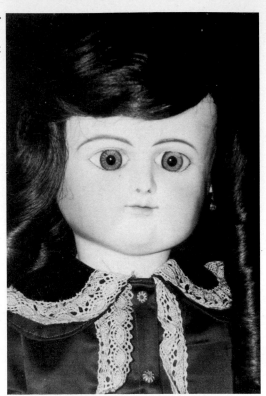

Petit & Dumontier--23" Socket head. Closed mouth. Pierced ears. Jointed wrists with metal hands. 23"--U-V. (Courtesy Ralph's Antique Dolls)

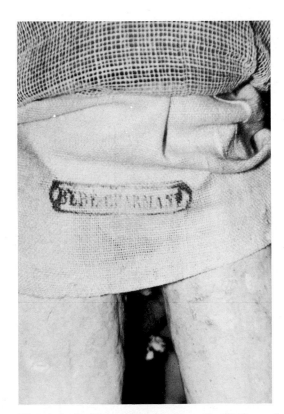

Pintel & Godchaux--12" "Bébé Charmant" 1892. Pápier maché body. Jointed at hips and shoulders. Closed mouth. Marks: H.P./1, on head. Stamped Bébé Charmant, on underclothes. All original. 12"--I-J. (Minter Collection)

Pintel & Godchaux--Stamp on underclothes of 12" "Bébé Charmant."

GRACE STOREY PUTNAM

Grace Storey Putnam was the designer and sculptor of the Bye-lo baby. The first was a cast in wax, painted with oil paints that was patted into the wax to give a transparent look. Milio of New York, who worked in wax, made this model up and they were sold to Madame Averill (Madame Henden), and soon Mrs. Putnam was under contract to the George Borfeldt Company. The dolls were made in all bisque rubber, celluloid, bisque heads, composition, and even vinyl. Grace Putnam obtained copyrights in 1922, two in 1923 and one in 1925.

Rumors have always been strong that the first wax model of the Bye-lo was actually a wax "death mask" of a dead 3-day old baby girl (colored) at the Bellview Hospital in N.Y.C. in 1921. This has never been confirmed in any manner.

The Bye-lo bisque heads were made by such companies as: Alt, Beck & Gottschalk, Kling, Kestner, Schwab & Co., Hertel, etc. The bodies were made by K & K Toy Co. (Kahl & Kohle) and were distributed by George Borgfeldt. The composition hands were made by the Cameo Doll Co., and Karl Standfuss made the celluloid hands. Wood hands were made by Schoenhut.

Grace Storey Putnam designed other dolls but non was successful like the Bye-lo, for example her "Fly-lo," and in 1938 a set of doll house dolls that were not produced.

Marks: © 1923 By
Grace S. Putnam
Made In Germany

Bye-lo Baby
K&K
Copyright 1922
By
Grace Storey
Putnam

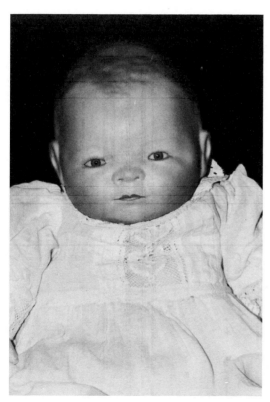

Grace S. Putnam--13" Cir. Bye-Lo Baby. 16"--H-I. (Minter Collection)

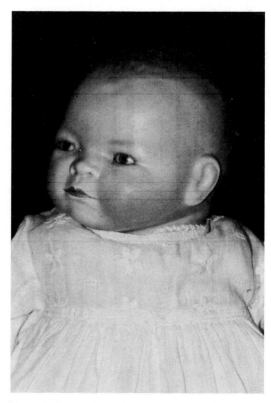

Grace S. Putnam--14½" long Bye-Lo baby. Cloth body. Celluloid hands. Marked on back. 14½"--F-G. (Walters Collection)

229

RABERY & DELPHIEU

In 1856 Jean Delphieu took out a French patent for using pink cloth instead of kid on doll bodies. This firm sold dolls with both linen and kid, with stationary and swivel bisque heads, then in 1881, added wooden bodies along with the kid. They won a silver medal at Amsterdam in 1883 and a silver medal in Paris in 1889.

The marks for this company: R.D. and "Bébé de Paris."

Rabery & Delphieu--17" This doll dates from 1881, as she has wooden arms and legs with Papier mache body. Cork plate. Papier mache feet molded onto wood legs. Pierced ears and very small feet. Closed mouth. Marks: R.OD. 17"--L-N. (Author)

Rabery & Delphieu--Full length view of R.D. child.

230

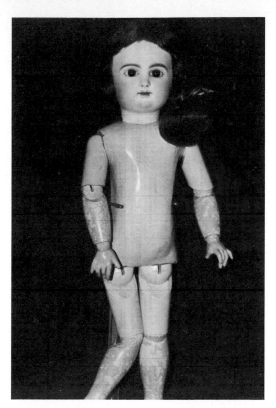

Rabery & Delphieu--Body of 17" R.D. The lower front of the body is almost cut flat.

Rabery & Delphieu--22" Socket head. Closed mouth. Oversized straight wrists. Made for Benoist Schneider (Paris). Marks: 1B/R.D. 22"--N-P. (Minter Collection)

Rabery & Delphieu--17" Socket head. Closed mouth. Marks: R.OD. 17"--L-N. (Minter Collection)

Rabery & Delphieu--17" Socket head. Closed mouth. Straight wrists. Marks: R.OD. 17"--L-N. (Minter Collection)

231

Rabery & Delphieu--20" Socket head. Closed mouth. Marks: R. 1D. 20"--M-O. (Courtesy Kimport Dolls)

Rabery & Delphieu--20" Socket head. Open mouth. Original wig. Marks: B/R9/0D. 20"--J-K. (Courtesy Ralph's Antique Dolls)

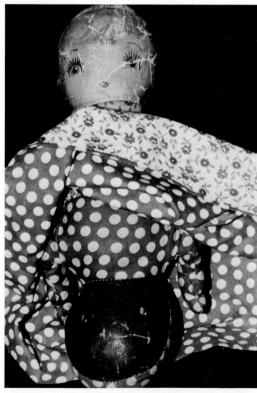

Rag Dolls--12" Maker unknown. 12"--$47.50. (Courtesy Kimport Dolls)

Rag Dolls--12" Topsy/Turvy. Colored and white. By Albert Bruckner. Patented July 9, 1901. 12"--$300.00. (Courtesy Kimport Dolls)

Rag Dolls--17½" Rag doll of the 1890's. 17½"--$100.00. (Courtesy Kimport Dolls)

Emma E. Adams Rag Dolls--19" "Columbian Doll." Rag doll made and painted by Emma E. Adams before 1900. Marks: Stamp: Columbian Doll/Emma E. Adams/Oswego Centre/NY. Sold at the 1893 Columbian Exposition in Chicago. 19"--$1,000.00. (Courtesy Kimport Dolls)

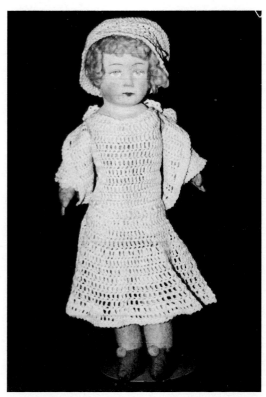

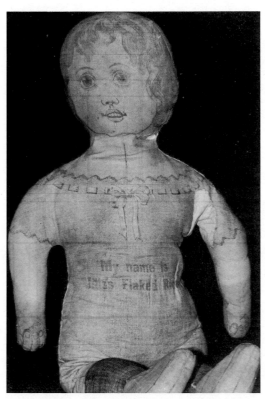

Rag Dolls-21" Germany "Lenci" type. Felt with sawdust filled body. 21"--$40.00. (Courtesy Kimport Dolls)

Rag Dolls-25" All stamped cloth. Cotton filled. Marks: My Name is Miss Flaked Rice, across stomach. 25"--$45.00.

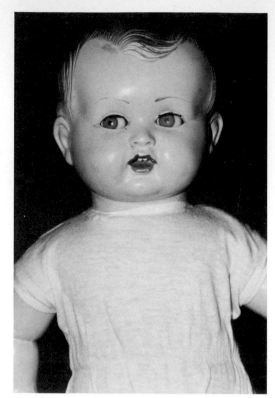

Raynal--14" Celluloid head, arms and legs. Stockinette body, with cryer. Flirty, blue sleep eyes. Open mouth/2 upper teeth. Molded brown hair. Marks: Raynal, on head. Raynal was located in Paris. ca. 1927. 14"--$38.50. (Courtesy Kimport Dolls)

RECKNAGEL OF ALEXANDRINETHAL

This company started as a hard paste porcelain factory. They produced dolls from 1886 through 1930.

Their porcelain marks: R.A.

Recknagel of Alexandrinethal--8" Bisque head. Blue set eyes. Pápier maché body with composition arms. Original clothes/ribbon. Marks: 21/Germany/R140A. 8"--A-B. (Maish Collection)

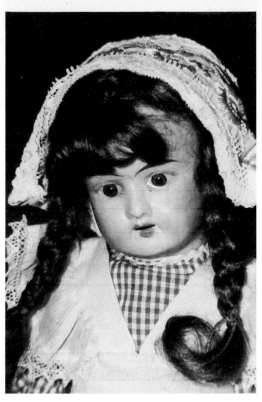

Recknagel of Alexandrinethal--8½" Bisque head. Composition body. Original Vollendam Costume. Open mouth/4 teeth. Marks: Germany/R15/0A/K1. 8½"--A-B. (Maish Collection)

Recknagel of Alexandrinethal--10" Socket head. Cardboard body with pápier maché limbs. Open mouth. Marks: 1914/Dep./R11/0A/#. 10"--A-B. (Walters Collection)

Recknagel--14" Socket head. Open mouth. Marks: 1909/Eep/R5/0A/13. 14"--B-C. (Clasby Collection)

Recknagel of Alexandrinethal--14" Socket head. Open mouth/4 teeth. Marks: R9/0xA. 14"--B-C. (Penner Collection)

A. Reich--6½" Baby with painted blue eyes.
Painted hair. Marks: Germany/N.K.2/A3/0-R.
Made by A. Reich (Coburg 1909-1915) for
Nehren & Kiko. ca. 1914. 6½"--A-B. (Walters
Collection)

OTTO REINECKE

Otto Reinecke--Otto Reinecke operated a hard
paste porcelain factory in Hof-Moschendorf,
Bavaria from 1878 through 1933. His dolls are
marked: "P.M." which stands for Porzellanfabrik Moschendorf.

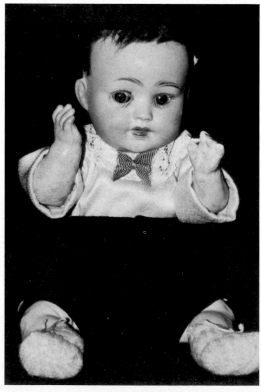

236

Otto Reinecke--11½" Bisque head with com-
position body. Black wig. Gray blue eyes.
Marks: Weber/Germany 22/P810M. Made by
Otto Reinecke and distributed by Franz Carl
Weber. ca. 1895. 11½"--A-B. (Maish Collection)

Otto Reinecke--8" Baby with open mouth/2
upper teeth. Sleep eyes. Marks: P.M./Dep/Ger-
many/5/0. 8"--B-C. (Gunnel Collection)

RHEINISCHE GUMME und CELLULOID FABRIK CO.

They have made celluloid (and rubber) dolls from 1873 and
are still in business making plastic/vinyl dolls. With the
outlaw of celluloid during the mid-1940's this company went
into a pressed paper construction until plastics came into
their own.

They made celluloid dolls for Kestner, Kammer &
Reinhardt and many others.

Their marks:

words: Schutz Marke

Rheinische Gummi und Celluloid Fabrik Co--9"
All celluloid. Painted eyes. Closed mouth. All
original. ca. 1935. Marks: Turtle, in a diamond.
9"--$22.50. (Clasby Collection)

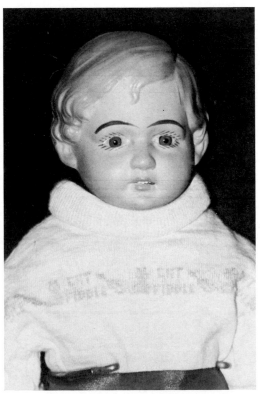

Rheinische Gumme und Celluloid Fabrik
Co.--14" One piece celluloid shoulder plate.
Molded blonde hair. Inset blue glass eyes. Open
mouth/5 teeth. Marks: Diamond with Turtle
mark/11. ca. 1889. 14"--$65.00. (Penner Collec-
tion)

237

Rheinische Gumme und Celluloid Fabrik Co.--15½" Brown glass eyes. Open mouth/teeth. 15½"--$65.00. (Courtesy Kimport Dolls)

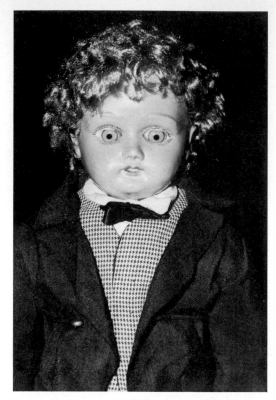

Rheinische Gummi und Celluloid Fabrik Co.--17" Celluloid shoulder head on kid jointed body. Sleep eyes. Open mouth/5 teeth. Marks: Germany/Turtle, in a diamond/Schutz Marke/11½. 17"--$70.00. (Clasby Collection)

Rheinische Gummi und Celluloid Fabrik Co.--21" Shoulder plate on a cloth body. Celluloid arms and legs. Glass eyes. 21"--$87.50. (Courtesy Kimport Dolls)

Seiberling--4½" Seven Dwarfs. All rubber and original. Marks: Walt Disney/Seiberling Latex/ Made in Akron, Ohio. U.S.A. Shown with a Madame Alexander's Snow White. Original. Alex. Doll--$65.00, Dwarfs--$22.00 each.

Rubber--6" All rubber. Wire jointed arms. Jointed neck and shoulders. Black mohair over molded hair. Painted blue eyes. Molded and painted on shoes. All original. Marks: Industria Argentina. ca. 1925. 6"--$30.00. (Author)

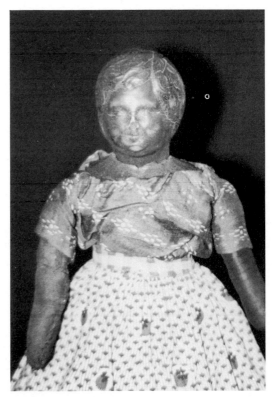

Rubber--11½" Goodyear Rubber doll of 1851. Applied ears. Shoulder head. Goodyear's patent was Mar. 6, 1851. 11½"--$1,000.00. (Courtesy Kimport)

CHARLES GOODYEAR

Rubber--Charles Goodyear of New Haven, Conn. was the one who invented vulcanized soft rubber, used for rubber dolls and in 1851, Nelson Goodyear, his brother invented hard rubber.

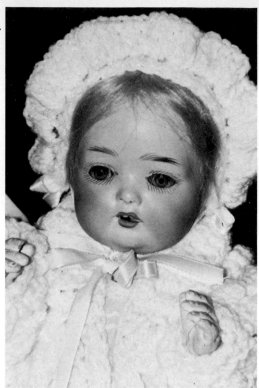

Phillip Samhammer & Co.--10" Socket head. Open mouth/2 upper teeth. Marks: P.S./23/Germany/0. Made by Simon & Halbig for Samhammer. Samhammer was in business from 1888 to 1916 and was one of the Grand Prize winners of the 1900 Paris Exposition. Samhammer's factories were in Sonneberg, Thur. 10"-- C-D. (Walters Collection)

Sannier & Caut--9" Sleep eyes. Closed mouth. Marks: 293/S&C/6/0. ca. 1889. 9"--B-C. (Clasby Collection)

BRUNO SCHMIDT

Bruno Schmidt--9" Socket head. Spring strung. Open mouth. Sleep eyes/top lashes. Lashes painted below only. Marks: B.S./4. ca. 1900. 9"-- B-C. (Gunnel Collection)

FRAN SCHMIDT & CO.

Fran Schmidt & Co. This company began in 1890 at Georgenthal, near Waltershausen, Thur and obtained an extremely interesting patent in 1891 (in England). It was for sleeping eyes made so the upper lids moved further and faster than the lower lids. It was in 1902 they registered the trademarks of crossed hammers with a doll between and "F.S.&Co."

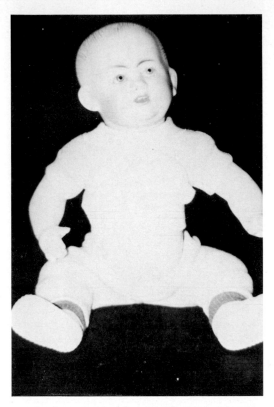

Fran Schmidt--10" long with 8" cir. head. Brush painted hair. Pierced nostrils. Marks: Germany/ F.S.&Co.2/1255/25/Deponiert. ca. after 1910. 10"--E-F. (Minter Collection)

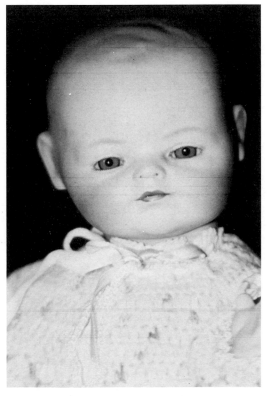

Fran Schmidt--16" Glass eyes. Marks: F.S.&C./ 1285/32. Low on neck and out of sight: S.S.&C. '17. Made for Societe Schiller, Rene & Cie (Paris). ca. 1917. 16"--J-K. (Author)

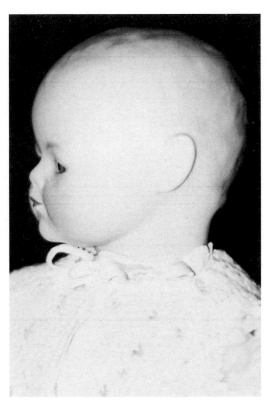

Shows profile of 16" Baby.

PAUL SCHMIDT

Paul Schmidt--A very late doll firm located at Sonneberg, Thur and operated for just 4 years, 1921-1925. Their registered trademark was "PSch, in an oval. Sample marks:

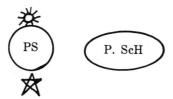

Paul Schmidt--15½" Shoulder plate. Open mouth/4 teeth. Marks: Germany/P.Sch./5/OM. 15½"--B-C. (Penner Collection)

Paul Schmidt--15" Socket head. Open mouth/2 molded teeth and factory white "paste" to make it look like two rows of teeth. Marks: Made in Germany/P.Sch./0. 15"--B-C. (Minter Collection)

21" Saucer crown (solid dome) with two stringing holes. Marks: 14, on head

SCHMITT & FILS (SONS)

Although this company seems to have been around since 1863, it was not until 1867 that the firm was listed as a toy maker. In 1877 they perfected a method of painting porcelain shoulder heads and took out a patent. They also patented all bisque bebes in 1879. In 1883 they had taken out a patent for a layer of wax to be applied over bisque doll heads, after the heads were removed from the kilns. They obtained several patents for eye movements, including one in 1885 (in Germany) for controlling eye movement by a knob on the back of the head.

Schmitt composition bodies generally have complete free motion balls at shoulders and hips, long feet and a very flat bottom of the rear torso, the front crotch area drops very low between the legs. The Schmitt mark is usually stamped on the flat bottom. On kid bodies the mark is generally located in between the rear joints of the hips.

Schmitt won a silver medal at Paris in 1878. From 1879 to 1890 they made the "Bebe Schmitt." They discontinued business in 1891.

Sample marks:

Schmitt & Fils--16" "X1" Composition/wood body. Very deep slice in pate. Straight wrists. Unpierced ears. Cork pate. Sleep, almost black eyes. Full closed mouth with dark red line between lips. Original. Head made by Simon & Halbig (most likely). Marks: Incised X1, on head. 16"--L-N. (Author)

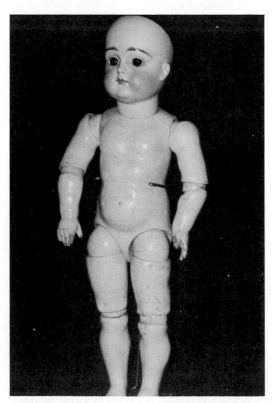

Schmitt & Fils--Body view of marked Schmitt & Fils body. Head marked X1 (incised)

244

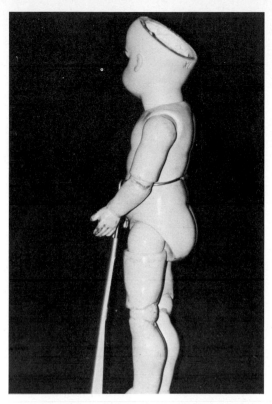

Schmitt & Fils--Side view of marked Schmitt "X1" body.

Schmitt & Fils--20" Socket head. Closed mouth. Marks: 10/ ⬡ . 20"--U-V. (Courtesy Ralph's Antique Dolls)

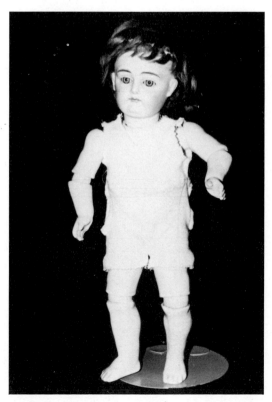

Schmitt & Fils--13½" Socket head. Straight wrists. Closed mouth. Paper weight set eyes. Stamped on flat part of underside of buttocks. 13½"--L-N. (Courtesy Kimport Dolls)

245

19" Laurent Marie Réné Péan (Péan Fréres), Criel, Oise France. 1962-90. Marks: P.F.

14" Kid body. Shoulder plate. Marks: Bru Jne R 5

Schoenau & Hoffmeister--This company entered
the doll making field "late." It was in 1901 and
they were located in Bavaria and also known as
"Porzellanfabrik Burggrub."

Sample marks:

Schoenau & Hoffmeister--6½" "Hanna Poly-
nesian" Painted bisque socket head. Papier
mache arms, legs and body. Black mohair wig.
Black sleep eyes. All original. Marks: ☆ /
Hanna/Germany. 6½"--B-C. (Maish Collection)

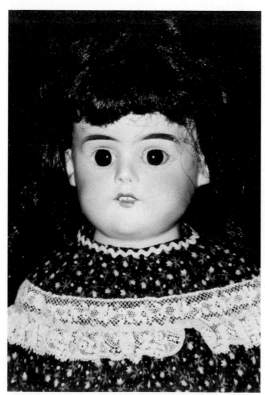

Schoenau & Hoffmeister--10½" Socket head.
Open mouth. Marks: S ☆ H/Germany.
10½"--B-C. (Walters Collection)

Schoenau & Hoffmeister--12" Socket head. Sleep
eyes. Open mouth. Marks: S ☆ H/1909/4/0/
Germany. 12"--C-D. (Clasby Collection)

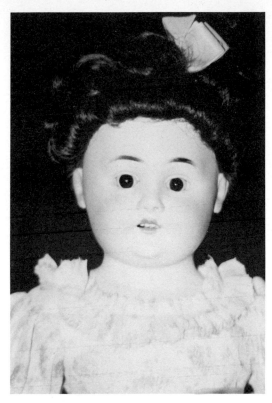

Schoenau & Hoffmeister--25" Socket head. Open mouth. Marks: 0½/S ☆ H/Dep/3D. 25"--C-D (Courtesy Ralph's Antique Dolls)

Schoenau & Hoffmeister--27" Socket head. Marks: S ☆ H/914/9. 27"-C-D. (Courtesy Kimport)

Schoenau & Hoffmeister--30½" Socket head. Sleep eyes/lashes. Open mouth. Marks: S ☆ : H/1906. 14"--B-C, 30"--E-F. (Courtesy Kimport Dolls)

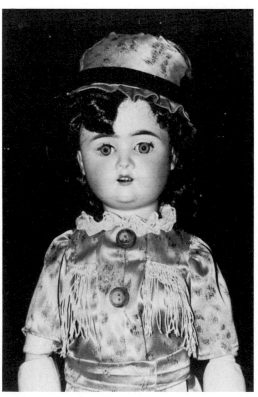

Schoenau & Hoffmeister--22" Socket head. Marks: S ☆ H/1909/4½/Germany. 14"--B-C, 30"--E-F. (Minter Collection)

249

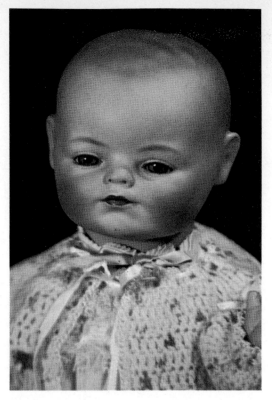

16" Franz Schmitt. Marks: 1285/32/F.S.&C. Made for French trade.

17" Open mouth. Marks: Tete Jumeau.

19" Marks: Depose/Tete Jumeau/Bte S.G.D.G./ 8, on head. Jumeau/Medaille D'or/Paris, on body.

15" Deep crown slice. Marks: B.6F.

Shoenhut--19" All wood, original. Label seal on chest: Schoenhut Doll/Pat. Jan. 17th 1911/USA. 19"--$260.00. (Minter Collection)

Schoenhut--21" All wood. Original. Label seal on chest: Schoenhut Doll/Pat. Jan. 17th 1911/USA. 21"--$260.00. (Minter Collection)

Schoenhut--18" Sleep decal eyes (part of decals missing). Open mouth with molded metal teeth. Marks: Schoenhut Doll/Pat. Jan. 17th 1911/USA. Top of pate stamped Patented/Sept. 1911. 18"--$260.00. (Clasby Collection)

Alfred Schroeder--19" Socket head strung with wires through 2 holes in back of head. Marks: Germany/C/3. 19"--C-D. (Esler Collection)

Schuetzmeister & Quendt--22" Socket head. Excellent quality bisque. Feathered brows. Marks: 301. Distributed by John Bing Co. The mold number 301 was used extensively by S.F.B.J. and Unis, after 1899 (S.F.B.J.) and 1922 (Unis). 22"--E-F. (Penner Collection)

Schuetzmeister & Quendt--16" Sleep eyes. Open mouth/4 teeth. Marks: 201/S inside a Q/Germany. Baby. 16"--C-D. (Gunnel Collection)

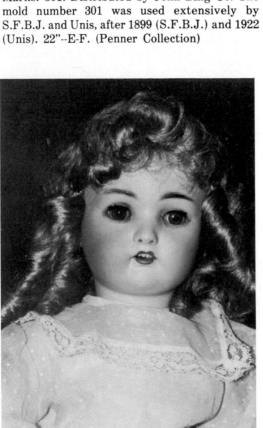

Schuetzmeister & Quendt--22" Socket head. Sleep eyes/lashes. Open mouth. Marks: 301/ Germany. 22"--E-F. (Courtesy Kimport Dolls)

SIMON & HALBIG

The Simon & Halbig firm operated from sometime in the late 1860's or early 1870's until the mid 1930's.

Some Simon & Halbig dolls have molded hair and untinted bisque and quite a few are found that are "bald" heads, generally lady types, that were so popular in the mid 1870's. Simon & Halbig was one of the largest German firms and supplied many heads/designs to French doll makers during the years of 1870's and 1880's.

In 1890 they obtained patents for movable eyes. One was a wire, with a loop, through a hole in the back of the head and later a wire with a handle to make the eyes move from right to left. They made dolls for many companies including, Fleischmann & Blodel, Gimbel Bros., Jumeau, Kammer & Reinhardt, Heinrich Handwerck, C.M. Begmann, Cuno & Otto Dressel, Bawo & Dotter, Hamberger & Co., George Borgfeldt & Co., etc.

In 1895 Simon left the firm (retired or deceased) and Carl Halbig took over as a single owner. Carl Halbig did not register "S&H" until 1905. Before then the dolls were marked with just "SH" or the full name of "Simon & Halbig."

Simon and Halbig had a "thing" about the number "9," and a large number of their molds contain a "9," and their most common doll (most often found) is #1079.

Sample marks:

		Halbig
C.M. Bergmann	S&H	K ✡ R
Simon & Halbig	1079	Germany
1299	S12H	1030
Simon & Halbig	949	Jumeau (body)

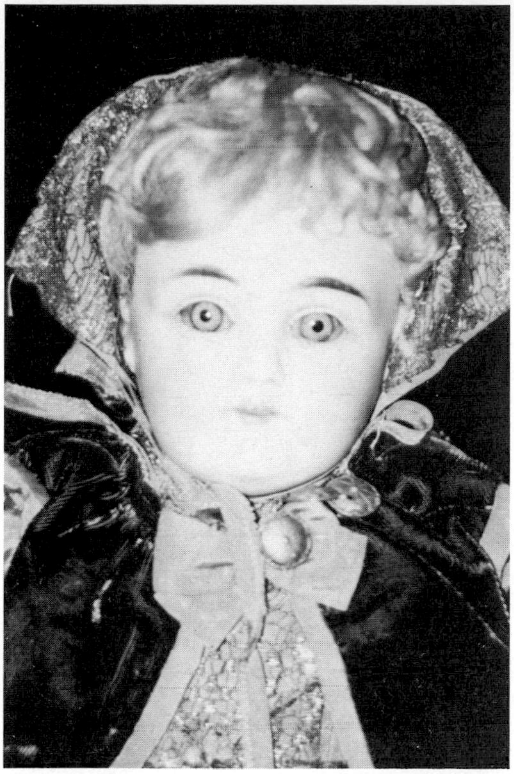

Simon & Halbig--18" Shoulder plate/kid. Marks: SH/Dep. 18"--C-D. (Courtesy Ralph's Antique Dolls)

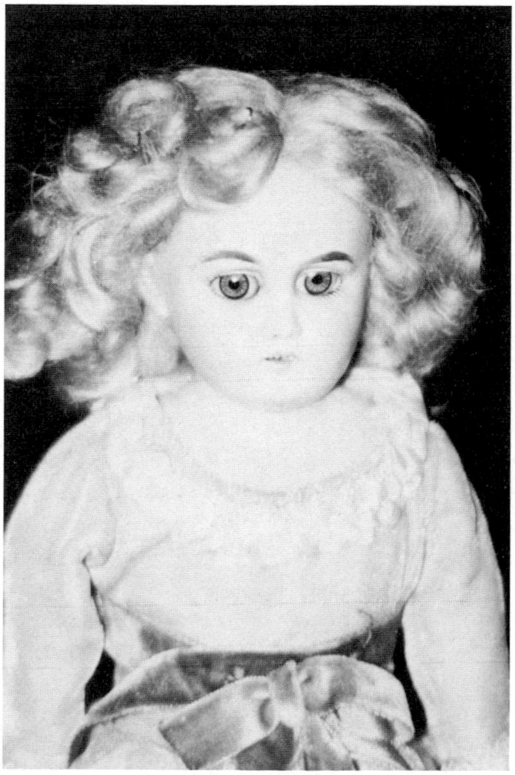

Simon & Halbig--16" Shoulder plate/kid. Marks: [mark] /Germany/3 𝓕 3-3. ca. 1890. Made for Henry Schwartz, Baltimore, Maryland, formerly of Herford, Germany and brother of F.A.O. Schwarz. 16"--C-D. (Courtesy Ralph's Antique Dolls)

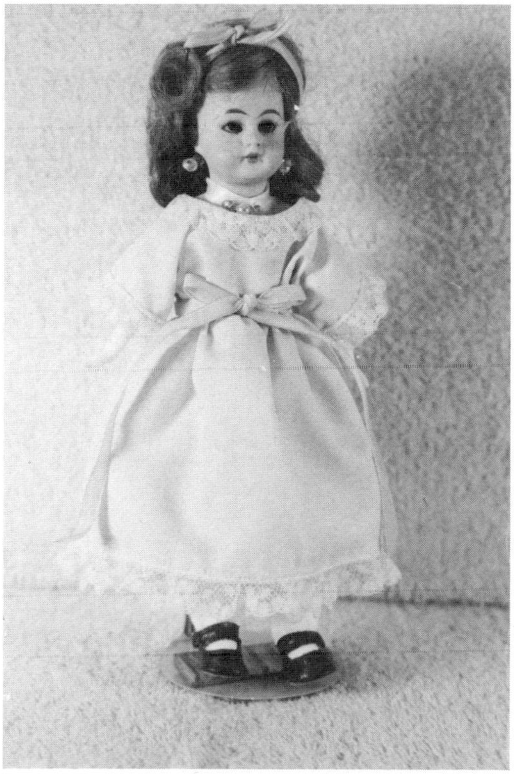

Simon & Halbig--10" Bisque head and half arms. Cotton body and legs. Dark blonde human hair wig. Grey blue sleep eyes. Open/closed mouth with incised teeth. Pierced ears. Marks: Simon Halbig/Germany. 10"--A-B. (Maish Collection)

Simon & Halbig--16" Socket head. Sleep eyes. Pierced ears. Open mouth. Marks: Dep. 7½. 16"--C-D. (Minter Collection)

Simon & Halbig--20" Socket head. Pierced ears. Sleep eyes/lashes. Marks: Dep. 20"--G-I. (Courtesy Ralph's Antique Dolls)

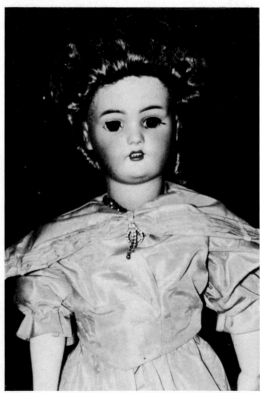

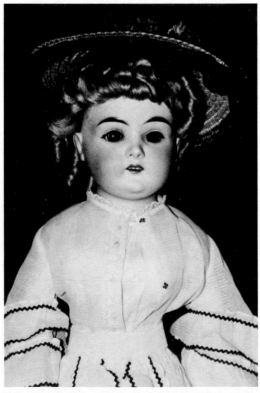

Simon & Halbig--26½" Socket head. Sleep eyes. Open mouth. Marks: Germany/Simon Halbig/ SH/10. ca. 1895. 26½"--D-F. (Courtesy Kimport Dolls)

Simon & Halbig--28" Socket head. Adult body. Sleep eyes/lashes. Open mouth. Marks: 30/130. 28"--G-I. (Courtesy Kimport Dolls)

Simon & Halbig--21" Socket head. Open mouth. Marks; 550/Simon & Halbig. 21"--C-D. (Walters Collection)

Simon & Halbig--22" Socket head. Marks: 550/ Germany/Simon Halbig/SVH. 22"--C-D. (Esler Collection)

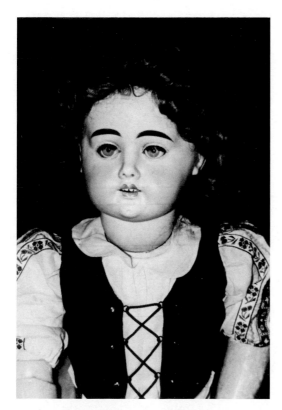

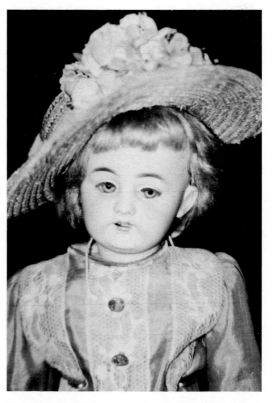

Simon & Halbig-32" Socket head. Marks: 1000-12. 32"--F-H. (Courtesy Kimport)

Simon & Halbig--16" Socket head. Pull string flirt eyes/lashes. Marks: SC½H1009/Dep/ST/ Germany. 16"--F-G. (Gunnel Collection)

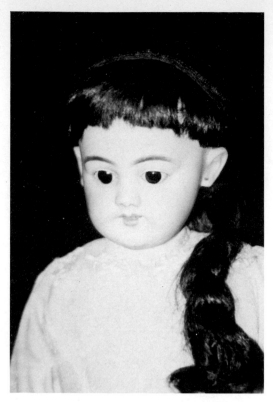

Simon & Halbig--21" Socket head. Marks: 10H 1009/Dep/SH. Open mouth. Pierced ears. 21"--F-G. (Courtesy Ralph's Antique Dolls)

Simon & Halbig--19½" Shoulder plate. Kid body. Open mouth. Marks: S.H.1010. This is the head they later used on the Edison Phonograph doll (1889). 19½"--D-E. (Walters Collection)

Simon & Halbig--7½" Blonde human hair dutch boy bob. Blue sleep eyes. Open/closed mouth. Painted on brown Mary Janes with knee socks. Composition arms, legs and body. All original. Marks: 410/1018/Simon Halbig/Company. 7½"--A-B. (Maish Collection)

Simon & Halbig--15" Socket head. Open mouth. Pierced ears. Marks: S&H 1039/6 Dep. ca. 1890. 15"--C-D. (Minter Collection)

Simon & Halbig--25" Shoulder plate/kid. Marks: S&H/1040. ca. 1891. 25"--E-F. (Courtesy Ralph's Antique Dolls)

Simon & Halbig--19" Socket head. Flirty eyes (do not sleep)/lashes. Marks: SH1059/Germany/Dep/8. 19"--E-F. (Gunnel Collection)

Simon & Halbig--37" Socket head. Sleep eyes. Open mouth. Marks: S&H/1079. ca. 1905. 37"--F-H. (Courtesy Kimport Dolls)

Simon & Halbig--12" Socket head. Open mouth. Marks: 1079/Dep/SH. ca. 1905. 12"--A-B. (Gunnel Collection)

259

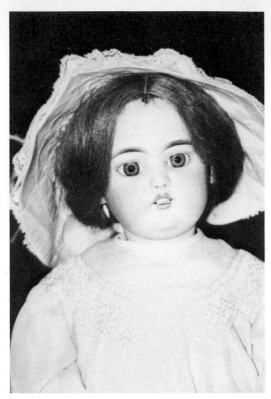

Simon & Halbig--21" Socket head. Marks: S.H. 1079 3½/Dep. 12"--A-B, 28"--D-E. (Gunnel Collection)

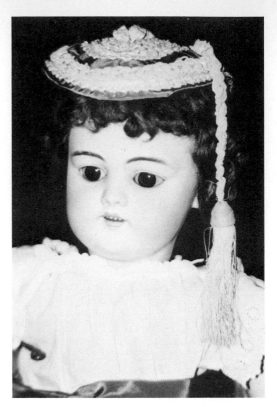

Simon & Halbig-- 28" Socket head. Marks: S&H 1079/Dep/12/Germany. ca. 1905. 12"--A-B, 28"--D-E. (Courtesy Ralph's Antique Dolls)

Simon & Halbig--21" Socket head. Pierced ears. Marks: S&H 1079/Dep/Germany/8. 12"--A-B, 28"--D-E. (Gunnel Collection)

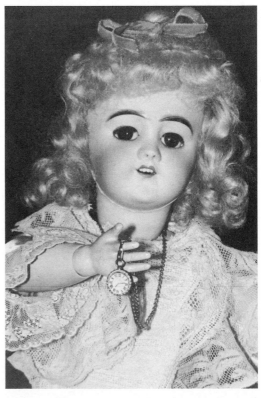

Simon & Halbig--22" Socket head. Open mouth. Marks: SH1079-10/Dep. 12"--A-B, 28"--D-E. (Gunnel Collection)

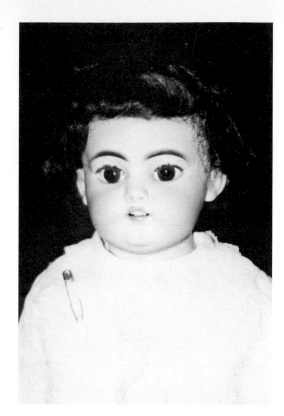

Simon & Halbig--22" Shoulder plate/kid. Almond shaped eyes/lashes. Marks: Dep/Wimpern/Gesetzel Schutz/SH1080-8. Wimpern means "eyelashes." 22"--D-E. (Author)

Simon & Halbig--10" Shoulder head. Cloth body. Glass eyes. Closed mouth. Marks: S&H/1160. 10"--C-D. (Clasby Collection)

Simon & Halbig--20" "Santa" body of composition/wood. Molded brows. Sleep/flirty eyes/lashes. Open mouth/4 teeth. Dark V in center of lower lip. Protruding pierced ears. Marks: 1249/Halbig/Germany/Santa/S&H. Some were made for the Hamburger & Co. in 1900-1910. Heubach also made a marked "Santa" that doesn't look like this doll at all. 20"--E-F. (Author)

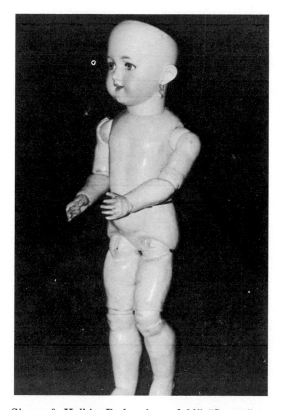

Simon & Halbig--Body view of 20" "Santa."

261

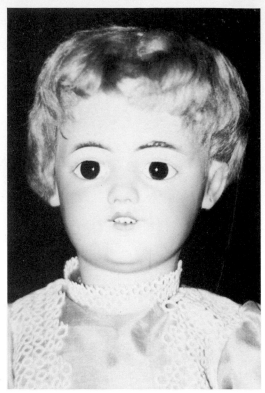

Simon & Halbig--23" "Santa" Socket head. Open mouth. Marks: Dep./Germany/Santa/10½. Made for Hamburger & Co. ca. 1900. 23"--E-F. (Courtesy Ralph's Antique Dolls)

Simon & Halbig--24" Shoulder plate. Open mouth. Marks: S&H 1250/Dep/Germany/9. 24"--E-F. (Courtesy Kimport Dolls)

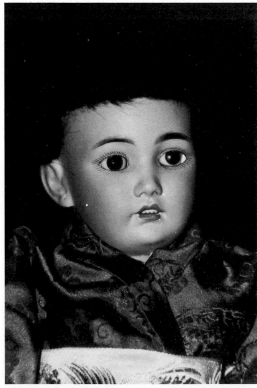

Simon & Halbig--16" Fashion kid body. Pierced ears. Shoulder head. Marks: SH1260/Dep/Germany/5½. On front (stamped) "Imperial." "Imperial" dolls were made for Hamburger & Co. 16"--D-E. (Clasby Collection)

Simon & Halbig--14" Socket head. Open mouth. Marks: 1329/Germany/Simon Halbig/S&H. Oriental. 14"--M-N. (Courtesy Kimport Dolls)

SOCIÉTÉ FRANÇAISE de FABRICATION de BÉBÉS et JOUETS

This society was formed in 1899 and known members were Jumeau, Bru, Fleischmann & Blodel, Rabery & Delphieu, Pintel & Godchaux, P.H. Schmitz, A. Bouchet, Jullien, Danel & Cie.

The society used the initials "S.F.B.J." and the most commonly found mold numbers are 60 and 301. There are some composition and celluloid S.F.B.J. dolls but the majority of them were bisque on composition bodies.

S.F.B.J. made many "character" dolls and these, generally are in the 200 mold number series.

In 1911 they registered, in France, the trademarks, "Bébé Prodige," "Bébé Jumeau," and "Bébé Francaise," in 1913, "Bébé Triomphe," in 1920, "Bébé Parisiana," "Bébé Moderne," "Le Seduisant" and "Bébé Parfait," in 1921, "Le Papillon."

In 1922 S.F.B.J. had 2,800 employees. This Society dissolved in the mid 1950's.

Sample marks:

  Depose S.F.B.J.

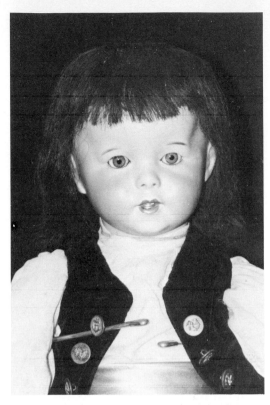

Société Française De Fabrication De Bébés et Jouets--24" "Twirp" 15" head. cir. blue sleep eyes. Open/closed mouth/2 molded teeth on rim. Socket head. Marks: 23/France/S.F.B.J./247/Paris/11. 24"--U-V. (Minter Collection)

Société Française De Fabrication De Bébés et Jouets--14" Called "Laughing Jumeau" Socket head. Open/closed mouth with molded upper teeth. Marks: S.F.B.J./230/Paris. 14"--J-L. (Minter Collection)

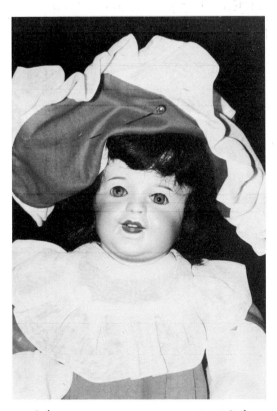

Société Française De Fabrication De Bébés et Jouets--14" "Laughing Jumeau" Socket head. Open/closed mouth with molded upper teeth. Marks: S.F.B.J./230/Paris. 14"--J-L. (Virginia Jones)

263

Société Française de Fabrication de Bébés et
Jouets--15" Socket head. Composition body.
Open mouth. Marks: S.F.B.J./301/Paris/3.
15"--C-D. (Walters Collection)

Société Française de Fabrication de Bébés et
Jouets--17" Socket head. Open mouth. Marks:
S.F.B.J./301/Paris/6. 17"--E-F. (Walters Collec-
tion)

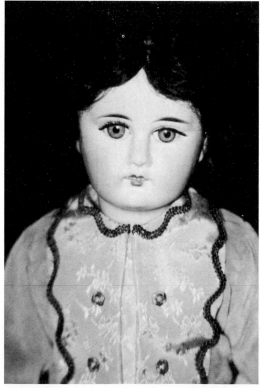

Société Française de Fabrication de Bébés et
Jouets--19" Socket head. Open mouth. Made
after 1899. 19"--F-G. (Gunnel Collection)

Société Française de Fabrication de Bébés et
Jouets--17½" Socket head. Open mouth. Set
eyes. Pierced ears. Marks: S.F.B.J./Paris. Body
marked Jumeau. 17½--F-G. (Courtesy Kimport
Dolls)

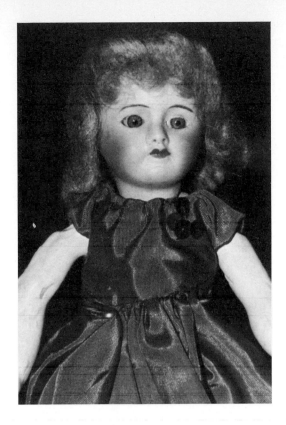

Société Française de Fabrication de Bébés et Jouets--8" Socket head on a papier mache stick body. Marks: S.F.B.J./60. 8"--A-B. (Courtesy Kimport Dolls)

Société Française Fabrication de Bébés et Jouets--15" Socket head. Open mouth/4 teeth. Marks: S.F.B.J./60/Paris/1/0. 15"--D-e. (Minter Collection)

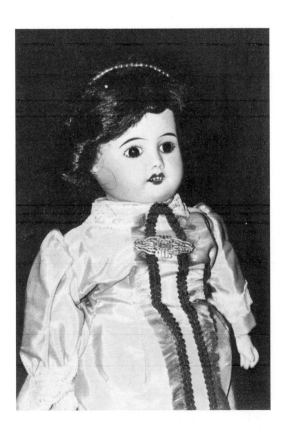

EDMUND ULRICH STEINER

Edmond Steiner came to the U.S. as a young man and during his lifetime, crossed the Atlantic 84 times. He worked for Horsman, L.H. Mace & Co., Strobel & Wilken and Louis Wolf & Co. It was in the 1890's that he went with Curman & Steiner and it was during this period that most of his dolls were made. After this company broke up he went back to and became the Doll Department Manager for the Strobel & Wilkens firm. From there he moved to manager at the Samstag & Hilder (about 1901) and was there until 1907. About 1915, he joined a glass company and died in 1917.

In 1902 he patented a walking and sitting doll and registered, both in Germany and U.S., the trademark "Majestic" and "Lilliput," which had both been used since 1894. In 1903 he registered "Daisy" as a trademark.

Sample marks:

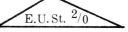

Edmund Ulrich Steiner--17" Shoulder plate. Marks: <E.U.St.> . 17"--C-D. (Gunnel Collection)

Edmund Ulrich Steiner--21" Shoulder plate. Marks: 25.5/6 170 K/Germany. 21"--C-D. (Gunnel Collection)

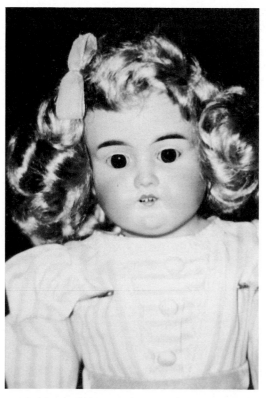

Edmund Ulrich Steiner--22" Shoulder plate. Marks: 25.7/Majestic/Reg'd/3/Germany. 22"--C-D. (Gunnel Collection)

HERMANN STEINER

Hermann Steiner--Hermann Steiner entered the doll makers field after World War I...1921...and made dolls at Neustadt, near Coburg & Sonneberg. Sample marks:

Hermann Steiner--13" Socket head. Open mouth. Marks: Germany/17/0, in a circle. ca. 1930. 13"--B-C. (Gunnel Collection)

Hermann Steiner--16" Socket head. Marks: Germany/Herm Steiner/0. . 16"--C-D. (Courtesy Ralph's Antique Dolls)

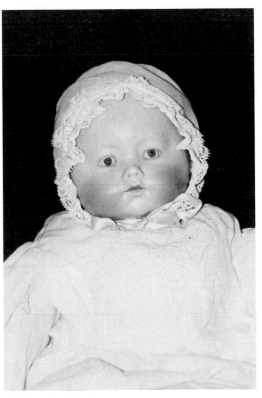

Hermann Steiner--19" with 13" head cir. Blue sleep eyes. Cloth body and feet. Composition hands. Bald head. Marks: X/Made In Germany/ 240/2. This mold number was also used for "Baby Phillis" by A.M. and this doll looks more like the Baby Phillis than a Herm. Steiner baby. 19"--F-G. (Minter Collection)

267

Jules Nichols Steiner operated the "Société Steiner" from 1855 to 1892 when the successor to the firm was Amedee Lafosse. A short time later the Widow Lafosse is listed. (1892-99). It was in 1895 that the Henri Alexandre firm (Maker of Bebe Phenix) and May Freres Cie (Maker of "Bébé Mascotte") merged with the Steiner company. It was in 1899 that Jules Mettais took over operating the company. In 1906 Edmond Daspres was the successor.

Steiner won a silver medal at Paris in 1878, a gold medal at Paris in 1889, received the Diplome d'Honneur in 1890 and, in 1891, received "Hors Concours" award. Almost all the awards were made during the time Jules Steiner was head of the firm.

The "wired eyed" Steiner was based on an 1880 patent. Many Jules Steiner dolls have a glass pupil and iris that are set into an opaque white eyeball. Also a separate big toe is a characteristic of Steiners. They seldom have cork pates but ones made of cardboard (pressed) that are sometimes purple, the same tone as the wash over the eyes. The mechanical Steiners and ones with two rows of teeth seldom have any marks. The mechanisms that operate the dolls usually are marked.

It was in 1889 that this firm registered a girl with a banner and the words "Le Letit Parisien." They introduced "Bebe Premier Pas" (walking doll) and "Bébé Marcheur" (walking doll) in 1890.

By 1892 Amedee Lafosse was head of the firm and registered the trademark "Le Parisien." He seems to have died shortly after taking over, and his widow ran the business until 1899 when Jules Mettais took over. It was 1899 when Jules Mettais registered "Phenix Bébé," "Bébé Liege" and "Poupée Merveilleuse." Mettais (Steiner) won a silver medal at the 1900 Paris Exposition and in 1901 registered "Bébé Modele" as a trademark and used the tradename "Mascotte." By 1906 Edmond Daspres was head of the Steiner firm and he advertised "La Patricienne" in 1908.

The Jules Nichols Steiner company had many mechanical dolls and Steiner heads are found on Motschmann & Huffner made bodies (bisque chest, upperarms, hips and lower legs) and it is not known if Steiner had the bodies made for them or if Motschmann & Huffner had the heads made for their bodies.

Considered the finest of the Steiner dolls are the "A" series of the dolls of the 1880's and 1890's.

The characteristic early Steiner dolls are of extremely white bisque, and these dates from 1855 into the 1860's. Sample marks:

Steiner Bte SGDG Ste C-4 Bourgoin	Steiner
Ste F2/0	SGDG
Bebe "Le Parisien"	Paris
Medaille D'or	A13
Paris	

Jules Nichols Steiner--13½"--Very early Steiner ca. 1855. Pressed bisque with flat slice on back of head. Composition/wood body. A very "heavy" little doll. Open mouth/2 rows tiny teeth. Rose-purple wash over eyes. Clothes and wig appear original (except shoes). Set pale blue eyes. Unpierced ears. Wire strung body. Unmarked head. Marked: "4" on bottom of feet. 13½"--L-N. (Author)

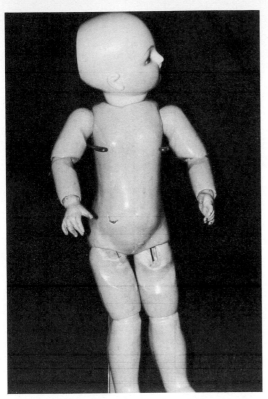

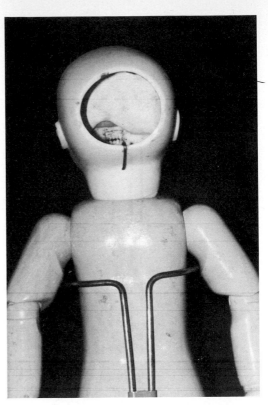

Jules Nichols Steiner--Shows body and head slice of 13½" Steiner.

Jules Nichols Steiner--Shows how head is "wired" to body and how teeth are set of 13½" Steiner.

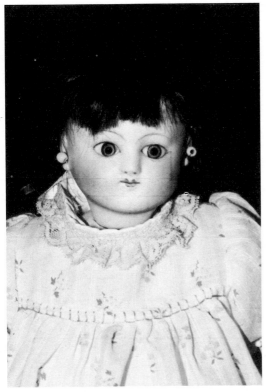

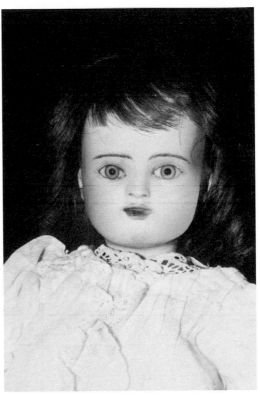

Jules Nichols Steiner--12" Socket head. Closed mouth. Early Steiner. 12"--K-L. (Courtesy Ralph's Antique Dolls)

Jules Nichols Steiner--11" Socket head. Open mouth with very small upper teeth. Ears pierced into head. Marks: 6, on head. An early Steiner should have 2 rows of teeth. 11"--I-J. (Courtesy Kimport Dolls)

269

Jules Nichols Steiner--11" "Bébé J. Steiner le Petit Parisien" Socke head. Closed mouth. Marks: J. Steiner/BTE S.G.D.G./Paris/FI re/A3. Flag sticker on body. 11" with box and wardrobe--M-N. (Minter Collection)

Jules Nichols Steiner--Shows box/clothes with "Bébé Steiner."

Jules Nichols Steiner--Flag sticker on back of 11" Steiner.

Jules Nichols Steiner--14" "Bébé Parisien" Pápier maché/wood body. Pierced ears. Closed mouth. Marks: Paris/A7-8. Body: Bébé "Le Parisien"/Medaille d'Or/Paris. 14"--M-O. (Author)

Jules Nichols Steiner--Close view of 14" "Bébé Parisien."

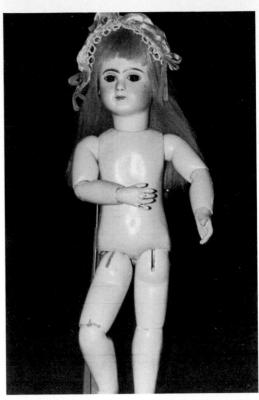

Jules Nichols Steiner--Body view of 14" "Bébé Le Parisien."

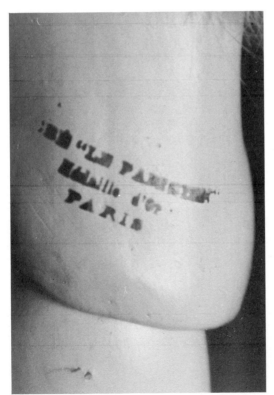

Jules Nichols Steiner--Stamp on body of 14" Steiner. Because of the curve of the body the first "Bé" of "Bébé" is missing.

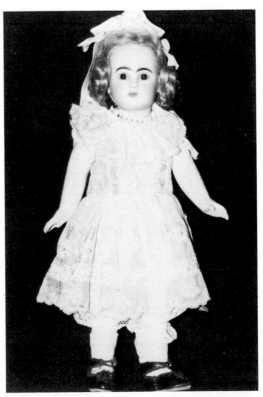

Jules Nichols Steiner--11" Pápier maché body with straight wrists. Closed mouth. Pierced ears. Brown eyes. All original. Marks: J. Steiner/BTE S.G.D.G./Paris/Fre A 3. Body: Medaille D'or/Paris. 11"--M-N. (Gregg Collection)

271

Jules Nichols Steiner--Close up of features of 11".

Jules Nichols Steiner--17" Socket head. Closed mouth. Marks: A9/Steiner. 17"--N-O. (Minter Collection)

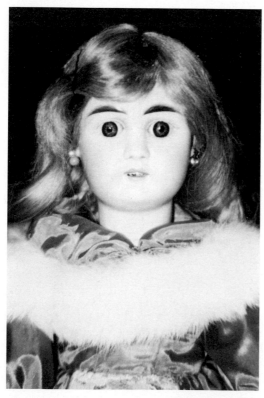

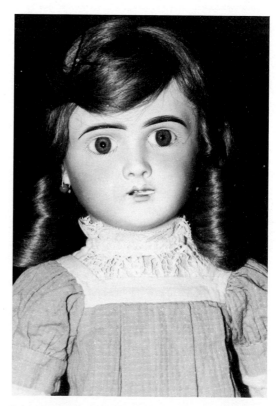

Jules Nichols Steiner--19" "Bébé Parisien" Socket head. Marks: 11 ⏚ . Body: Bébé "Le Parisien"/Medaille D'or/Paris. 19"--J-K. (Gunnel Collection)

Jules Nichols Steiner--19" Socket head. Open mouth. Marks: V10S, on head. Body marked "Le Parisien." Made for Vallee & Schultz (Paris) 1892. 19"--J-K. (Courtesy Ralph's Antique Dolls)

Jules Nichols Steiner--19" Socket head. Closed
mouth. All original. Marks: Steiner/Paris/FA11
Body: Medaille D'or/Paris. 19"--N-P. (Minter
Collection)

Jules Nichols Steiner--21" Socket head. Pierced
ears. Closed mouth. Marks: J. Steiner/BTE
S.G.D.G./Paris/F1re/A13. 21"--P-R. (Minter
Collection)

Jules Nichols Steiner--21" Socket head. Closed
mouth. All original. Marks: J. Steiner/BTE
S.G.D.G./Paris/F1reA13. 21"--P-R. (Minter
Collection)

Jules Nichols Steiner--22" Socket head. Closed
mouth. Marks: A-15/Paris/Le Parisien, on head.
Body: Petite Le Parisien/Medaille d'or/Paris.
Original. 22"--Q-S. (Minter Collection)

273

TERRA COTTA

Terra Cotta--Terra Cotta is actually "earthenware." A kiln low fire material. It is much less durable than porcelain and was used before the discovery of ways to make china. Terra Cotta dolls were shown in the Berlin Exhibition of 1844.

Terra Cotta--23½" Italian Terra Cotta Creche figure. All original. ca. 1800. 23½"--$450.00. (Courtesy Kimport Dolls)

UNICA

Unica--18" Painted Pápier Maché. Glass eyes. Open mouth with very dark red lips. Marks: Unica/Couraria/Belgium, in a circle with 56 in center. 18"--$135.00. (Minter Collection)

UNION NATIONALE INTER-SYNDICALI

"Unis, France" was a type of trade association, a kind of "seal of approval" for trade goods, to consumers from manufacturers. Often the guide rules of this group of business men, who were supposed to watch the quality of French export goods, were overlooked and some rather poor quality dolls escaped them. There are some very nice "Unis France" dolls, also.

Unis started right after World War I and is still in effect today. Two doll companies are members, Poupée Bella and Petit Colin. There are other types of manufacturers in this group and they include makers of toys, sewing machines, tile, etc.

Sample marks:

Union Nationale Inter-Syndicali--10½" "French Lacer" Composition body jointed only at shoulders and hip. Pupiless black eyes. Open mouth/4 teeth. Lace on underclothes same as lace in box. All original. Painted on pale brown boots. Marks: Unis France, in oval/71 149/60. 10½"--B-C. (Author)

Union Nationale Inter-Syndicali--23" Open mouth/4 teeth. Lashes not original. Marks: 71 Unis 149/France/301. With the Unis France in an oval. 9"--A-B, 23"--D-E. (Penner Collection)

275

Union Nationale Inter-Syndicali--9" Socket head. Open mouth/5 teeth. Sleep eyes. Made after 1922. Marks: Unis/France, in oval/301/0. 9"--A-B, 23"--D-E. (Minter Collection)

Union Nationale Inter-Syndicali--22" Socket head. Open mouth. Marks: Unis/71/France/149/301/ ® /B. 9"--A-B, 23"--D-E. (Gunnel Collection)

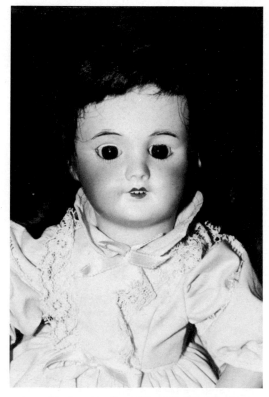

Union Nationale Inter-Syndicali--14" Socket head. Open mouth. Sleep eyes. Marks: Unis/France. 14"--C-D.

Union Nationale Inter-Syndicali--22" Socket head. Open mouth. Marks: 71 Unis 149/France/60. The Unis France is in an oval. 9"--B-C, 22"--D-E. (Minter Collection)

Union Nationale Inter-Syndicali--9" Socket head. Open mouth. Marks: 71 (Unis France) 149/60. 9"--B-C, 22"--D-E. (Courtesy Kimport Dolls)

Union Nationale Inter-Syndicali--24" Socket head. Sleep eyes/lashes. Open mouth. Marks: Unis/70, on head. Body marked Jumeau. 24"--E-F. (Gunnel Collection)

Union Nationale Inter-Syndicali--20" Sleep/ flirty eyes. Socket head. Closed mouth. Marks: 71 Unis 149/France/247. The Unis France is in an oval. Original clothes and wig of a boy. 20"--F-G. (Courtesy Irene Henderson)

J. Verlingue--12½" French child. Bald head. Shoulder pate with 3 sew holes. Kid body. Glass inset eyes. Marks: Lutin ⚓ . J. Verlingue operated 1915-1921, both at Boulogne-sur-Mer and Montreuil-sous-Bois, France. 12"--G-H. (Courtesy Kimport Dolls)

J. Verlingue--24" Socket head. Open mouth. Pupiless eyes. Marks: Petite Francaise/ ⚓ / France/8/ Liani. 24"--F-G. (Gunnel Collection)

WAX DOLLS

Wax dolls are recorded as early as the 1690's. The wax used for modeling was mostly beeswax with additives but the earliest dolls were made from a solid lump of wax and sculptured into shape.

Limbs and heads of the most expensive wax dolls, by 1850, were made by pouring wax into molds and are referred to as "poured wax" dolls.

As to the makers, many were in the field of making wax dolls but the two best known are the generations of Pierotti and Montanari. The last of the Pierotti doll makers retired in 1935. These two "leaders" of the wax making area had dolls that generally had glass eyes, embedded hair and often, hair eyelashes and eyebrows. A great number of wax dolls had hemp used for "hair."

It was was Madame Augusta Montanari who made the first real baby dolls in wax (about 1850). Before this the bodies were adult forms with narrow waists. In 1851 Madame Montanari was awarded a prize for her dolls in London. She showed dolls from infancy to adulthood. It is odd that it was almost 60 years later before the "baby" body was really accepted.

The cheaper type of wax dolls were papier mache or composition dipped in wax. They were painted either before the dipping or after. They had wigs either glued on or inserted in a slit on the top of the head. Wax over composition dolls do not, as a general rule, last as long as the poured wax.

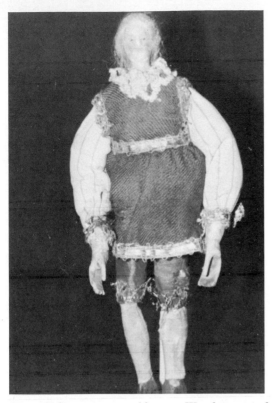

Wax--6" German wax nobleman. Wood arms and legs. ca. 1810. 6"--$65.00. (Courtesy Kimport Dolls)

Wax--8" Early 1830's English wax (Beeswax). Original. 8"--$300.00. (Courtesy Kimport Dolls)

Wax--9" Wax over Pápier maché. Cloth body with wood limbs. Painted eyes. 9"--$135.00. (Courtesy Kimport Dolls)

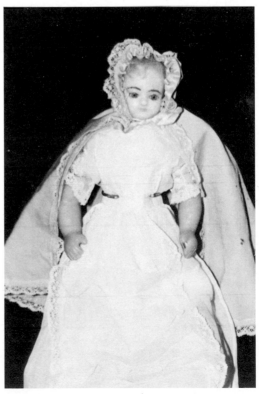

Wax--15" English wax baby with rooted hair. 15"--$325.00. (Courtesy Kimport Dolls)

Wax--16½" Wax over mache. ca. 1880. Cloth body. Glass eyes. Pierced ears. Closed mouth. 16½"--$250.00. (Courtesy Kimport Dolls)

Wax--16½" "Pumpkin" head wax. Molded blonde hair. Sleep eyes. Composition limbs with cloth body that is sawdust filled. 16½"--$175.00. (Courtesy Kimport Dolls)

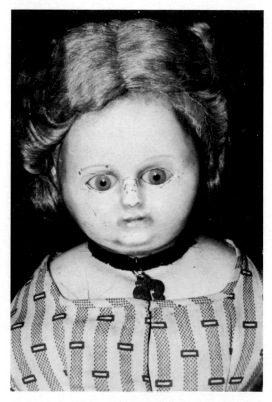

Wax--16½" Wax over papier mache. Sleep eyes. 16½"--$225.00. (Courtesy Kimport Dolls)

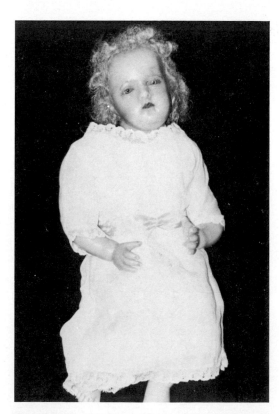

Wax--18" Creche baby. Blue glass paperweight eyes. Shoulder plate, lower arms and bent lower legs are wax also. Body filled with chips of wood. Embedded hemp hair. Open mouth/teeth. Unmarked French figure. 18"--$325.00. (Minter Collection)

Wax--18" Poured wax, turned shoulder plate. Wax limbs. Cloth body. Glass eyes. ca. 1870's. 18"--$450.00. (Courtesy Kimport Dolls)

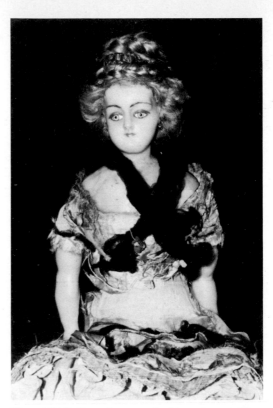

Wax--18½" French wax fashion type. Glass eyes. Pierced ears. 18½"--$300.00. (Courtesy Kimport Dolls)

Wax--19" Wax of the 1870's. Glass eyes. Glued on hair, except where embedded along part line. 19"--$235.00. (Courtesy Kimport Dolls)

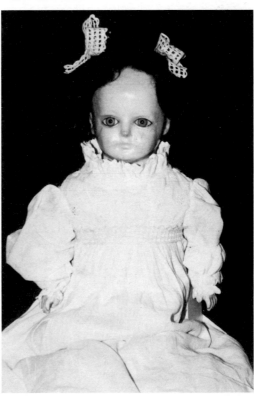

Wax--20" Wax over mache. Cloth body. Glass inset eyes. ca. 1880. 20"--$135.00. (Courtesy Kimport Dolls)

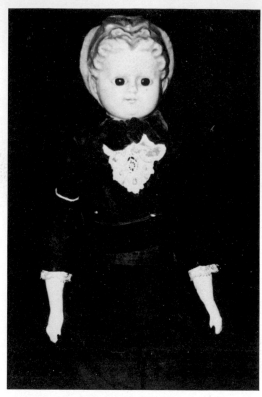

Wax--20" "Pumpkin" head wax with molded blonde hair and hair ribbon. Black glass eyes. 20"--$200.00. (Courtesy Kimport Dolls)

Wax--20" Cloth body with wax limbs. Turned wax shoulder plate. Glass eyes. Glued on hair. ca. 1880's. 20"--$200.00. (Courtesy Kimport Dolls)

Wax--21½" "Pumpkin" wax of the 1880's. Shoulder plate on cloth body with wax lower limbs. Painted eyes. 21½"--$250.00. (Courtesy Kimport Dolls)

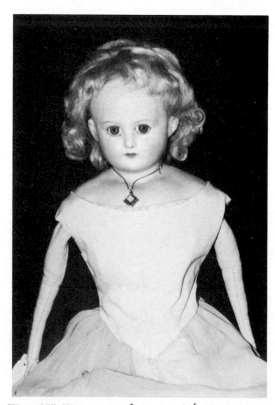

Wax--22" Wax over pápier maché. Cloth body with leather arms. Glued on wig. Glass eyes. 22"--$175.00. (Courtesy Kimport Dolls)

Wax--22" German wax over mache of 1885. Inset eyes. Hair embedded only along part line. 22"--$185.00. (Courtesy Kimport Dolls)

Wax--23" German wax over mache. ca. 1880. Glass eyes. 23"--$175.00. (Courtesy Kimport Dolls)

Wax--23" "Pompadour" wax over mache. Glass eyes. Glued on wig. 23"--$185.00. (Courtesy Kimport Dolls)

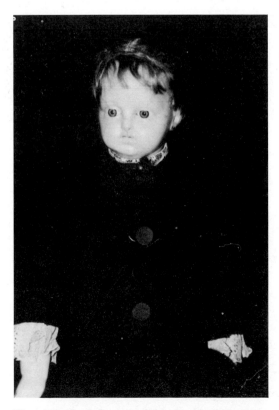

Wax--24" English wax child. Inset glass eyes. 24"--$275.00. (Courtesy Kimport Dolls)

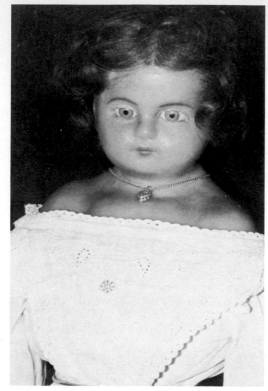

Wax--24" Slightly turned wax shoulder head. Cloth body and wax limbs. Embedded hair. Glass eyes. 24"--$675.00. (Courtesy Kimport Dolls)

Wax--24½" German wax over mache of 1880. Glass eyes. Open mouth/teeth. Sawdust filled cloth body. 24½"--$235.00. (Courtesy Kimport Dolls)

Wax--25" English wax of the 1830's. Blue leather arms. Cloth body and feet. Her hair is rolled in leather curlers. Pupiless black glass eyes. 25"--$325.00. (Courtesy Kimport Dolls)

Wax--25½" Early wax "pumpkin head" with snood. Wax over wood arms and legs. Sawdust filled body. ca. 1850. 25½"--$325.00. (Courtesy Kimport Dolls)

Wax--26½" "Pompadour" wax over mache of 1880. Inset eyes. Cloth/papier mache limbs. 26½"--$200.00. (Courtesy Kimport Dolls)

Hermann Wegner--11" Painted bisque with brown sleep eyes. Open mouth. Marks: Germany/733/H1W. Hermann Wegner had a doll factory in Sonneberg, Thur and operated from 1909 through 1936. 11"--C-D. (Gunnel Collection)

White Bisque--27" Blonde. Deep molded shoulder plate. Marks: none. 27"--$300.00. (Gunnel Collection)

White Bisque--27" "Highland Mary" child. Spoon hands. Flat painted on boots. Marks: 1000 11. Glass eyes. 27"--$575.00. (Courtesy Kimport Dolls)

White Bisque--21" Turned blonde, decorated shoulder plate. Printed "ABC" cloth body. Doll by Hertwig & Co. Dress is made from the draperies from the Green Room of the White House. 21"--$280.00. (Minter Collection)

White Bisque--14½" White bisque bonnet doll with gold luster ribbon. 14½"--$295.00. (Courtesy Kimport Dolls)

White Bisque--13" White bisque child. Brown glass eyes. 13"--$675.00. (Courtesy Kimport Dolls)

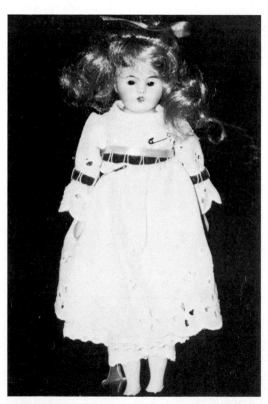

White Bisque--11" White bisque head, arms and legs. Excelsior filled body. Inset black eyes. Open mouth. One piece shoulder plate. Marks: 1910, on shoulder plate. 11"--$80.00. (Minter Collection)

White Bisque--9" White bisque bonnet doll. Excelsior filled body. 9"--$275.00. (Courtesy Kimport Dolls)

White Stone Bisque--17" Bonnet doll of white stone bisque. 17"--$325.00.

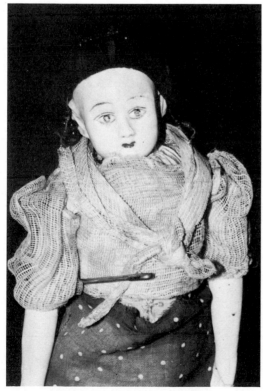

Manufacturer Unknown--14" White stone bisque. Cut in painted blue eyes. Black painted pate. Original wig of thin string yarn. Earrings attached to wig. Original clothes. 14"--$200.00. (Clasby Collection)

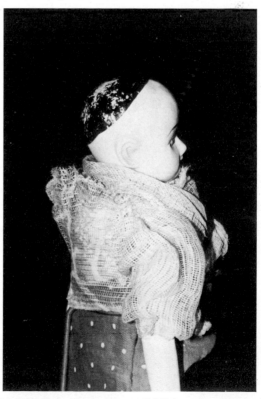

Manufacturer Unknown--14" White stone bisque doll with painted pate under yarn wig. (Clasby Collection)

287

White Bisque--9½" White stone bisque. Cloth body and upper limbs. Stone bisque lower arms and legs. Painted eyes. Marks: 114/10/0, on shoulder. 9½"--$80.00. (Courtesy Kimport Dolls)

White Bisque--8¼" Turbin type bonnet white stone bisque. Molded on shirt front. 8¼"--$185.00. (Courtesy Kimport Dolls)

White Bisque--4" White stone bisque. Marks: Germany. 4"--$35.00. (Gunnel Collection)

ADOLF WISLIZENUS

Adolf Wislizenus--Adolf Wislizenus started by
making Pápier maché dolls in 1851. He started
to use the trademark "Old Glory" in 1900 and
registered it in 1902.

Sample marks:

Germany
A.W.

AW-2
GERMANY
4

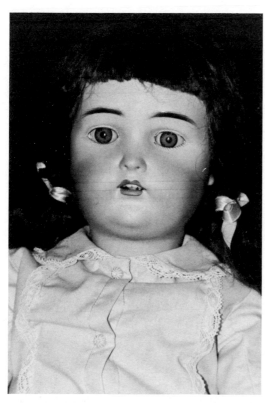

Adolf Wislizenus--23" Socket head. Composition
body. Open mouth. Marks: A.W./W/Germany.
23"-C-D. (Walters Collection)

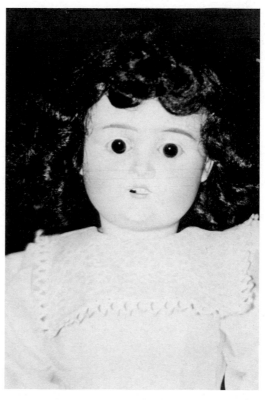

Adolf Wislizenus--24" Socket head. Marks:
AWs/Germany/II. 24"--C-D. (Gunnel Collection)

289

WOOD DOLLS

Because of its availability and cheapness, wood has been used for making dolls for centuries.

"Queen Anne" is the name given to the early wood dolls (1700-1780) although Queen Anne only reigned from 1702-1714. It is odd the name "stuck," for although Queen Anne bore seventeen children, all died in infancy but one, a boy, the Duke of Gloucester survived. It is unlikely dolls were items in the royal nursery.

The earliest wood dolls had eyes carved into the wood and were painted black and were pupiless, but soon after the year 1700, glass eyes were used. These early woods have eyelashes and eyebrows painted by a series of small dots. By 1780 some wood doll's eyes were painted blue and had pupils. The expensive woods had carved fingers of wood on wooden arms where the cheaper ones had arms of cloth or leather.

Germany began making wood dolls in the 1700's and these were known as "peg wooden dolls" or "Dutch" dolls due to the tiny wooden pegs that made the limbs articulated. The peg wooden dolls were made from a tiny half inch to 3 feet.

The quality of wood dolls declined in the mid-1800's and began to become very crude and did not reflect the former quality and artistry.

Wood--52" Georgian English wooden household figure. All wood with jointed shoulders. Painted eyes. Original clothes, with many jewels. ca. 1680. 52"--$4,750.00. (Courtesy Kimport Dolls)

Wood--22½" Early wooden Portrait Creche figure. Gesso finish with inset glass eyes. Cloth with wood limbs. Late 1700's. 22½"--$795.00. (Courtesy Kimport Dolls)

Wood--10" Painted wood doll of 1910. Jointed shoulders. 10"--$25.00. (Courtesy Kimport Dolls)

Wood--11" "Wooden Penny" Fully jointed all wood. Painted black hair. This doll is old but Shackman and others of Japan are reproducing them. 11"--$30.00, 11" Reproduction--$5.00. (Penner Collection)

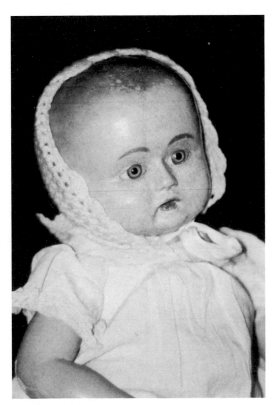

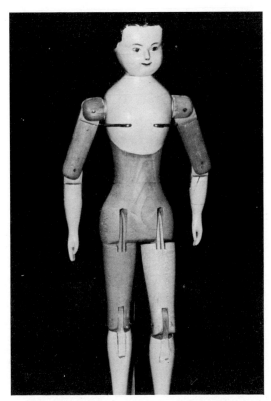

Wood--16" French wood baby. Inset glass eyes. Open mouth. Has hole drilled through one hand. 16"--$350.00. (Courtesy Kimport Dolls)

Wood--18" Springfield wood of the Ellis type. 18"--$495.00. (Courtesy Kimport Dolls)

Wood--18½" "Queen Anne" wood of 1700. Inset glass eyes, cloth arms. 18½"--$1,500.00. (Courtesy Kimport Dolls)

Wood--20" Early wooden Creche type. Inset eyes. ca. 1500's. 20"--$750.00. (Courtesy Kimport Dolls)

Wood--21½" Early 16th Century religious figure. Inset glass eyes. Gesso over wood. 21½"--$695.00. (Courtesy Kimport Dolls)

REPRODUCTIONS

Normally I would not include photographs of reproduction dolls in an antique doll book but would include them into a modern manuscript. But since there are unsigned reproductions and a greater than ever interest in reproductions, I decided to include a very few.

Good reproductions are worthy of their price, and it does not take an expert to learn to judge them on their workmenship and quality of bisque and to know if the doll is worth the price that is asked.

Reproduction dolls come in every quality that the antique ones do...from Par Excellence (example of the finest of bisque: Judi Kahn, Rene McKinley, etc.) to above average, fair and poor.

Most artists sign their work.. but some do not and not because they are trying to fool anyone. They just don't sign their work..but here again it does not take an expert to determine that they are reproductions except in a few areas: Parian/China, where if they are not artist-signed a great amount of caution is advised, as unscrupulous persons even make their dolls look old by adding red lines above the eyes, making scuff marks on the heads and all the rest of it to make a doll appear old. The finest and most difficult to spot are the Bonnet Dolls. Even the new ones made by the Schackman Co. of Japan are being made to look old by burying them for a week or so.

The finest of all "put on" reproductions discovered to date are the dolls marked "F+G." They are nothing but good!!! I owned one and have seen three. Two were "fashions" and the other a child doll on a composition body. They are really beautiful in their own right and, if the parties making them had introduced them as reproductions, they would still warrant a place in the finest of collections.

For information on the F+G dolls I would refer you to an article in the Sun Flower Antique Doll Club Regional Souvenir Book, U.F.D.C. Doll News Nov. 1967, U.F.D.C. Boston Convention Book (1967 and to Virginia Chrostowski's article in Yesterday's Children, Region 14 Souvenir Book (1974).

The makers of the F+G dolls are reported to be living in Finland and a friend of mine in Ireland who just returned from Europe advises me that both makers (mother and son) are in prison..so I don't know which is true but I do suspect that they also made other dolls besides the F+G!

Reproduction--17" Marked F+G. Made in France in the 1960's. $320.00.

Reproduction--16" All bisque with open mouth. 1974 by Ruby Stuart. Incised 224. Artist signed. $75.00. (Gunnel Collection)

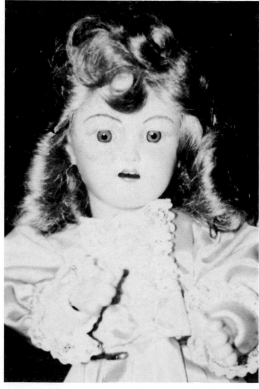

Reproduction--14" All bisque. Open mouth. By Ruby Stuart. Incised Handwerck. Artist signed. $75.00. (Gunnel Collection)

Reproduction--21½" China by Grace Lathrop. 1957. Artist signed. $225.00. (Kimport Dolls)

Reproduction--19½" Parian by Emma Clear. Artist signed. $185.00.

Reproduction--20" Snood Parian by Emma Clear. Artist signed. $185.00. (Gunnel Collection)

Reproduction--25" Modern China. Incised R.B.F. Pierced ears. $40.00. (Courtesy Kimport Dolls)

Reproduction--14" Modern bonnet China. Maker unknown. $30.00. (Courtesy Kimport Dolls)

Reproduction--14" Modern China doll. Maker unknown. $125.00. (Courtesy Kimport Dolls)

Reproduction--11" Bonnet doll by Carrie Kerr. Artist signed. $45.00. (Penner Collection)

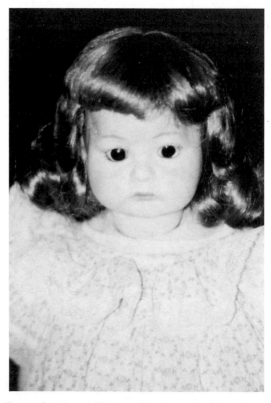

Reproduction--12" Bonnet doll by Lydia Hill. Artist signed. $45.00. (Penner Collection)

Reproduction--14" Pouty by Lydia Hill. Artist signed. $85.00. (Gunnel Collection)

Reproduction--12" Socket head. Bru Jne. Artist unknown. $70.00 (Gunnel Collection)

Reproduction--10" Googly by Marilyn Mosser. Artist signed. $80.00. (Minter Collection)

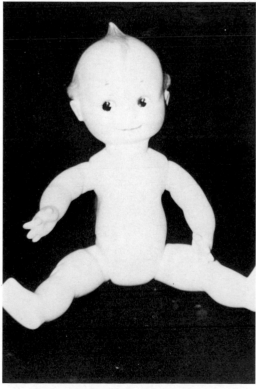

Reproduction--14" Heubach (Gebruder). Incised. 5/Germany/Carrie Kerr. $65.00. (Penner Collection)

Reproduction--10½" All bisque Kewpie type. Incised Lydia Hill. Artist signed. $65.00. (Gunnel Collection)

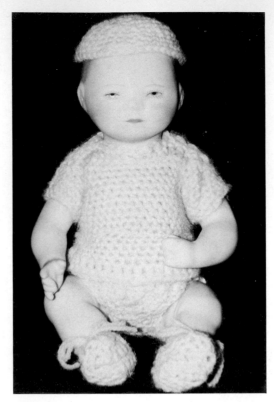

Reproduction--7" Bye-lo incised Lydia Hill. Artist signed. $35.00. (Penner Collection)

Reproduction--5" Colored Bye-lo. All bisque. Incised Gertrude Zigler. Artist signed. $38.00. (Minter Collection)

Reproduction--5½" Bonnet doll. All bisque. Being reproduced by Shackman of Japan. There is only a small paper sticker on the doll. $45.00. (Gunnel Collection)

Reproduction--6½" All bisque googly by Lydia Hill. Artist signed. $80.00. (Gunnel Collection)

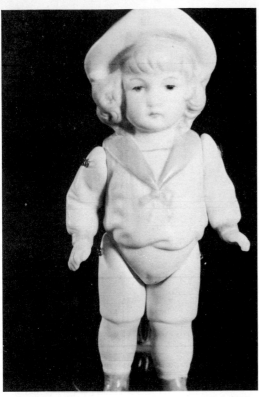

Reproduction--5" All bisque sailor boy signed Edith. $45.00. (Gunnel Collection)

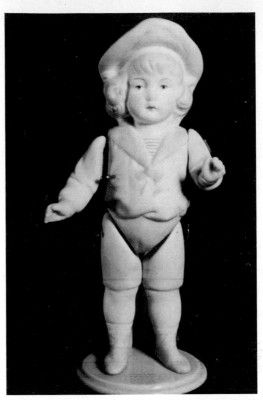

Reproduction--6" Sailor boy. All bisque by Lydia Hill. Artist signed. $45.00. (Gunnel Collection)

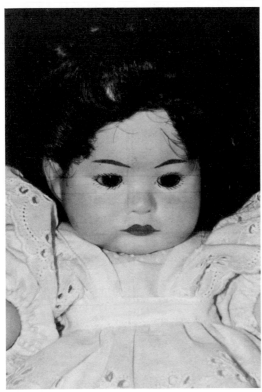

Reproduction--11" Pouty by Ida Mae Staples. Artist signed. $85.00. (Gunnel Collection)

Bibliography

A Scrapbook About Old Toys: 1964, Margaret Marshall Lehr and Margaret Patti Follett

A Scrapbook About Old Dolls: 1964 Margaret Marshall Lehr and Margaret Patti Follett

The Collector's Library Dolls: 1927 Esther Singleton

Dolls, Toys-Miniatures 1900-1930

A Book Of Dolls & Doll Houses: Flora Jacobs and Estrid Faurholt

Seattle: 1968 (N.F.D.C.)

The Age of Dolls: Coleman

The Doll Collectors of America: 1940, 1942, 1946, 1949, 1956-57, 1964, 1973

Speaking Of Old Dolls: 1964 Margaret Marshall Lehr and Margaret Patti Follett

Dolls: Max Von Boehn

Weitere Beitrage zur Forensischen Bedeulung des Puppen-fetischismus 1916 K. Boas

Porzellanfiguren 1929: Josten H.H. Fulder

Toymaking In Germany 1911 Harper's Bazaar, Merriam

Revelution In Kosener Puppenstaat 1923 Westermann

Monalshefte: E. Warburg

The New Era Of Dolls: 1916: The World's Work

A Doll's Family Album 1937: Edna Knowles King

Dolls & Puppets: Max Von Boehn

Classics Of The Doll World: Nina S. Davies

Guegmol du grand Cercle (Aix-les-Bains 1912) E. Delaunany

Puppen 1908 Neue Reveue Berlin: R. Breuer

A Study of Dolls (Pedogogical Seminary, iv, Worchester, Mass. 1896-97) Ellis, A.C. & Hall, G.S.

Antique Journel: Apr & May 1962

Toy Trader: June-Oct. 1962, Oct. 1965

The Jumeau Doll Story: Nina S. Davies

Handbook of Collectable Dolls: Merril & Perkins (3 Vols.)

Doll News (U.F.D.C.) May, 1962, Aug. 1967, Aug. 1969

Part IV Directory Of United States Doll Trademarks: L. Hart

Same: French

Same: German

Composition Dolls, Cute & Collectable: (Vol. 1&2) R. Shoemaker

The Doll: Carl Fox

The Armchair Museum of Dolls: O. Tavares

Region 4 1974 Souvenir Booklet (Victorian)

24th Annual Convention Book (U.F.D.C.) Louisville, Ky.

Region 9 1973

Region 14 1974

Region 3 1973

Region 2 1974

Once Upon A Time: Ralph Griffith

Doll Home Library Series: Marlowe Cooper (Vol. 1, 8, 15)

Dolls of Three Centuries: Eleanor St. George

All Color Book Of Dolls: Kay Desmonde

Silver Ann. Convention-U.F.D.C. Miami 1974

The Story Of Old Dolls & How To Make New Ones: Winifred H. Mills & Louise M. Dunn

Dolls In Color: Marjorie Merritt Darrah

Dolls: John Noble

Open Mouth Dolls: LaVaughn C. Johnston

China Heads: Martha Cramer

Heirloom Dolls: Brenda South

Dimples & Sawdust: Marlowe Cooper (Vol. 2)

The Collector's Book Of Dolls & Doll Houses: Roger Baker

The Dolls Of Yesterday: Eleanor St. George

Dolls A New Guide For Collectors: C.H. Fawcett

Portrait Of Dolls Vol. 1&2: Carol Jacobson

Blue Book Of Dolls And Values: Bateman & Faulke

Old Dolls: Elenore St. George

Research On Kammer & Reinhardt Dolls: P. Schoonmaker

Further Research On Kammer & Reinhardt: P. Schoonmaker

Rijksmuseum Book: Holand

Histoire des Jouets: H. d'Allemagne

Die Puppe In Wandel der Zeiten: E. Lehmann

Handbook Of German Toymakers: P. Nickermann

European And American Dolls: Gwen White

Ancient & Modern Dolls: Gwen White

Les Jouets a la World's Fair en 1904: H. d'Allemagne

An A.M. Picture Book: The Heart Of Ohio Doll Club

A Book Of Pottery Marks: W. Percival Jervis

Altes Spillzeug: Julianna Roh

Kinderspielzeug aus Alter Zeit: Karl Grober

Toys Of Other Days: F.N. Jackson

Tageslaug In Puppenhaus: Leonie von Wilckens

Doll Marks Clues: Ralph Shea (Vol. 1,2,&3)

The Many Heads Of Armand Marseille: Hobbie Nov. 1970: Mary Mooris

The Collector's Encyclopedia Of Dolls: Dorothy, Elizabeth and Evelyn Coleman

Porcelain & Pottery Marks: O&L Allard/Urban Hartman

Index

Numbers and Symbol Index

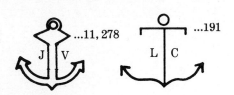
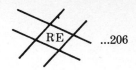
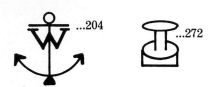

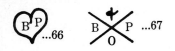
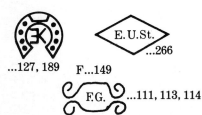

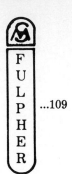

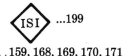

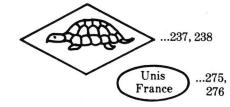
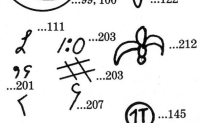